Media, Terrorism, and Theory

Critical Media Studies
INSTITUTIONS, POLITICS, AND CULTURE

Series Editor
Andrew Calabrese, University of Colorado

Advisory Board

Recent Titles in the Series

Media, Terrorism, and Theory

A Reader

EDITED BY

ANANDAM P. KAVOORI AND TODD FRALEY

ROWMAN & LITTLEFIELD PUBLISHERS, INC.
Lanham • Boulder • New York • Toronto • Oxford

ROWMAN & LITTLEFIELD PUBLISHERS, INC.

Published in the United States of America
by Rowman & Littlefield Publishers, Inc.
A wholly owned subsidary of The Rowman & Littlefield Publishing Group, Inc.
4501 Forbes Boulevard, Suite 200, Lanham, Maryland 20706
www.rowmanlittlefield.com

P.O. Box 317, Oxford OX2 9RU, UK

British Library Cataloguing in Publication Information Available

Library of Congress Cataloguing-in-Publication Data

Media, terrorism, and theory : a reader / Anandam P. Kavoori and Todd Fraley.
    p.   cm. — (Critical media studies)
   Includes bibliographical references and index.
   ISBN-13: 978-0-7425-3630-2 (cloth : alk. paper)
   ISBN-10: 0-7425-3630-0 (cloth : alk. paper)
   ISBN-13: 978-0-7425-3631-9 (pbk. : alk. paper)
   ISBN-10: 0-7425-3631-9 (pbk. : alk. paper)
   1. Terrorism—Press coverage.   2. War—Press coverage.   3. Terrorism in
mass media.   I. Kavoori, Anandam P.   II. Fraley, Todd, 1972–   III. Series.
PN4784.T45M44 2006
070.4′49303625—dc22

                                             2005012635

Printed in the United States of America

∞™ The paper used in this publication meets the minimum requirements of
American National Standard for Information Sciences—Permanence of Paper for Printed
Library Materials, ANSI/NISO Z39.48–1992.

Contents

Preface

It was a defining moment for us as citizens, students, and scholars of global television: Live coverage of the first Gulf War, where the world became compressed into the life-space of the CNN crew in Baghdad. In the years since, numerous books have been written and documentaries produced on how that war changed all the rules around Media and War. Today, we can see the effects of these new rules—a global news environment, a 24-hour news cycle, the growth of sectarian broadcast media, a deeply polarized political leadership, and the emergence of new technologies of information. Now, the events of 9/11, the unfinished second Gulf War, and the open-ended "War on Terrorism" have brought into sharp relief the contradictions and processes put into motion by the first Gulf War. As students, scholars, and media practitioners, we are immersed every day in trying to understand how to make sense of the daily events and find a vocabulary—both professional and scholarly—that will make sense.

This volume is an attempt to provide that vocabulary—that sense of how to contextualize the daily cycle of violence and spin, to frame "military action" and "terrorism," to assess "news coverage" and "commentary." We invite you to read these chapters collectively or singly; use the discussion questions at the end of each part to frame your understanding of these topics and begin an open-ended conversation that creates the critical vocabulary that is needed around issues of media, terrorism, and theory.

Part 1, Orientations, tries to meet just that goal—to *orient* the reader to both the scope and conceptual context of the chapters. This first section has the chapters "Televising the 'War on Terrorism': The Myths of Morality" by Daya Kishan Thussu and "Mediatizing the Global War on Terror: Television's Public Eye" by Simon Cottle.

Daya Thussu's chapter draws on the mythmaking function of global news to present a series of legitimizing narratives about the war on terrorism. He argues that the myths circulated by television news help consumers of mass media to construct a worldview that plays into the values and interests of U.S. and British corporate media and the political interests they represent. Drawing on the late Marjorie Ferguson's work on the "mythologies of globalization," he argues that there are five dominant myths that structure our understanding of the war on terrorism: the myth of Islamic terrorism, the myth of madness, the myth of nuclear threat, the myth of atrocities, and the myth of (American) morality. He contrasts these myths with the complexity that underlies reality, and his chapter concludes with a call to accountability and a refocus on the disjunctures that have appeared in events such as the global protest movement and the numerous studies that have called into question both U.S. foreign policy and an uncritical news media.

Simon Cottle's chapter examines the process of "mediatization"—the very specific ways in which the "communicative architecture" of television journalism functions to shape public perception of the war on terrorism. Drawing on an analysis of news content from six different countries, twenty-seven television channels, and four international service providers, Cottle's chapter accomplishes an enviable task: Providing a theoretical accounting of "television's Janus-faced relation to systems of domination *and* democracy." His findings examine the processes of mediatization through the communicative frames of conflict (namely, *dominant, contest, contention, campaigning*, and *exposé/investigation*) and consensus (*community service, collective interests, cultural recognition*, and *mythic tales*). Cottle invites us to reconsider the democratizing possibilities that inhere within television journalism's existing communicative architecture, which is now routinely deployed in countries and by satellite TV around the world, as well as the systematic use of communicative structures that permit dominant views to go unchallenged.

These two chapters structure the overall collection—one oriented to discursive closure (along lines of global political power, corporate interests, and the power of media technology) and the other to those of disruption (along lines of disjunctive reception, internal ruptures in discourse, local and regional readings, and the democratic potential in both mainstream and alternative media). These two themes are elaborated in the chapters that follow in the next section—organized around a single genre or medium—and then reworked in the final section of the book through their connections to contemporary social theory, media literacy, and international communication.

Part 2, Genres and Contexts, contains the chapters "Prime Time Terror: The Case of *La Jetée* and *12 Monkeys*" by Marion Herz, "Mediated Terrorism in Comparative Perspective: Spanish Press Coverage of 9/11 vs. Coverage of Basque Terrorism" by Teresa Sádaba and Teresa La Porte, "National Politics of Belonging and Conflicting Masculinities: Race and the Representation of

Recent Wars" by Antje Schuhmann, and "Terrorism and the Exploitation of New Media" by Bruce Klopfenstein.

The chapter by Marion Herz is a reading of two films, *12 Monkeys* (starring Bruce Willis) and an avant-garde film, *La Jetee*. Drawing on the theoretical work of Freud, Lacan, and Foucault, the chapter offers an original insight: "The producers of catastrophe films *are* of course terrorists, simply in a milder form." Herz argues that the quality of terrorism exists in the ability to turn a TV image into a medium of terror that "unites the extradiegetic reality of the spectators with the intradiegetic reality of the incident, and which suspends the distinction between fictionality and factionality." He explores this distinction by a close reading of both films and offers an analytic for the understanding of contemporary terrorism whose impact lies not just in the realm of politics but also in the personal realm that the films deal with. He suggests that we understand the relation between media and terrorism by examining issues of phantasm and fantasy, dreams and trauma, personal agency and responsibility.

Sádaba and La Porte's chapter examines Spanish press coverage of the events of 9/11 and that of Basque terrorism. Framed within the theoretical framework of "glocalization," the chapter eschews any "national" or essentialist framework for the comparative reception of these two realms of reporting on terrorism but rather articulates a nuanced reading based on issues of local/national party affiliation, competing media ideologies (referenced to Spanish politics and global corporate culture), and localization. Stories from *El Pais*, *ABC*, *El Mundo*, *El Correo*, and *Gara* are examined with an eye for examining the problematics of traditional categories of local/global and of a homogenous globalization (Americanization). In one instance, for example, the localization tendency is examined in the use of Basque language to make puns, plays on words, and punch lines, framing Basque leaders such as Batasuna as members of the Taliban. In sum, the chapter is a counterpoint to much contemporary discourse about how the events of 9/11 "changed everything." Issues of local reception (such as the Spanish one) orient the rest of the world much differently from how mainstream American political and media corporate narratives have defined terrorism in recent months.

Antje Schuhmann's essay explores the idea of localization with a different conceptual lens: Gender politics and issues of feminism and masculinity as they relate to the German experience with terrorism. The chapter examines both sides of how nation-states are constructed through mass media—internally and externally. Internally, issues of German identity are discussed through examples of German national politics, immigration, and Bavarian identity. External constitution of German identity is examined through a wide range of examples, from the war in Iraq and the Abu Ghraib prison scandal to

German concentration camps to the conflicts in Kosovo and Afghanistan. In each case, the focus of the analysis is on how gendered notions of whiteness and masculinity/femininity are used in the articulation of German identity, furthering a national politics of belonging.

The concluding chapter of this part by Bruce Klopfenstein is a context-setting one—articulating an overall framework of how we can understand "new media" and "terrorism"—both terms that are used in a range of ways, with little in the way of systematic accounting. Klopfenstein examines both terrorist organizations' use of new media and the role of such media in the war in Iraq and develops a model examining how the medium constructs messages with different conceptual/cultural vocabularies for internal and external audiences.

The concluding section, part 3, Frames and Contexts, contains the chapters "Critical Media Theory, Democratic Communication, and Global Conflict" by Todd Fraley and Elli Lester Roushanzamir, "Terrorism, Public Relations, and Propaganda" by Nancy Snow, "September 11, Social Theory, and Democratic Politics" by Douglas Kellner, and "International Communication after Terrorism: Toward a Postcolonial Dialectic" by Anandam P. Kavoori.

The chapter by Fraley and Roushanzamir sets the tone for this part of the book, which takes the task of theoretical redirection of "media and terrorism" as a defining theme. Their focus is not directly on terrorism but on its reflection in the realm of democratic communication under current conditions of global conflict and global corporate media. Fraley and Roushanzamir offer a model for critical media consciousness in place of the traditional models of critiquing corporate media content, and they suggest alternative ways of gathering information, different organizational arrangements, and so forth. Using evidence such as the role of alternate production and delivery (for example, in the Iranian Revolution) and the role media continue to play in the current pan-Islamicism, they highlight how the application of critical media consciousness may show ways of organizing outside the dominant corporate paradigm.

Nancy Snow parses the relationship between terrorism, public relations, and propaganda and provides a framework for understanding these often-misunderstood terms. Drawing on a range of theoretical material and examples from the world of media coverage, public diplomacy, advertising, public relations, and strategic information campaigns, Snow articulates both a descriptive and prescriptive set of criteria that can be used while evaluating the range of media messages that make up public relations, public diplomacy, and propaganda. Her perspective eschews an unproblematic critique of public relations or a simplistic analysis of propaganda but rather draws on her extensive work experience with the U.S. Information Agency and her status as a well-known scholar of propaganda to articulate ways out of the current quagmire of understanding media reporting and public diplomacy.

Douglas Kellner's chapter suggests how certain dominant social theories were put in question during the momentous and world-shaking events of September 11. He takes up the claim that "everything has changed" in the wake of September 11 and attempts to indicate both changes and continuities to avoid one-sided exaggerations and ideological simplicities.

Kellner examines the dominant dualistic theories—those of Huntington, Barber, Fukuyama, and neoconservative thinkers—that posit a fundamental bifurcation between the West and Islam and argues that they are analytically suspect in that they homogenize complex civilizations and gloss over the differences, hybridizations, contradictions, and conflicts within these cultures. Kellner argues that by positing inexorable clashes between bifurcated blocs, they fail to illuminate specific discord within the opposing spheres and the complex relations between them and also fail to articulate the complexity in the current geopolitical situation, which involves highly multifaceted and intricate interests, coalitions, and conflicts that shift and evolve in response to changing situations within an overdetermined and constantly evolving historical context.

Kellner's chapter frames the terms of an alternate theory by suggesting that local, national, and global democratic movements should be for democracy, peace, environmentalism, and social justice and against war, militarism, and terrorism, as well as the multiplicity of injustices that social movements are currently fighting. He replaces "neoliberal globalization" with a genuine multilateralism that is multipolar, involves autonomous partners and alliances, and is radically democratic, and he suggests that a democratic and multipolar globalization would be grounded philosophically in Enlightenment cosmopolitanism, democracy, human rights, and ecology, drawing on notions of a cosmos, global citizenship, and genuine democracy.

Kavoori's concluding chapter focuses on "postcolonial" theory in the fields of cultural studies, comparative literature, anthropology, and historiography and its relevance for a cultural perspective for the study of media and terrorism. Postcolonial analytical strategies are discussed and related to the subject matter of terrorism by critiquing the semantic and political field behind traditional categorizations of international communication (culture, nation, and theory) and suggesting how these are reworked in the mediated space of contemporary terrorism. Kavoori concludes with a sustained treatment of issues of globality, identity, and reflexivity and a look at how issues of terrorism are implicated in these concerns.

Each section of this volume thus has a thematic unity, and the overall book is held together by the thrust of the theoretical work that is being done by each chapter as it relates to the links between media, terrorism, and theory. Needless to say, the import and impact of this volume must, in the end, begin with you, the reader.

Part 1

Orientations

Televising the "War on Terrorism": The Myths of Morality

Daya Kishan Thussu

The U.S.-led "war on terrorism" has tended to dominate foreign news on television screens around the world. The open-ended nature of the conflict and its global reach, coupled with the Bush doctrine of preemptive strikes, has led to concerns about a deteriorating international security environment that appears to be fraught with dangers. Almost impervious to the growing unease among educated opinion internationally about U.S. unilateralism, U.S.-dominated international television news has generally presented the war on terrorism in mythical terms and in a highly moralistic language. Exploring some of these myths, defined here as a "fiction or half-truth, especially one that forms part of an ideology," this chapter focuses on how the war on terrorism—part of the wider U.S.-led pattern of military interventions in the post–Cold War era—is being framed by international television news. Given the power and reach of the 24/7 English-language news networks such as CNN and BBC World, as well as the dependence of broadcasters on Western-supplied footage of foreign news on television news agencies such as APTN and Reuters Television, such framing has a global impact.

MEDIA AND MYTHOLOGIES

Myths have been associated with human history from "creation" onwards. With the growing secularization of social relations, the traditional mythmaking and communicating institutions, such as religion, have made way for mass media to become the primary site for mythic narratives. With growing expansion of television, the transition from the pulpit to the mythic box seems to have taken place across the world. Arguably, one of the key functions of mass media is to create, codify, and circulate stories, narratives, and myths, and given the primacy of television, the visual varieties of mythologies have a much wider circulation than printed ones and therefore correspondingly greater impact, especially if they are on a serious and fact-based genre of television such as news. A study conducted in the United States for the Project for Excellence in Journalism found that, in 2003, as many as 79 percent of Americans received "most of their news about national and international issues" from television. TV was followed by newspapers (45 percent), the Internet (19 percent), radio (16 percent), and magazines (5 percent) (Project for Excellence in Journalism 2005). In other countries too, television remains the main source for information and entertainment, particularly among developing countries, many of which have made a drastic jump from an oral to a visual medium, largely skipping the epoch of the print medium.

The myths circulated by television news help consumers of mass media to construct a worldview. This worldview in the long run can make the consumers accept as being "natural" something which in fact is a manufactured reality, created to mask the real structures of global power. Thus global television news, controlled in this era of privatized airwaves by powerful corporate interests, can construct a mythical reality and encourage conformity to the value systems of the dominant groups in society. In this sense, the mass media play a crucial ideological role, promoting the values and interests of dominant groups and implanting beliefs and representations that sustain and legitimize their domination.

As cultural theorist Terry Eagleton (1991, 5–6) astutely observed:

> A dominant power may legitimate itself by promoting beliefs and values congenial to it; naturalizing and universalizing such beliefs so as to render them self-evident and apparently inevitable; denigrating ideas which might challenge it; excluding rival forms of thought, perhaps by some unspoken but systematic logic; and obscuring social reality in ways convenient to itself. Such "mystification," as it is commonly known, frequently takes the form of masking or suppressing social conflicts, from which arises the conception of ideology as an imaginary resolution of real contradictions.

Myths have been part and parcel of modern media almost since its inception and not just in the Western world. For decades, Soviet propaganda machinery promoted the myth of a socialist utopia based on the notions of class, ethnic, and gender equality. However, one has to look very hard to find any women in the highest echelon of power and even harder to spot a non-European face in the Politburo of the Soviet Communist party, despite the fact that a large part of the Union was outside Europe. During the years of the Cold War, the mainstream Western media kept peddling the line that the Soviet Union was going to take over the world, especially controlling the newly emergent nations of Asia and Africa. Informed opinion in the West knew that even by the early 1980s, it was becoming increasingly clear that the USSR was on the brink of bankruptcy as it failed to keep up with the arms race initiated by the United States. The media mythmakers maintained that the Cold War was a period of peace and tranquility when in fact more than 20 million people died across the "Third World" in Cold War–related conflicts—from Korea to Vietnam, from Indonesia to Angola, and from Iran to El Salvador.

Mythologizing media discourses is not just an issue for the Northern Hemisphere. In Asia too, media-induced myths have played a crucial role in recent history. In China, during Cultural Revolution, for example, the myth of the purity of Chinese peasants was exploited by the state propaganda machinery to devastating effect, while—despite widespread myths of India's nonviolence, peace, and spirituality as the land of Buddha and Mahatma Gandhi—violence arising from caste, class, or communal antagonisms is endemic in India.

In the Islamic world, the 1980s war between Iran and Iraq (the only conflict that can justifiably be called a Gulf War—the subsequent "wars" of 1991 and 2003 were disproportionately one-sided invasions) destroyed the myth of Islamic brotherhood; more than a million died in the decade-long war during which Muslims massacred others of the same faith. The atrocities committed by what was then West Pakistan on East Pakistan (later to become the independent nation of Bangladesh in 1972) and the barbarity and cruelty witnessed during internecine warfare within various Afghan mujahideen factions are further examples of the fragility of this myth.

ISLAMIC TERRORISM: A TRANSNATIONAL THREAT?

In the contemporary world, the myth about Western aid to developing countries is sustained by the mass media. The general assumption is that Third World countries, especially in Africa, are totally dependent on Western largess, when the reality is that the net flow of resources is from the South to the North. However, as Ziauddin Sardar and Merryl Wyn Davies (2004, 117–18) note:

> Myths have their own storyline that come complete with stock characters and familiar scenarios. The function of myth is to facilitate understanding and negotiate changing events and circumstances in the real world by reading them against its own familiar ideas, values and morals. In this way the world around us is shaped, it becomes coherent, manageable and meaningful. Myths create a sense of identity and help to identify who are the good guys, who the baddies, and why.

This good guys vs. bad guys dichotomy is at the heart of current circulation of televised myths and the most dangerous myths making the media headlines concern the so-called war on terrorism.

The myth is being created that in the post–Cold War era, a radicalized Islam has replaced Communism as the preeminent transnational threat to Western interests, exemplified by shadowy networks such as al-Qaeda, with its alleged links to "rogue" states such as Iran.

In this version of international politics, influenced by the discourse of the "clash of civilizations" and strengthened by the events of September 11, 2001, militant Islam has characteristics that are inimical to a modern, secular, and rational market-democracy. This terrorism is being undertaken by "irrational," "bigoted" Muslims and this type of violence can only be reciprocated by force, as they seem to be unwilling and, more importantly, incapable of taking part in reasoned debate and discussion.

This view of Islamic militancy is undifferentiated: Lebanon's Hezbollah, Palestinian Hamas, Indonesia's Jemaah Islamiyah, the Abu Sayyaf Group in the Philippines, Hizbul-Mojaheddin in Kashmir, Abu Musab al-Zarqawi's supporters in Iraq, and Chechen rebels are all linked as part of a seamless transnational terror network. The fear that weapons of mass destruction may fall into the hands of such networks is at the heart of the U.S. security agenda. The U.S.-led global and open-ended war on terrorism is part of the grand strategy to make the world a safer place. The corollary of this narrative is that the West, led by the United States, the world's only hyperpower, is committed to bringing democracy and protecting human rights around the world, even if it requires preemptive strikes or "regime change"—and that military interventions in the post–Cold War era have been undertaken largely for humanitarian reasons.

These myths have been presented in the media in a highly moralistic tone and the discourse has been played up for international consumption mainly through 24/7 news networks, given the primacy of television as a medium for near-global dissemination and consumption of information.

GLOBAL CIRCULATION OF MYTHS ON 24/7 TELEVISION NEWS

The multiplication of dedicated news channels—as a result partly of deregulation and privatization of airwaves globally and partly of the rapid innovations in information and communication technologies, particularly digitalization—have made 24/7 news a reality of contemporary journalism. In this market-driven broadcasting environment, scores of news channels operate round-the-clock, replicating the formula of "real-time news" broadcasting pioneered by the Cable News Network (CNN), "the world's news leader." After CNN, the most significant global actor in 24/7 news is BBC World, the commercially run 24-hour global news and information channel of the British Broadcasting Corporation. In recent years, Fox News, part of Rupert Murdoch's media empire—with its sister news organizations Sky News in Europe, headquartered in London, and Star News Asia, beamed from Hong Kong—has also emerged as a powerful rival to CNN.

Though there is an obvious domination of the English-language television journalism, news in other languages too is being globalized. The French government has pledged more than $35 million to launch CII (International Information Channel)—a kind of "CNN à la Française"—a joint venture between the government-owned television group France Televisions and the main private broadcaster TFI (Henley 2004). China's CCTV and India's Star News broadcast news to international audiences in Mandarin and Hindi, respectively. Brazil's Globo News, part of the TV Globo conglomerate, and the Qatar-based pan-Arabic network al-Jazeera, which has transformed broadcasting in the Arab world, are some other notable examples of transnational 24/7 news broadcasting.

The increasingly pluralist international television newsscape may give the impression of a multiplicity of languages and perspectives, but the English-language news networks continue to have a privileged position in the production and distribution of global TV news. The structural reality of the global flow of television news footage remains unchanged: broadcasters across the world continue to depend for international news footage mainly on two Anglo-American television news agencies: Reuters Television, a part of Reuters news agency; and Associated Press Television News (APTN), part of the U.S.-based Associated Press, the world's biggest news agency (Boyd-Barrett 1998; Thussu 2000).

No respectable broadcaster can manage without access to the World News Service of Reuters Television, given the "breadth and depth" of its "global reporting infrastructure," with journalists and camera crews in more than eighty locations globally (Reuters Television 2005). Similarly, APTN's Global Video Wire service, fed to more than five hundred broadcasters, major portals, and websites with video from APTN's eighty-three bureaus, is indispensable for television journalists covering foreign affairs. Since 2003, the agency has also been operating APTN Direct, live news coverage to cater to 24/7 networks (APTN 2005).

In addition, global round-the-clock news networks are also dominated by the British and U.S. media. In 2005, through fifteen cable and satellite television networks across the world and a global team of four thousand "news professionals," CNN International was reaching more than two hundred countries and territories. In addition, it also operates CNN Newsource, the world's most extensively syndicated news service (CNN 2005). BBC World, the international twenty-four-hour news and information channel, claimed to be reaching 254 million homes in more than two hundred countries and territories worldwide, drawing on the BBC's 58 international news bureaus and 250 correspondents (BBC World 2005).

In conjunction with the CNN/BBC presence, the third arm of the English-language TV news troika—Fox-Sky-Star—effectively leads to what has been called a "U.S./U.K. news duopoly" (Tunstall and Machin 1999, 88). This duopoly can ensure that the media myths perpetuated by the U.S./British myth-making machinery—the nexus of journalists, public relations companies, and government and military "spin doctors"—can reach a global audience. It has been argued that networks such as CNN and BBC World have a small audience internationally and therefore their influence in setting the news agenda is often widely exaggerated. While it is true that most consumers of news prefer to watch their own national news, the small number of viewers for CNN are in fact what the company itself defines as "influentials"—the business and political elite. It is scarcely surprising then that CNN or BBC is a regular presence in television newsrooms around the world, as well as in information and foreign ministries, for information bureaucracies to keep abreast of developments, especially at a time of man-made or natural international crises. Admittedly, there are variations in broadcasting norms between the U.S. and British news networks, the latter steeped in the public service broadcasting ethos of Western Europe, but the differences may have more to do with style than substance, especially on stories that impinge upon sensitive geopolitical or economic issues. Thus how the U.S. and British television networks frame the war on terrorism becomes a crucially important site for inquiry.

MEDIA MYTHOLOGIES AND THE WAR ON TERRORISM

The mythologies associated with the televisual representations of the war on terrorism need to be analyzed within the broader context of post–Cold War U.S. military interventions, undertaken ostensibly to protect human rights and export market democracy. An analysis of U.S. operations, from the regime change in Panama in 1989 to the installation of a new regime in Iraq in 2004, demonstrates that the representations of these invasions almost invariably were framed in a discourse couched in the language of humanitarianism and high moral rectitude.

This is reflected also in the way the operations were named by the Pentagon. From the first post–Cold War military intervention—Operation Just Cause, the 1989 invasion of Panama to depose President Manuel Noriega—to Operation

Iraqi Freedom, launched in 2003 to "liberate" Iraq from the dictatorship of Saddam Hussein, a moral element was integral in the selling of the proposition. Other examples of such moralistic nomenclature include Operation Provide Comfort, the intervention in Iraqi Kurdistan in 1991; Operation Restore Hope, the 1992 invasion of Somalia; the 1994 Operation Uphold Democracy undertaken ostensibly to restore to power Haiti's democratically elected President Jean-Bertrand Aristide; and Operation Enduring Freedom, the 2001 invasion of Afghanistan.

These and other military actions were undertaken in Pentagon-speak primarily to promote peace, stability, and democracy across the world, following what has been called the myth of "democracy for export via American TV" (Ferguson 1992). The general tone and tenor were moralistic and the responsible behavior of the U.S. troops was constantly underlined; the capacity of superior U.S. weaponry, especially the "smart bombs" with their almost mythical precision and pinpoint accuracy, was routinely emphasized. In the cloak of moralistic humanitarianism, the U.S. government has advanced its geostrategic and economic interests. The "war on terrorism," it would appear, is the logical next step in this agenda for global hegemony. We can discuss the myths associated with the war of terrorism under five headings.

The Myth of Islamic Terrorism

In the discourse on Islam, a tendency is evident to present the world's one billion Muslims as potential terrorists. "Islamic fundamentalism" seems to receive a disproportionate amount of airtime on global television networks in comparison with Christian, Jewish, or Hindu verities of religious fundamentalisms. Often the distinction between "political Islam" and "Islamic fundamentalism" is collapsed in media coverage. As political scientist Mohamood Mamdani (2004) has argued, there is a long history of the U.S. government harnessing and cultivating radical Islamic groups fighting "communism" in Afghanistan during the 1980s. Profoundly influenced by Cold War thinking, it was normal to see the Afghan mujahideen routinely labeled in Western media reports as "freedom fighters." These fighters for freedom have now become enemies of freedom and apparently form part of a transnational terror network, bent upon destroying Western interests. Al-Qaeda, reputedly led by Saudi fugitive Osama bin Laden—himself a creation of the CIA—may have more to do with "the politics of fear" of the U.S. government to justify the war on terrorism than any tangible global organization, as Adam Curtis's series, broadcast on the BBC, has argued (Curtis 2004).

There is also a worrying tendency in conservative sections of mainstream Western media to use the term "islamofascism," bracketing Islamic militancy with Nazi political legacy. Western involvement in the Islamic world has a long and complex history steeped in medieval Crusades and modern colonial conquests, as Rashid Khalidi (2004) has shown. In recent years, Western support for the creation of Israel and its suppression of Palestinian aspirations has contributed to anti-Western sentiment. However, the U.S./British discourse, given its global reach and influence, can affect how other non-Muslims view Islam. The growth of anti-Islamic sentiment in India (home to the second largest Muslim population after Indonesia) in the past ten years is a testimony to this. It is instructive to note that—despite Western-influenced propaganda in Indian news media about the tentacles of "Islamic" terrorism gripping India, condoned by Indian Muslims—when U.S. forces entered Afghanistan in October 2001, not one Indian Muslim was found in the terrorist training camps, though other nationalities, including Arabs, were present.

It is true that sections of Islamic militant groups—whether in Palestine, Chechnya, or Kashmir—have used terrorist activities as an extreme manifestation of political protest and some "Islamist" groups have descended into extortion and blackmailing rackets and criminal syndicates, as evident in occupied Iraq. However, the vast majority of Muslims want to get on with their lives and have nothing to do with terrorism. However, the "war on terrorism" may have in fact *brought* Islamic militancy to secular Iraq. A report by the National Intelligence Council, a CIA think tank, describes how foreign terrorists entered Iraq after the U.S. invasion and how the insurgency against the occupation was viewed by radical Muslims as a war against a foreign occupier, thus enmeshing it with the occupation of Palestine by Israel. "Iraq and other possible conflicts in the future," the report warns, "could provide recruitment, training grounds, technical skills and language proficiency for a new class of terrorists who are 'professionalized'" (quoted in Goldenberg 2005).

The Myth of Madness

Television can be very effective at framing conflicts within a context of binary opposition—an us-versus-them dichotomy, in which Islamist opposition is projected as irrational and fanatical, pitted against a firm, rational, and reasonable U.S. leadership. Demonization of Islamic leadership can be eased by television's proclivity for the exotic and the unusual. A turbaned, bearded, one-eyed Mullah Omar, the former leader of Taliban in Afghanistan, or a gun-wielding Osama bin Laden fits the image of a villain in popular Western imagination, influenced in no small way by the stereotyping of the Islamic East, which has deep cultural and historical roots (Said 1978, 1997).

The demonizing of a supposedly bigoted leader can be an effective tool for propaganda, as it helps to personalize an invasion by reducing the entire country and its population to one person. The powers of Iraqi dictator Saddam

Hussein were exaggerated in the media coverage to such an extent that he was seen not only as a major threat to the Middle East region but to the world at large. The allegation that this avowedly secular Arab leader had links with Islamic terror groups put his power in a different scale of danger in the post-9/11 world. Saddam's apparent megalomania was staple fare in his Western media portraits. Veteran BBC journalist John Simpson noted after the "regime change" in Iraq that "Saddam was never the crazed dictator of Western imaginings. He was rational, highly intelligent and thoroughly well-informed" (2003, 134). However, during Saddam's reign it was very rare to find such language used in Western media reports to describe the Iraqi dictator.

The Myth of Nuclear Threat

Media coverage of the war on terrorism is littered with concerns about the possibilities of Islamic terrorist groups gaining access to nuclear bombs to wreak havoc on Western targets. In the post-Soviet era, this discourse has been given respectability by numerous high-powered reports, academic articles, and conferences, although there has been no evidence of any nonstate actors acquiring nuclear weapons. The claim that "rogue states" such as Iran, Syria, and Iraq (which has ceased to belong to this category after its "liberation" by the United States in 2003) were risking the proliferation of nuclear weapons, remains a key security concern for the United States.

The argument that Iraq was in possession of nuclear weapons and had the capacity to deploy them within 45 minutes notice was presented in the media as a compelling reason for invading that country. A great deal of skepticism about these claims was expressed by many, including such senior international bureaucrats as Hans Blix, head of the UN Monitoring, Verification, and Inspection Commission (Blix 2004). Yet most television networks gave short shrift to any dissenters and kept representing these threats as real. However, as the subsequent events showed, this claim was without any basis whatsoever. In his interim report to the U.S. Congress in October 2004, Charles Duelfer, who led the CIA-sponsored Iraq Survey Group, conceded that the Iraqi government had destroyed its last weapons of mass destruction more than a decade ago and had little capacity to build new ones.

Since the conquest of Iraq, the focus of nuclear and other weapons of mass destruction has turned to neighboring Iran and its nuclear weapons program. Television coverage is full of alarming reports about the "nuclear threat" posed by Iran, with concerns voiced about the amount of enriched uranium the Iranians possess to build a bomb. Although Mohammed el Baradei, the head of UN's International Atomic Energy Agency, has given a clean chit to Iran's nuclear program, in Western media reports Iran is constantly projected as a dangerous country. American journalist Seymour Hersh reported in the *New Yorker* magazine in January 2005 that the Pentagon has sent special operations teams into Iran to locate nuclear weapons sites. Hersh, a veteran investigative reporter, wrote that the Bush administration "has been conducting reconnaissance missions inside Iran at least since last summer . . . . The goal is to identify and isolate three dozen and perhaps more (nuclear, chemical and missile sites) that could be destroyed by precision strikes and short-term commando raids" (Hersh 2005).

The revelations tally with pronouncements at the highest level. In his State of the Union address delivered on February 3, 2005, President George W. Bush warned that "Iran remains the world's primary state sponsor of terror—pursuing nuclear weapons while depriving its people of the freedom they seek and deserve" (Bush 2005).

The high moral ground adopted by the United States in the debate is disingenuous given that the United States is the only country to have used nuclear weapons—not once but twice, against Japan in 1945—and has not hesitated in deploying unconventional weapons in its military interventions in recent years.

The Myth of Atrocities

Double standards define television's portrayal of atrocities committed in the name of the war on terrorism, with terrorist groups receiving maximum opprobrium and the state-sponsored terrorism often being ignored.

The atrocity story has been central to propaganda efforts in modern warfare. Western television was full of atrocities committed by the Taliban in Afghanistan, though the equally gruesome record of local supporters of Western powers, namely, the Northern Alliance, did occasionally make it to global TV news bulletins as well. The horrendous abuse and torture of Iraqi citizens in Abu Ghraib prison and elsewhere takes atrocities to a different level. Baathist brutality received prominent coverage, while the massacres in Fallujah—a city of 350,000 people that was razed in November 2004 and its people forced to flee and live as refugees in their own country—received scant coverage on television.

When Iraqi doctor Ali Fadhil visited the ghost town of Fallujah in December 2004, more than a month after the biggest U.S. military operation in occupied Iraq, to report for Britain's Channel 4 News, he found rotting bodies scattered in empty homes in the town (Channel 4 News 2005). A study published by the British science journal *The Lancet*, based on surveys comparing mortality before and a year after the U.S. invasion of Iraq, claimed that "invasion violence" may have cost more than 100,000 Iraqi lives (Roberts et al. 2004). Despite repeated and televised assurances of peace, the spiral of violence has continued and even intensified. The routinization of suicide bombings and other varieties of violence has become such that Iraqi deaths are not even counted as a statistic in Western reports, while U.S. troops or civilians killed or kidnapped in Iraq receive prime-time prominence.

Apart from these physical acts of violence, there are other types of atrocities committed that can have long-term effects on the Iraqi psyche—the destruction of ancient cultural sites in the cradle of civilization. One example of such an atrocity is the construction of a U.S. military base in the ruins of the ancient city of Babylon, described by the *Guardian* in an editorial as "one of the most reckless acts of cultural vandalism in recent memory" (*Guardian* 2005, 21).

The Myth of Morality

The most important myth being televised around the world is about the U.S. crusade to spread democracy, freedom, and human rights in the world. It has been proposed that force may be needed to democratize the international community. However, the undermining of democracy in the United States and Britain was evident during and leading up to the Iraqi invasion. A historically unprecedented number of ordinary citizens—as many as eight million—marched on the streets of five continents on February 15, 2003, demonstrating against the U.S.-British plan to invade Iraq, and yet the democratically elected governments chose to ignore popular sentiment. Noting this irony, historian Eric Hobsbawm wrote: "Other than creating complex problems of deceit and concealment, electoral democracy and representative assemblies had little to do with that process. Decisions were taken among small groups of people in private, not very different from the way they would have taken in nondemocratic countries" (Hobsbawm 2004).

The "force of freedom" is now central to U.S. foreign policy rhetoric. The U.S. government wants to transplant freedom and liberty to "outposts of tyranny." In his twenty-minute State of the Union Address, President Bush exhorted "the expansion of freedom in all the world," using the word "freedom" or "free" no less than twenty-seven times (Bush 2005).

However, this penchant for exporting democracy does not include democratizing international institutions such as the United Nations Security Council, which sixty years after its inception still does not have any veto-wielding representation from Latin America, Africa, or the Arab world (it may be worth remembering that until 1972, Taiwan was a veto-wielding Security Council member, while China, representing one-fourth of all humanity, was excluded from the UN system). With occasional disagreements from Russia and China and sparingly from France, as during the 2003 Iraq debate, the United States seems to set or manipulate the agenda and, when the world body does not suit its political interests, to totally undermine the United Nations.

DEMYSTIFYING THE MORALITY OF THE WAR
ON TERRORISM

With the support of a largely compliant media, the U.S. government has arguably succeeded in transforming its myths about the war on terrorism, coated in a firebrand moral discourse, into reality. In the process, it has almost unilaterally redrawn the rules of international military intervention to further its own geostrategic and economic interests. The unilateralist ideology propounded by the so-called neoconservatives is increasingly shaping U.S. foreign policy. Former CIA director James Woolsey, a member of the Project for the New American Century, described the invasion of Iraq as the onset of the "Fourth World War" (the third being the Cold War), indicating that this is likely to continue for years if not decades to come. It may even spread to other parts of the world, just as the Cold War was globalized. Hersh quoted a former top U.S. intelligence official as saying: "This is a war against terrorism, and Iraq is just one campaign. The Bush Administration is looking at this as a huge war zone. Next, we're going to have the Iranian campaign. We've declared war and the bad guys, wherever they are, are the enemy. This is the last hurrah—we've got four years, and want to come out of this saying we won the war on terrorism" (Hersh 2005).

However, there are indications that these myths of morality are being punctured by a growing chorus of discontentment, paralleled with the declining credibility of mass media. Disjunctures seem to be appearing within the moral discourse, and there are indications of a growing resentment against military adventures around the world. A major international survey in the United States released in January 2005 found: "In seven out of nine nations surveyed in 2004, majorities of those who doubt U.S. sincerity in the war on terror said America is seeking to control Mid-east oil. Nearly as many respondents believe America's ultimate aim is nothing less than world domination" (Pew Center 2005).

The survey, part of the Pew Center's Global Attitudes Project, noted:

> Anti-Americanism is deeper and broader now than at any time in modern history. It is most acute in the Muslim world, but it spans the globe—from Europe to Asia, from South America to Africa. And while much of the animus is aimed directly at President Bush and his policies, especially the war in Iraq, this new global hardening of attitudes amounts to something larger than a thumbs down on the current occupant of the White House. (Pew Center 2005)

These sentiments have been echoed by other opinion polls. As George W. Bush was elected for a second term, a BBC poll conducted in twenty-one countries on five continents reported that 58 percent felt that his reelection would have a negative influence on peace and security in the world (MacAskill 2005).

How can one make sense of such antagonism? Have the mythmakers failed to deliver? Has the morality of the "war on terrorism" been exposed for what it is—a cloak for U.S. imperialism? What is the role of journalists in this process? The study *State of the News Media, 2004* by the Project for Excellence in Journalism in the United States reports: "Those who would manipulate the press and public appear to be gaining leverage over the journalists who cover them. Several factors point in this direction. One is simple supply and demand. As more outlets compete for their information, it becomes a seller's market for information" (Project for Excellence in Journalism 2005).

This dependence for information on official U.S. sources and the live broadcast of press conferences by American military commanders—often shown in their entirety on networks such as CNN—has been a key reason for the Pentagon's version of the war on terrorism being globalized. As a study of the *New York Times*'s coverage of foreign policy issues shows, this paper of record mainly recorded the official line on the Iraq situation, supporting the case for invasion by depending on unattributed and dubious sources. The editorial page of the newspaper, the study reports, never mentioned the words "UN Charter" or "international law" in any of its seventy editorials on Iraq from September 11, 2001, to March 20, 2003 (Friel and Falk 2004).

"Journalism," *The State of the News Media* notes, "is in the midst of an epochal transformation" (Project for Excellence in Journalism 2005). Advances in news technology, making dissemination of information cheaper, can ensure that other media outlets may challenge the U.S. myths about the war on terrorism. The growing importance of al-Jazeera, which has been used not only to expose the myths of Western morality but also to give space to Islamic myths about martyrdom, afflicting many a youth in the Muslim world, has made the global news space more complex (Seib 2004). The multiplicity of blogs and the talk of a "blogosphere" as an alternative site for global communication have further complicated the picture, changing the way many people produce and consume news (Hamilton and Jenner 2003; Welch 2003).

However, as the media outlets proliferate, the audience too is fragmenting and the gap between mediated and social realities remains as wide as before. With more than 150,000 of its troops stationed in Iraq and the expenditures on the invasion and occupation of that country reaching $200 billion, the United States seems to be in for a long haul in the name of "combating terrorism." More than half a century after the end of the Korean War, U.S. soldiers continue to be based in South Korea. In terms of loss of life, on the U.S. side the invasion and occupation of Iraq has been relatively easy to manage—139 American troops were killed and 542 wounded during the invasion (March 19–April 30, 2003); the number of troops killed since May 2003 stood at 1,226 as of January 2005, while 9,960 had been wounded (*Time* 2005, 29). On the plus side, the United States now has control over the world's second largest reserves of oil. It has successfully restructured Iraq's industrial infrastructure, privatizing it to suit mainly U.S. corporate clients (Ali 2003; Chatterjee 2004), and with the possibilities of extending the war on terrorism to Iran and elsewhere in the Muslim world, it can ensure that the need to create and circulate televised myths about "freedom from fear" will continue to dominate its public diplomacy. After all, "journalism is how people learn about the world beyond their direct experiences" (Project for Excellence in Journalism 2005), and if journalism—especially its televised version—is hijacked by U.S./British corporate–government synergy, one can be assured that the myths about the "war on terrorism" will continue to dominate media discourse.

REFERENCES

Ali, Tariq. 2003. *Bush in Babylon: The recolonisation of Iraq*. London: Verso.

Associated Press Television News (APTN). 2005. http://www.aptn.com.

BBC World. 2005. http://www.bbcworld.com/content/template_about.asp.

Blix, Hans. 2004. *Disarming Iraq*. New York: Pantheon.

Boyd-Barrett, Oliver. 1998. Media imperialism reformulated. In *Electronic empires: Global media and local resistance*, ed. Daya Kishan Thussu, 157–76. London: Arnold.

Bush, George W. 2005. State of the Union Address. Delivered to the U.S. Congress, Washington, D.C., February 2. Available at http://www.cnn.com/2005/ALLPOLITICS/02/02/sotu.transcript.7/index.html.

Channel 4. 2005. *Channel 4 News* (U.K.), special report on Fallujah, broadcast January 11, 7:00 P.M.

Chatterjee, Pratap. 2004. *Iraq, Inc.: A profitable occupation*. New York: Seven Stories Press.

CNN. 2005. http://www.cnn.com.

Curtis, Adam. 2004. *The power of nightmares*. Broadcast on BBC2, October 20, October 27, and November 3.

Eagleton, Terry. 1991. *Ideology: An introduction*. London: Verso.

Ferguson, Marjorie. 1992. The mythologies about globalization. *European Journal of Communication* 7:69–93.

Friel, Howard, and Richard Falk. 2004. *The record of the paper: How the* New York Times *misreports U.S. foreign policy*. London: Verso.

Goldenberg, Suzanne. 2005. Iraq breeding a new generation of professional terrorists, warns CIA report. *Guardian* (London). January 15.

Guardian. 2005. Babylon: Cultural vandalism. Editorial, *Guardian* (London), January 15.

Hamilton, John Maxwell, and Eric Jenner. 2003. The new foreign correspondence. *Foreign Affairs* 82, no. 5 (September/October).

Henley, Jon. 2004. "French CNN" to challenge U.S. view of world affairs. *Guardian* (London), December 10.

Hersh, Seymour M. 2005. The coming wars: What the Pentagon can now do in secret. *New Yorker*, January 24. Available at http://www.newyorker.com/fact/content/?050124fa_fact.

Hobsbawm, Eric J. 2004. Spreading democracy. *Foreign Policy*, September/October. Available at http://www.foreignpolicy.com/story/cms.php?story_id=2666.

Khalidi, Rashid. 2004. *Resurrecting empire: Western footprints and America's perilous path in the Middle East.* Boston: Beacon Press.

MacAskill, Ewen. 2005. World fears new Bush era. *Guardian* (London), January 20.

Mamdani, Mahmood. 2004. *Good Muslim, bad Muslim: America, the Cold War, and the roots of terror.* New York: Pantheon.

Pew Center. 2005. *Trends 2005.* Pew Research Center for the People and the Press, Washington, D.C. Available at http://people-press.org/commentary/display.php3?AnalysisID=104.

Project for Excellence in Journalism. 2005. *The state of the news media, 2004: An annual report on American journalism.* Washington, D.C.: Project for Excellence in Journalism. Available at http://www.stateofthenewsmedia.org/2005/index.asp.

Reuters Television. 2005. http://about.reuters.com/tv/tv/wns.htm.

Roberts, Les, Riyadh Lafta, Richard Garfield, Jamal Khudhairi, and Gilbert Burnham. 2004. Mortality before and after the 2003 invasion of Iraq: Cluster sample survey. *Lancet* 364, no. 9445 (October 30).

Said, Edward W. 1978. *Orientalism.* London: Routledge and Kegan Paul.

———. 1997. *Covering Islam: How the media and the experts determine how we see the rest of the world.* 2nd ed. New York: Vintage.

Sardar, Ziauddin, and Merryl Wyn Davies. 2004. *American dream, global nightmare.* London: Icon Books.

Seib, Philip. 2004. *Beyond the front lines: How the news media cover a world shaped by war.* New York: Palgrave Macmillan.

Simpson, John. 2003. Saddam: A dictator of mass destruction. In *The battle for Iraq: BBC news correspondents on the war against Saddam*, ed. Sara Beck and Malcolm Downing. London: BBC Books.

Thussu, Daya Kishan. 2000. *International communication: Continuity and change.* London: Arnold.

Time. 2005. Iraq: A status report. *Time*, January 31, p. 29.

Tunstall, Jeremy, and David Machin. 1999. *The Anglo-American Media Connection.* Oxford: Oxford University Press.

Welch, Matt. 2003. Blogworld: The new amateur journalists weigh in. *Columbia Journalism Review*, no. 5 (September/October).

2

Mediatizing the Global War on Terror: Television's Public Eye

Simon Cottle

On September 20, 2001, nine days after the 9/11 atrocities in the United States, President George W. Bush announced in his State of the Union Address his intentions to engage in a global "war on terror." He stated, "Our war on terror begins with al Qaeda, but it does not end there. It will not end until every terrorist group of global reach has been found, stopped and defeated" (cited in Tuman 2003, 96). This ill-defined but infinitely elastic definition of "war on terror" has, to date, led to wars in Afghanistan (2001) and Iraq (2003), with the ousting of the Taliban and Baathist regimes and the deaths of many thousands of combatants and innocent civilians. Acts of indiscriminate terror around the globe have continued since, including bombings in Bali (2002), Madrid (2004), Jakarta (2004), London (2005), and many other countries. The improbable links alleged between Saddam Hussein and al-Qaeda, like the existence of Iraqi weapons of mass destruction (WMD)—prominent justifications for the 2003 invasion—subsequently proved without foundation. The "successful" invasion of Iraq by the "coalition of the willing" has, however, unleashed a continuing reign of terror, including unspeakable acts of mediatized inhumanity by insurgents videoing hostages pleading for their lives and their beheading, assassinations, and suicide bombings. The Coalition, for its part, has become ensnared in protracted and deadly military operations aimed at quelling the continuing insurgency amid revelations of torture by military personnel in Abu Ghraib prison and elsewhere and the continuing incarceration of more than six hundred "terrorist suspects" without trial, in defiance of international law, at Guantanamo Bay. Condoleeza Rice, the new U.S. secretary of state, has publicly referred to the "long war" aimed at the "virulent threat" of global terrorism.

The 9/11 attacks and the U.S. government's self-declared war on terror, it seems, have decisively moved the world into a new and dangerous phase of globalized terror. State-sanctioned or "wholesale" terror has always accounted for the bulk of political killings, in comparison to insurgency or "retail" terror that includes, but is not confined to (much less explained by), the terrorism tactic of deliberately producing scenes of human carnage designed to shock, disseminate fear, and mobilize state responses. But the war on terror and its aftermath are in many respects unprecedented and speak to a new era best characterized perhaps as the global "migration of dreams and nightmares" (Nassar 2005). The U.S. war on terror, as much as its asymmetric enemies, has positioned "terror" at the center of the new world (dis)order—and global news agendas.

In this chapter I want to examine how television journalism has communicated this bloody and dangerous turn in world history. Specifically, I want to know how the "communicative architecture" of television journalism, its established cultural forms and communicative frames, has variously shaped the public representation and elaboration of this globalized conflict—a conflict often said to be conducted in our name and under the rubric of democracy.

But first, what do we know about the mediatization of terror? We know from detailed research that oft-heard assertions of the media "causing" terrorism, giving "oxygen to terrorism," or generating a terrorism "contagion effect" are simplistic and are often invoked as part of a state propaganda war that seeks to publicly depoliticize and delegitimize the aims of insurgents. This may be understandable given the threat posed by insurgents to the state's own existence and its monopoly of legitimate violence within a given territorial jurisdiction (Schlesinger 1991; Paletz and Schmid 1992; Cottle 1997). The semantic politics of "terrorism" and ascribed labels of "terrorist," inevitably, become a key part of this propaganda war, as can the deliberate tactic of terror designed to capture media attention and exposure (Tuman 2003; Nassar 2005). We also know that the media come under the most intense pressures from governments and military in times of insurgency (Curtis 1986; Rolston and Miller 1996; Miller 1994; Cottle 1997; Liebes 1997; Philo and Berry 2004) and war (Morrison and Tumber 1988; Glasgow University Media Group 1985; Kellner 1992; Taylor 1992; Harris 1994; Pedelty 1995; Knightley 2003; Hoskins 2004). The post 9/11 War on Terror, uneasily straddling both, has already proved to be no exception (Zelizer and Allan 2002; Thussu and Freedman 2003; Allan and Zelizer 2004; Miller 2004; Tumber and Palmer 2004; Van Der Veer and Munshi 2004; Kamalipour and Snow 2004).

A powerful confluence of controls and constraints helps explain the media tendency to succumb to cheerleading and consensual support of government aims in times of war and counterinsurgency. These include direct and indirect censorship, often involving military controls imposed on journalists in the field; routine news deference to political and military elites; deep-seated news values of drama, conflict, violence, human interest, and in the case of TV, visual spectacle; the commercial and competitive logics of the media and the pursuit of readers, ratings, and revenue; and the nature of "war" itself, which lends itself to cultural myths and the established "war genre" rich in narrative, drama, and marketable potential.

We also know that political dynamics, unfolding events on the ground, and the contingencies of particular wars also impact media representations. "Total wars" and "limited wars," "civil wars" and "insurgencies," "our wars" and "other people's wars," "humanitarian wars" and "degraded wars" all shape the nature of media representations (Carruthers 2000; Van Der Veer and Munshi 2004; Sonwalker 2004), as can reporting from different fronts, whether home, international, or the enemy's (Hallin 1997). The changing and/or fragmenting nature of elite consensus also opens up or closes down what Daniel Hallin has termed the media's "sphere of legitimate controversy," and this too conditions the extent to which the media publicly airs dissenting and oppositional views (Hallin 1986, 1994). This more politically dynamic and contingent view, in turn, has paved the way for interrogation of the complex interactions among political elites, the media, and various publics and how these can shift through time and condition media performance (Bennett 1990; Butler 1995; Wolfsfeld 1997; Robinson 2002; Entman 2004).

Less well explored is how established media forms "mediatize," that is, shape, facilitate, and condition the communication of conflicts, sometimes in the most decisive of ways. Only a few studies have sought to examine how different media, genres, and formats enact the public display and deliberation of opposing interests in times of war, insurgency, and terror. Fewer still have sought to seriously consider how some of these may provide opportunities for enhancing and deepening public understanding of the issues, interests, and identities at stake. Seminal studies here include analyses of the heavily symbolic and ritualized forms of press performance in the Troubles in Northern Ireland (Elliott 1980) and television's "discourses of terrorism" mediated through the more "open" spaces granted to oppositional voices and the discursively less predetermined or "tight" formats found in current affairs, documentary programs, and dramas (Elliott, Murdock, and Schlesinger 1986). David Altheide has also reported how "event-type" reports associated with regular evening news broadcasts tend to focus on the visuals of the aftermath and tactics of terrorism, while "topic-type" formats associated with interviews and documentary presentation are more likely to include materials about purposes, goals, and rationales, again pointing to the complexities and impact of media formats (Altheide 1987).

More recently, a study of British current affairs programs in the aftermath of 9/11 demonstrates how significant opportunities for public speech and wider deliberation were enacted by a minority of British programs, and how these constituted rare but meaningful "agorae" for the public airing and engagement of opposing views and did so at a time when a culture of fear and an emerging fortress mentality were influencing political discourse and legitimizing U.S. military responses (Cottle 2002). For example, exceptionally, one program used live satellite linkups to facilitate intercultural exchanges across geopolitical, cultural, and religious divides and momentarily brought together studio audiences based in New York and Islamabad not long after 9/11 and prior to the U.S. invasion of Afghanistan. Such rare moments proved electrifying and were "democratizing" in their provision of images and ideas, rhetoric and reasons, arguments and affect, emotions and experiences, discourses and debate silenced elsewhere.

Such programs, then, can potentially provide necessary resources for wider deliberation and contribute to deepening public understanding of conflicts and their contexts, consequences, and contending claims. They can perform an indispensable role in the "democratization of violence" (Keane 2004). When democracies are challenged by transnational "apocalyptic" terror, as well as by more traditional nationally based insurgency, it is imperative that state responses are measured and reasoned and that violent reactions which can lead to the exacerbation of terror and undermine democracy itself are publicly scrutinized and held to account. Public deliberation and debate at such times is vitally necessary if democracies are not to forfeit their democratic legitimacy by disproportionate or misjudged violence. John Keane argues convincingly that the democratization of violence requires, first and foremost, that we "always try to understand the motives and context of the violent" (2004, 167). What part, if any, has television journalism and its communicative forms played in "democratizing the violence" of the war on terror?

Let me state my position clearly at the outset. Contemporary television journalism, I believe, is Janus faced. As institution and industry, television is embedded within commercial logics and structures of dominance that often implicate it in times of conflict, as we have heard, in "propaganda war" (Herman and Chomsky 1988). Even so, in liberal democracies, a combination of normative expectations deeply embedded in civil societies, regulatory requirements, and the professional raison d'être of journalism itself, all mandate a central responsibility in the communicative enactment of democracy. This claim cannot be dismissed as entirely rhetorical or chimerical only, though it may well need to be bolstered and deepened in practice (Cottle 2005). In today's mediatized societies, where politics and conflicts are often played out on the media stage, television journalism matters and it may yet contain unrealized possibilities for deepening forms of democratic engagement.

I will now report on findings from a wider study of television journalism practiced in and across six "democracies" and by global satellite news providers and examine how the communicative architecture of contemporary television journalism has mediatized the war on terror and the contemporary maelstrom of terror around the globe.[1]

THE COMMUNICATIVE ARCHITECTURE
OF TELEVISION NEWS

At the heart of television journalism are a number of "communicative frames" routinely structuring the presentation and elaboration of news stories. These frames have become naturalized through time and, as we shall see, are widely (probably universally) deployed by television journalists around the world. They exhibit a communicative complexity that has yet to be recognized and properly assessed by researchers, and this proves consequential for the communication of conflicts and dissent generally, as well as the mediatized war on terror.

The communicative frames of television journalism serve to demonstrate a number of liberal-democratic claims embedded in the canons of journalism professionalism and practice, including providing information and social surveillance; demonstrating independence, balance, and impartiality; acting as a critical watchdog; and facilitating public discussion and opinion formation. They also permit much else besides, including giving voice to the powerful, occluding or marginalizing dissent, constructing consensus, championing causes, recognizing cultural differences, telling mythic tales, and bearing witness. This (Janus-faced) complexity will be demonstrated below and explored as it impacts on the mediatized war on terror. Conventional ideas about news "frames" are invariably discourse dependent and issue specific and, as such, are insufficiently cognizant of the communicative structures that routinely structure television news. These communicative complexities (and democratizing possibilities) are often lost from view, for example, by a reductionist understanding of news frames as necessarily involving a "preferred point of view" or "dominant discourse." As we shall see, the communicative frames of television journalism in fact exhibit far more complexity (and democratizing potential) than this—which is not to say that it is always enacted.

MEDIATIZING THE WAR ON TERROR:
COMMUNICATIVE FRAMES

Not surprisingly, television news deploys a number of communicative frames oriented to conflict. While each frame routinely structures the communication of conflicts in different ways, each principally does so in terms of propositions,

claims, contending claims, and arguments. Conflicts thereby assume propositional and analytical form, and these resources become available for wider
public deliberation. These communicative frames can be differentiated analytically as *dominant, contest, contention, campaigning*, and *exposé/investigative*
frames . Not all news is about conflicts and framed in such propositional ways
however, and some conflicts—the war on terror is no exception—can be communicatively structured consensually. These more consensual communicative
frames are based more on "cultural display" than "analytic deliberation" and
can be differentiated as *community service, collective interests, cultural recognition*, and *mythic tales*. While the content of some of these news presentations
may be premised on structural or hidden conflicts, these communicative frames
position them consensually with no obvious issue or contending perspective
in play. Unlike the conflict-driven and analytical frames, they tend to work
expressively or "culturally," moving from the semiotic to the symbolic and
mythic in keeping with their more "expressive" communicative mode. Finally,
two further news frames, *reporting* and *reportage*, can variously draw upon
both analytic/propositional and aesthetic/expressive or deliberative and display
modes of communication (see fig. 2.1).

To help illustrate how these conventionalized communicative frames impact the mediatized War on Terror and their possible contribution for, or denial
of, the necessary "democratization of violence," we can now turn to examples drawn from a large sample of television news programs broadcast in six
different countries over a two-week period, comprising 27 television channels, 4 international satellite providers, 56 different news programs, and 560

Figure 2.1. The Communicative Architecture of Television News

broadcast news programs. The sample consisted of 1,662 terror-related news items—17.2 percent of the total news sample of 9,662 broadcast news items gathered.[2]

Reporting

At the core of the historical evolution of television news and its current communicative architecture is the "classic" *reporting frame*. This instantly recognizable frame functions principally in terms of information conveyance and surveillance of current events consonant to the daily production cycles of television news. The events reported here can be conflictual or consensual in nature but they are communicatively framed in terms of providing up-to-date information and are generally, though not always, of short duration. This stock reporting frame, then, serves to ground journalism's professional mission "to inform" as well as lending some factual support to ideas about accuracy and even objectivity. It delivers, however, at best thin accounts of events, often without context, background, explanation, or competing definitions and accounts. Communicatively it privileges an epiphenomenal and disaggregated view of reality in which violent events and reactions, rather than underlying conditions, possible causes, or motivations, become the focal point. How this frame impacts the mediatization on the war on terror can be clearly seen in the following two illustrations.

ANCHOR: Overseas anti-government forces unleashed a powerful car bomb in the heart of Baghdad killing forty-seven people. More than one hundred others were wounded, many of them Iraqis waiting to apply for jobs on the police force. In another attack in Baquba, gunmen fired on a van carrying police home from work; twelve men were killed. Two groups linked to Al-Qaeda and led by Abu Mussab Al-Zarkawi are claiming responsibility. (*ABC News* [U.S.], September 14, 2004).

ANCHOR *(visuals: mug shots of several suspects, footage of the embassy blast)*: Indonesian police have arrested two men suspected of being involved in the bombing of the Australian embassy in Jakarta earlier this month. They have been identified as Isnu and Idnu. An Indonesian newspaper says an anti-terror squad arrested them in a coastal town in West Java on Friday. Officials are now looking for a third suspect who went through bomb-making training with the two. Their arrests bring to sixteen the number of people detained for questioning over the embassy blast. The suicide car bombing is blamed on the Al-Qaeda-linked Jemaah Islamiah. Nine people were killed and more than a hundred and eighty wounded. Police have named Malaysians Ashari Hussein and Noordin Mohammad Top as the main suspects. Both are still at large. (*CNA Asia Tonight* [Singapore], September 26, 2004).

Dominant

Closely aligned to, but deliberatively developing beyond the news-controlled reporting frame, is the *dominant frame*. This frame refers to news stories that are clearly dominated, that is, defined by a single external news source. This source may derive from authority, challenger, or other groups within the social hierarchy, but it is their perspective or views that clearly "dominate" the communicative frame and remains unopposed or receive, at most, token challenge. In the latter case, challenges are typically confined to responses that are prefigured by the agenda set by the dominant "framing" source. This frame, then, comes closest to the classic view of "primary definition" elaborated by Stuart Hall and his colleagues (Hall et al. 1978). While it need not in principle be taken to be dominated by institutional and political elites, in practice this is generally so, and by this means alternative or opposing views and arguments are communicatively occluded and silenced, as illustrated in the following.

ANCHOR: Meanwhile the top weapons inspector in Iraq, giving new details about the WMD Saddam did and did not have. Bret Baiere, the national security correspondent, and a Fox Report live now from the Pentagon. Bret.

REPORTER *(visuals: Saddam Hussein before and after capture, weapons inspectors, weapons found)*: U.S. officials told Fox News the Iraq Survey Group, the experts that had been hunting for weapons of mass destruction inside Iraq, will publish a final report soon. That report, the draft of that report, is still classified, but intelligence sources say it will state stockpiles of weapons have not been found but small laboratories have. Officials say there is no hard evidence yet that weapons were buried or transported out of the country. Sources tell Fox the ISG will conclude that Saddam Hussein had every intention to restart weapons production after international inspection subsided. In an exclusive interview with Fox's Sean Hannity, Secretary of State Colin Powell said that had always been understood inside the Bush administration, Hussein was the same animal.

SECRETARY OF STATE COLIN POWELL *(video clip)*: That Saddam Hussein never changed his spots. The man who gassed five thousand people one Friday morning in 1988 is the same man we took out of power last year. He never changed his spots. He had the intention; he had these mini laboratories that were humming away. He was keeping intact the infrastructure. Why? To make pesticides later or to make chemical weapons and biological weapons later. What would you put your money on?

REPORTER: Powell said President Bush refused to put the American people at that risk. You can see that exclusive interview with Secretary of State Powell on tonight's Hannity and Colmes, Nine, eastern time. *(Fox Report,* Fox News [Satellite], September 18, 2004).

Contest

Television news also presents news stories in terms of a *contest frame*. Here conflictual news stories are framed in terms of binary opposition, with opposing views and arguments generally given approximately equal weight or representation and structured in adversarial terms. While comment and criticism may also be delivered on these "contests" by accessed experts or "arbitrators," the frame nonetheless presents the conflict in terms of a fundamental opposition between two opposing sides or interests, and this structures the communicative frame.

> ANCHOR: A key campaign issue in the United States is Iraq and in a strong attack John Kerry has called the decision to attack Iraq a huge mistake. President Bush has hit back accusing his opponent of changing his position way too often.
>
> REPORTER: Just a day before George Bush spells out key foreign policy goals at the UN, Democratic presidential rival John Kerry is using his platform in New York to launch his most scathing attack yet on Bush's Iraq War.
>
> SENATOR JOHN KERRY *(video clip)*: The President misled, miscalculated and mismanaged every aspect of this undertaking and he has made the achievement of our objective, a stable Iraq secure within its borders with a representative government, far harder to achieve than it ever should have been.
>
> REPORTER: Senator Kerry reminded his audience a thousand Americans had died in Iraq and that Bush's task is to get the international community to ease America's burden. With only six weeks until the Presidential vote, polls show Bush inching ahead of Kerry so the President decided to hit back.
>
> PRESIDENT GEORGE W. BUSH *(video clip)*: Today my opponent continued his pattern of twisting in the wind. With new contradictions of his old positions on Iraq. He apparently woke up this morning and has now decided, no, we should not have invaded Iraq after just last month saying he still would have voted for force, even knowing everything we know today. Incredibly, he now believes our national security would be stronger with Saddam Hussein in power not in prison.
>
> REPORTER: For now the world will be watching to see if President Bush has more to offer than the political sparring on Iraq during his speech. (*NDTV Evening News* [India], September 21, 2004).

Contention

Further conflictual complexity is encapsulated within the television news *contention frame*. Here an increased array of voices or perspectives may be represented, in contrast to only two opposed views as above. The contention frame is not confined to the elaboration of conflictual currents that circulate within or around deep oppositions and "contests" but also serves to capture the more nuanced and qualifying engagements of different interests and identities that variously debate, criticize, or contend, without necessarily fundamentally opposing some state of affairs, interest, or perspective. The following item about the kidnapping of Ken Bigley in Iraq was presented in terms of a contention frame where different political views and perspectives became canvassed amid the confusion of developments on the ground. The item began as follows:

ANCHOR: Good evening. This is the time of night the families of those kidnapped in Iraq have learned to dread, the time when we start to get first reports that a captive has been killed with great brutality. But tonight the gunmen chose a different, clearly political, ploy. They forced British hostage Ken Bigley publicly to plead with Tony Blair to save his life. The recording was then put on an extremist website.

KENNETH BIGLEY *(video recording)*: I don't want to die. I don't deserve it and neither do the women who are imprisoned. . . . Please, please release the female prisoners that are held in American prisons. Please help them. I need you to help me, Mr. Blair, because you are the only person now on God's earth that I can speak to.

ANCHOR: One of Ken Bigley's brothers, Paul, said tonight that at least the video proves Ken is still alive. The day has also been one of confusion with one Iraqi ministry saying two women prisoners would be released and the Americans asserting quite the opposite.

Robin Denselow reports on the day's events and on the underlying question of "Who really runs Iraq?" *(Newsnight,* BBC2 [UK], September 22, 2004).

Exposé/Investigation

The *exposé/investigation* frame conforms to the idealized liberal democratic role of journalism as public watchdog and self-proclaimed champion of the Fourth Estate. Here journalists actively set out to investigate, expose, and uncover information and practices that would not otherwise be revealed within the public domain. This frame includes, therefore, traditional investigative journalism based on intensive research and exploratory fact-finding as well as exposé journalism of public or private affairs. The sample included very few examples of exposé/investigation, notwithstanding the enormity of government spin and misinformation that has attended the war on terror and an earlier major exposé that had challenged the legitimacy of the British government and ricocheted through other Coalition governments. The David Kelly affair, it will be recalled, had brought to light allegations that the British government had deliberately "sexed up" intelligence reports about the existence of WMD in Iraq as a way of legitimizing an invasion, allegations vehemently resisted by the government and which eventuated in the suicide of Dr. David Kelly, an expert witness who had been interviewed by the BBC. Such investigative journalism, as we shall see, is statistically rare indeed. The following example develops on a newspaper undercover operation, exposing the lack of security in the British Houses of Parliament.

REPORTER *(visuals: postcards of London, security officers, front page coverage of* Sun *reporter)*: The Houses of Parliament, the iconic view of London and a thousand postcards, the seat of democracy and, precisely because of that, a target for terrorists. The leader of the House was told when he took over his job last year that Al Qaeda operatives had been focusing on Parliament. Officials told him they were seriously worried about an anthrax or ricin attack. Yet today another breech of security has emerged. Even as policing at Westminster was being tightened following the invasion of hunt protesters, a *Sun* reporter claimed that yesterday he could have blown up the Commons from inside. It was the culmination of a four-month undercover investigation. . . .

Back in May just days after the purple flour demonstration by the Fathers for Justice campaigners prompted a review of security in the House of Parliament, the *Sun* reporter, Anthony France, applied for a job as a waiter in the Commons through a catering recruitment agency. Asked at the interview for past catering experience, he named two fictitious restaurants. As referees, he gave the mobile phone numbers of two journalist colleagues. No contact was made with them. But on the common security questionnaire Mr. France, who has a press pass issued by the police, listed correct details of his name, date of birth, and past addresses. *(Channel 4 News* [UK], September 17, 2004)

Campaigning

A further communicative frame also rarely deployed in the mediatized war on terror is the *campaigning frame*. This frame, often more closely associated with the partisan press (and consumer campaigns headed by populist TV news magazines), involves the media actively and explicitly campaigning for a cause or issue and advocating action or change beyond the world of journalism. The lack of campaigning frames in this sample is not to suggest, of course, that supportive or critical views have not been deliberately marshaled by the news media in support of a particular viewpoint (see, for instance, examples from the Fox News Channel).

Emergent elements of a possible campaigning frame deployed by some sections of the media can be detected in the following, though this falls short of a full-on, media-led campaign.

ANCHOR: Well, on the line now from Amsterdam, Paul Bigley, brother of Ken Bigley, that British subject being held hostage in Iraq. Thanks very much for joining us; I know this is a very difficult time for you so we appreciate this enormously. Mr. Bigley, how are you coping and how have the two developments in the last twenty-four hours, the killing of Jack Hensley and the release of a woman prisoner in Iraq, affected your hopes and fears?

PAUL BIGLEY: May I first take this opportunity to offer my deepest condolences to the family of Eugene and Jack for this horrible slaying. To answer your question, this is a step in the right direction. It's a step that should have been taken days ago. . . .

ANCHOR: Do you consider this as an adequate response to you and your family's desperate appeal to Prime Minister Tony Blair to intervene?

PAUL BIGLEY: I have great respect for Mr. Blair. I understand his diplomacy factors and things like that, but at the end of the day there are lives at stake here. . . . And I have been speaking through people I know in the Middle East and they have been kind enough to translate my pleas and my statements to Arabic and these have flooded the airways in the whole of the Gulf, so I am just hoping and praying that our efforts, including your kind efforts and also the press's in the UK will bring about a gram of decency and offer some salvage for Ken. (*World News Asia*, CNN International [Satellite], September 22, 2004)

Community Service

Also going beyond the classic news reporting frame is the *community service frame*, where the news media explicitly advise the audience on what new information actually means and how it impacts on them. Here the news media may take on a more advisory or service-oriented role. Information that is essentially consensual (as opposed to conflictual, which would suggest a media-led exposé/investigative frame) is represented as useful or "good advice" and may be presented in a pedagogic fashion. Often associated with consumer issues, here it is deployed in respect of the War on Terror:

ANCHOR: The State Attorney General's Office and the University of Medicine and Dentistry of New Jersey are offering new support services for any resident still suffering trauma, anxiety and other problems from the September 11 terrorist attacks. Desiree Taylor has the story:

REPORTER *(visuals: firefighters clearing debris of 9/11 attacks)*: For some people feelings of shock, horror and fear still persist three years after the terrorist attacks. Health professionals say it is not just those who lost loved ones that day who are impacted, even people with an indirect connection may have been traumatized.

ASSISTANT STATE ATTORNEY GENERAL PATRICIA PREZIOSO: What happened at the World Trade Center on September 11th, 2001, was the largest crime scene that this country has ever had, and much like when we service all victims who witness violent crimes the victims, the New Jersey residents, the New York City residents, need assistance, too.

REPORTER *(visuals: footage of help center, people answering phones assisting callers)*: Any resident looking for assistance can now find it through a new 24-hour hotline. The phones are manned by health professionals . . . who can make clinical assessments and refer callers to counseling services if needed. All free of charge. (*NJN News*, PBS [U.S.], September 13, 2004)

Collective Interests

Like the community service frame, the *collective interests frame* also structures representation consensually. However, here news stories do not simply report on news events or provide advice but rather elaborate and visualize collective interests through their identification of "common interest" subject matter, often embodying and/or prescribing shared communal values and sentiments. This too was put to work in the mediatized war on terror.

ANCHOR 1: Christians and Muslims were united in prayer tonight in Ken Bigley's hometown of Liverpool where the agonizing wait for news continues. . . .

ANCHOR 2: The local newspaper, *The Echo*, has been inundated with hundreds of messages of support for Ken, not just from Liverpuddlians but from people across the world.

ANCHOR 1: Tim Rogers is in Liverpool for us tonight. Tim.

REPORTER *(visuals: call to prayer and service at a Liverpool mosque)*: Well, it is the eighth day of the endurance test that this family is facing. But time probably has very little meaning for them. Every hour willing Ken Bigley home; a sentiment shared today by a city's prayers. In this city the Muslim call to prayer today was also a call for Ken Bigley's freedom. Here the faithful were reminded that Islam is a religion of peace and mercy forbidding kidnapping, torture or murder and that their prayers should include Ken Bigley and his family.

REPORTER *(visuals: text of newspaper)*: In the local newspaper this evening there are expressions of sympathy from around the world. From Canberra, Australia, this, saying, "With thousands and thousands of others, I am praying continuously for Ken and all of you." And this from Norway, "I only hope that the captors show as much compassion for Ken as the zeal in which they fight for their cause." But it is in Liverpool tonight where the family's plight is most keenly felt and where, in the quiet moments of contemplation, the silent prayers continue to be for the safe return for this city's son . . . . (*ITV News* [UK], September 24, 2004)

Cultural Recognition

The *cultural recognition frame* serves to evoke and appeal to notions of cultural identity and cultures of difference by, inter alia, acknowledging and/or celebrating the events, individuals, or groups represented. This consensual frame, then, can variously be deployed to display and endorse views of multicultural difference (very broadly conceived) or implicitly reassert monocultural conceptions of cultural homogeneity. While the war on terror readily draws lines between "Us" and "Them" and threatens to further marginalize minority groups already distanced as "Other" within imagined national communities, the cultural recognition frame works to recognize and affirm their cultural position consensually.

> ANCHOR: A new kind of must-see TV, a brainstorm that quickly became a broadcasting reality but might never have happened at all had there never been a September 11. It is called "Bridges TV." It is named that for a reason. It is the very first American Muslim television network to be broadcast in the English language.
>
> NBC's Ron Allan tonight.
>
> REPORTER: Broadcasting to the world, it's the TV industry's newest experiment, "Bridges TV," billing itself the American Muslim lifestyle network. Featuring movies, documentaries, cartoons 24 hours a day in English about Islam and life for America's estimated 8 million Muslim citizens. Often poking fun at stereotypes. . . .
>
> It's the brainchild of Asia Zubair, an architect, and her husband Muzzammil Hassan, a banker, who are disturbed that negative images of Muslims seem to dominate TV especially since 9/11.
>
> ASIA ZUBAIR *(visuals: Osama bin Laden, violence in the Middle East)*: I did not want my kids growing up to watch Muslims being portrayed as terrorists.
>
> MUZZAMMIL HASSAN: I hope, long-term, Bridges TV can play a role towards a better understanding between America and Islam. (*NBC Nightly News* [U.S.], December 9, 2004)

Mythic Tales

The *mythic tales frame* displays and activates cultural myths that have resonance for contemporary cultures. This communicative frame, then, is not principally about imparting new information but communicating, often through heavy symbolism and emotion, preexistent values and narratives that draw from the deep cultural reservoirs that exist within all communities. These mythic tales may focus on individuals, groups, places, or objects that symbolize values or ideals that are exceptional or extraordinary in some way or that are felt, normatively, to be culturally meaningful. The mediatized funeral of Chris Engledrum, a U.S. soldier killed in Iraq, was communicatively framed to display and discharge such feelings.

ANCHOR *(visuals: funeral procession, coffin draped in American flag)*: Here in New York today an emotional funeral for a man who, as a firefighter, answered the call on 9/11 only to die as a soldier fighting for his country. NBC's Mike Taibbi tonight on a man who was a hero to his family and to his band of brothers both here and overseas.

REPORTER *(visuals: Engledrum steadying the American flag, fighting in the Gulf war, Engledrum posing with fellow firefighters)*: They gathered by the thousands to pay their last respects, most of them firemen but scores of national guardsmen, too, because 39-year-old Chris Engledrum wore both uniforms with gusto and honor. He was the steadying hand in a famous photograph of exhausted firemen raising a tattered flag into the ruins of the Trade Towers and he was a Gulf War veteran who chose to fight in another war a dozen years later and who, on one of Baghdad's especially bad days last week, was killed by a roadside bomb.

No one who knew Chris Engledrum was surprised that he put on his other uniform again, even at his age. In fact, more than a hundred New York City firemen, not all of them young, have now seen active duty in Iraq. Among them, Fire Department Lieutenant and Army Reserve Colonel Neil Scarrow, eleven months in Iraq.

FELLOW SOLDIER/FIREFIGHTER: Doing that as a military, or firefighter or police officer to me basically serves the same purpose.

REPORTER: Which made the loss the same for whoever wore either of Engelwood's uniforms.

FELLOW FIREFIGHTER PAUL ALLEN: This is a family, an extended family, um, I lost a brother. *(Allen gets very emotional has difficulty continuing sentence.)*

REPORTER: A Senator, a Governor, a Mayor and an ex-Mayor all paid their respects for a father of two whose wife is pregnant with a third child and whose oldest son Shaun seemed to speak the thoughts of so many others.

SHAUN ENGLEDRUM *(visuals: son's emotional speech at his father's funeral)*: My Dad was always there when I needed help.

REPORTER: The first out of the rig, the last to leave the scene.

FELLOW FIREFIGHTER DAN FINNEGAN: Every time an alarm comes across you wish he was right there with you.

REPORTER: And the first New York firefighter to die in a war he believed began two Septembers ago. A final journey tomorrow to Arlington National Cemetery, where only heroes are laid to rest. *(NBC Nightly News* [U.S.], December 9, 2004)

Reportage

The *reportage frame* can represent issues and events either conflictually or consensually and can communicatively do so through display/expressive and/or deliberative/analytic modes of representation. Here, however, the communicative frame serves to provide the means for generating deeper understanding by going behind the scenes of "thin" news reports and providing "thick" descriptions of reality (Geertz 1973; Cottle 2005). The reportage frame, given its affinity with documentary modes (Nichols 1991), invariably makes use of film and visuals as well as personal testimonies and thereby positions itself (and us as viewers) as "bearing witness." Reportage often "moves"—performatively, diachronically, and emotionally—from the *indicative* to the *subjunctive* in its story treatment, from "what is" to "what ought to be." Communicatively, this represents a relatively elaborate and often powerful frame for the exploration of conflicts and their origins, dynamics, and impact. Two short extracts suffice here to help illustrate this analytical and expressive capacity.

REPORTER *(visuals: ambulance pierced with shrapnel, large bloodstain on the pavement)*: In Fallujah, residents picked through the aftermath of what was supposed to be a strike on associates of suspected Al-Qaeda operative Abu Mussab Al Zarkawi. Locals say many innocent people were caught up in the carnage, including five patients, two nurses and a driver—all killed when an American missile hit an ambulance.

To the north of the country, there is frustration as American marines and Iraqi forces prevent residents returning to their homes in the besieged city of Tal Afar.

IRAQI GUARDSMAN *(translated with voiceover by reporter; visuals: roadblock at Tal Afar, guardsman)*: "Brothers, leave this location," says an Iraqi guardsman by loud hailer. "We allow residents to get out but we don't allow them in."

REPORTER *(visuals: injured man taken away on stretcher)*: It's unclear how many have been killed here, but corpses reportedly litter the streets and essential services such as water and electricity have collapsed. The U.S. says the town, populated mainly by ethnic Turkmen, is a base for foreign militants but Turkey insists that excessive force is being used against the civilian population.

TURKISH FOREIGN MINISTER ABDUL AGU *(translated with voiceover by reporter; visuals: interview)*: "We have been in contact with American authorities at the highest level for the operations to stop," says Turkey's Foreign Minister Abdul Agu. "If it continues, Turkey's cooperation on issues regarding Iraq will come to a total halt."

REPORTER: If Turkey did end cooperation with the U.S., it could have a serious impact. As well as supplying logistical help, Turkey is a major trade and supply route into the country. (*SBS World News* [Australia], September 14, 2004).

ANCHOR: Iraq's turbulent history has left the country with a large group of orphaned children and with a government in the middle of a tough transition. Its institutions are also changing as well. Diana Muriel visited a shelter in Baghdad to learn more about Iraq's street kids. . . .

AHKMED *(translated with voiceover by reporter)*: "I was locked up," he says. "They would beat us. We went hungry. There was nothing, no food. . . ."

REPORTER *(visuals: other street kids in Baghdad, Dohah huddled with her buddies in the bushes just out of range of the police)*: But here [at the shelter]

Ahkmed can relax. But hundreds of kids here in Baghdad haven't been as lucky as Ahkmed. The reality for the rest of them is the daily hustle on the street in a struggle just to survive. Seven-year-old Dohah is taking a break from begging with her buddies. But the game comes to an abrupt halt when the police show up. Stiff with fright, the kids wait it out. Baghdad street kids live in constant fear of the authorities. In fear, too, of their parents, if they have them. Bahdle says he ran away from home after his father beat him.

BAHDLE *(translated with voiceover by reporter)*: "They said I had to work every day to bring us money," he says. "They wanted ten bucks a day and I just couldn't get that." (*World News*, CNN International [Satellite], September 17, 2004)

MEDIATIZING THE WAR ON TERROR: GLOBAL NEWS ARCHITECTURE

As we can see there is considerable complexity in the communicative frames of television news and how these have communicatively impacted the mediatized war on terror. We can now pursue this further with the help of table 2.1, which documents comparatively the general patterns of communicative frames deployed across the sample and with respect to the war on terror. Television news, evidently, is communicatively structured by a common architecture that is internally and complexly differentiated and exerts consequences on the mediatization of conflicts.

The reporting frame, delivering "thin" updates and information on events in the war on terror, accounts for half of all news terror items (50.7%)— 10 percent less than news generally. This difference, however, is mostly accounted for by the increased use of the dominant frame (23.6%). Together these two communicative frames produce a predominance of news oriented within the sphere of event coverage and dominant definitions (74.3%). All countries have deployed the dominant frame in the war on terror considerably more often than they have across their general news coverage. Given the global importance and profound consequences of the war on terror for so many combatants, civilian populations, and countries around the globe, as much as its essentially conflictual nature, such systematic closure to wider perspectives, accounts, and arguments can only be seen as injurious to democracy.

Contest and contention frames, at 8.7 percent and 10.3 percent, respectively, indicate that most of the conflict and contention infused in the war on terror and securing explicit public engagement is confined, for the most part, to 19.0 percent of all news items. Exposé/investigation and campaigning frames comprise a mere 0.3 percent of all news items, notwithstanding the urgent need to dig deeper into the policies, practices, and public claims that inform the war

Table 2.1. Mediatized Terror and Global News Architecture

Communicative Frames	Australia War on T Freq	%	Australia All Items Freq	%	USA War on T Freq	%	USA All Items Freq	%	UK War on T Freq	%	UK All Items Freq	%	India War on T Freq	%	India All Items Freq	%
Reporting	194	56.2	1,352	60.6	114	42.7	641	56.4	100	42.0	612	52.7	58	48.3	588	56.6
Dominant	53	15.4	187	8.4	54	20.2	114	10.0	82	34.5	195	16.8	45	37.5	198	19.1
Contest	39	11.3	173	7.8	31	11.6	86	7.6	6	2.5	22	1.9	5	4.2	39	3.8
Contention	50	14.5	122	5.5	37	13.9	89	7.8	39	16.4	126	10.8	5	4.2	63	6.1
Exposé/Investigation	0	0.0	6	0.3	1	0.4	5	0.4	2	0.8	4	0.3	0	0.0	1	0.1
Campaigning	0	0.0	9	0.4	0	0.0	3	0.3	0	0.0	5	0.4	0	0.0	1	0.1
Community Service	0	0.0	53	2.4	2	0.7	44	3.9	0	0.0	17	1.5	0	0.0	9	0.9
Collective Interests	3	0.9	249	11.2	3	1.1	84	7.4	3	1.3	121	10.4	1	0.8	105	10.1
Cultural Recognition	0	0.0	8	0.4	3	1.1	12	1.1	1	0.4	8	0.7	0	0.0	16	1.5
Mythic Tales	0	0.0	42	1.9	13	4.9	14	1.2	0	0.0	30	2.6	2	1.7	9	0.9
Reportage	6	1.7	30	1.3	9	3.4	45	4.0	5	2.1	22	1.9	4	3.3	10	1.0
Total	345	100.0	2,231	100.0	267	100.0	1,137	100.0	238	100.0	1,162	100.0	120	100.0	1,039	100.0

Communicative Frames	Singapore War on T Freq	%	Singapore All Items Freq	%	South Africa War on T Freq	%	South Africa All Items Freq	%	Satellite TV War on T Freq	%	Satellite TV All Items Freq	%	Total War on T Freq	%	Total All Items Freq	%
Reporting	96	56.8	651	56.2	30	54.5	389	58.7	250	53.4	1,507	66.3	842	50.7	5,740	59.4
Dominant	47	27.8	147	12.7	9	16.4	71	10.7	102	21.8	246	10.8	392	23.6	1,158	12.0
Contest	9	5.3	44	3.8	2	3.6	24	3.6	53	11.3	162	7.1	145	8.7	550	5.7
Contention	13	7.7	51	4.4	11	20.0	67	10.1	16	3.4	48	2.1	171	10.3	566	5.9
Exposé/Investigation	0	0.0	0	0.0	0	0.0	0	0.0	0	0.0	0	0.0	3	0.2	16	0.2
Campaigning	0	0.0	1	0.1	0	0.0	2	0.3	2	0.4	4	0.2	2	0.1	25	0.3
Community Service	0	0.0	51	4.4	0	0.0	5	0.8	0	0.0	33	1.5	2	0.1	212	2.2
Collective Interests	4	2.4	196	16.9	0	0.0	71	10.7	5	1.1	100	4.4	19	1.1	926	9.6
Cultural Recognition	0	0.0	7	0.6	0	0.0	8	1.2	1	0.2	18	0.8	5	0.3	77	0.8
Mythic Tales	0	0.0	5	0.4	0	0.0	13	2.0	0	0.0	11	0.5	15	0.9	124	1.3
Reportage	0	0.0	5	0.4	3	5.5	13	2.0	39	8.3	143	6.3	66	4.0	268	2.8
Total	169	100.0	1,158	100.0	55	100.0	663	100.0	468	100.0	2,272	100.0	1662	100.0	9,662	100.0

on terror. A further 2.4 percent of all items are framed in respect of consensual frames of community service, collective interests, cultural recognition, and mythic tales, often domesticating and privatizing and lending, as we have seen, "human interest" to dominant agendas and definitions. While the essentially conflictual nature of the war on terror is unlikely to lead to a similar use of community service and collective interests frames as in general news coverage, it is noticeable that precisely at the moment when cultural recognition of difference is likely to come under threat by a social imaginary of exclusion and "Othering," the frame of cultural recognition finds reduced use.

Though still in a minority, an increased number of news items are communicatively framed within the deeper parameters of reportage (4.0%), and here international satellite providers have noticeably provided more (8.3%) than other country-based news services. This communicative frame, as we have begun to see above, is capable of providing on-the-ground accounts, deeper analysis, and humanistic insights—all much needed if we are to better understand, make sense of, and politically respond to the contemporary maelstrom of terror. Perhaps here are seeds of hope, of the "democratization of violence"? Here at least the ontological view of violence produced in the reporting frame—visualized as incessant, universal, ahistorical without political context or motivation—combined with the tendency of dominant frames to relay elite views that often delegitimize, pathologize, and demonize insurgents, finds a possible counterbalance. In such communicative frames, a politics of pity—or a politics of shame—may even find sustenance: "By portraying uncivil acts as deeply contingent, as 'man-made' events with culprits and victims, they encourage audiences to live for a while in the subjunctive sense" (Keane 2004, 197), and when deployed alongside more obviously analytical and argumentative frames of contest and contention, possibilities for deliberation and the democratization of violence may be at hand.

These general patterns, then, point both to the internal complexities and differentiations of television news as a globally deployed architecture as well as its delimitations and democratizing possibilities when used to communicatively frame the war on terror.[3]

MEDIATIZING THE WAR ON TERROR: EXPANDING THE PUBLIC EYE?

Notwithstanding the existence of communicative frames that, potentially at least, could serve to expand and deepen the public eye of television, we have seen how these have found marginal deployment within and across television news journalism in six countries and global satellite providers. But there is

Table 2.2   Current Affairs/Documentaries and the War on Terror

Country	Programs	Items	War on Terror Items
Australia	48	143	21 (14.7%)
India	21	39	6 (15.4%)
Satellite	100	238	69 (28.9%)
Singapore	9	21	5 (23.8%)
South Africa	38	71	5 (7.0%)
United Kingdom	48	138	18 (13.0%)
United States	40	90	18 (20.0%)
Total	304	740	142 (19.2%)

Source: Summary of all current affairs/documentary programs broadcast September 13–26, 2004. Percentages refer to percentage of items within each country or the combined satellite providers CNN International, BBC World, Sky News, Fox News.
Note: Some programs comprise more than one item.

more to television journalism than television news, so here we must attend, if only briefly, to other communicative forms of television journalism and see how these too may have opened up, or closed down, the public eye on the war on terror. Across the two-week sample collected from our six selected countries and satellite services, all current affairs programs and documentaries broadcast were recorded. This produced the sample shown in table 2.2.

As with television news and its massive weighting toward the war on terror (17.2%)—with one war-related news item, on average, encountered out of every five or six news items—this theme finds great prominence in our sample of current affairs and documentary programs. Here program items comprise nearly a fifth of all current affairs and documentary items (19.2%). These programs and program items, based on this two-week sample, serve to demonstrate something of the available variety and communicative forms of established program genres and how these too have informed the mediatization of global terror. Clearly these individual programs deserve more qualitative and typological analysis than is possible here, and these also need to be pursued comparatively across countries, time, and the changing contexts of public service and commercial broadcasting (the majority of these program forms having been produced by satellite and national public service channels). Nonetheless, something of the range, diversity, and communicative shaping of the mediatized war on terror can be addressed, and here we can usefully compare to what extent and how such program forms have departed from or reinforced dominant news agendas and possibly opened or closed television's public eye on globalized terror.

The majority of the sample programs have pursued dominant news agendas and focused on international terrorism and the perceived threat that it poses to civilian populations. These have done so through the use of studio interview and discussion formats (*Insight*, ABC [Australia], September 14) and have frequently debated with politicians and so-called terrorism experts the threat posed by regional terrorist networks (*Insight*, CNA [Singapore], September 22). Documentary biographies of wanted terrorists such as Abu Musab al-Zarqawi (*60 Minutes*, CBS [U.S.], September 26), as well as docudramas enacting hypothetical scenarios of terrorist attacks, sustain similar agendas (*Dirty War*, BBC1 [UK], September 26). Some documentaries, however, have departed from this dominant agenda by returning to earlier terrorist outrages, such as the IRA bombing of the Conservative party conference in Brighton twenty years earlier, and explored the bombers' motives (*The Brighton Bomb*, BBC1 [UK], September 14), while others have pursued the human consequences for the victims of earlier IRA bombings and how some of these victims now feel about the convicted perpetrators (*Storyville: My Terrorist*, BBC2 [UK], September 15).

Other documentary and current affairs programs explored the contemporary contexts and sense of injustice felt by many and which leads them to take up insurgency and commit terrorist acts (*Inside Ramallah*, NDTV [India], September 16; *Storyville: This Is Palestine*, BBC2 [UK], September 14), and others, also based on personal testimonies and experiential accounts, explore personalized military experiences and perspectives (*Now by Bill Moyers*, PBS [U.S.], September 17). A few programs also reflexively consider the media's own response to the war on terror both in the West and the Middle East (*International Correspondents*, CNNI [U.S.], September 26).

These and other programs, then, have collectively begun to expand the range of accessed voices and views and thereby to provide different perspectives on the war on terror. They have done so through the established and evolving communicative architecture of contemporary television. While many of these programs take their lead from dominant news agendas, as illustrated in the dominant frame example provided earlier, embedded in the communicative architecture of different program forms are nonetheless opportunities that can, and sometimes do, help to expand the public eye on the war on terror. Four examples will suffice to indicate something of the ways in which this variegated communicative architecture has been deployed in practice and how it can sometimes produce invaluable resource for deepening public understanding.

Increasingly, television programs make use of new interactive capabilities—e-mail, phone-ins, polls—and deliberately encourage audience feedback and response to topics in the news or following studio discussion with invited guests. These formats invariably set the agenda through defining (and thereby delimiting) the topic under consideration as well as controlling "turn-taking" and the different qualitative opportunities for dialogue and speech. Even so, these same formats, as in the example below, can sometimes contribute to an expanded array of opinions which may even, on occasion, agenda-shift or recontextualize the informing political and program presuppositions. Consider the following from the BBC World program *Talking Point* (September 26, 2004):

> HOST: Welcome to *Talking Point*, I'm Robin Lustig and we are broadcasting on BBC television, radio and the Internet. Our subject this week, the kidnappings in Iraq. More than a hundred foreigners have been abducted in the past six months and more than twenty of them have been murdered. Among them two Americans, Eugene Armstrong and Jack Hensley, both killed within the past week. Still being held, their colleague Ken Bigley, two French journalists, two Italian aid workers, Macedonians, Jordanians and people from many other countries. What do you think can be done? Should governments be more prepared to negotiate or would negotiation only encourage more kidnaps? This is your chance to have your say, here's how *(information appears on screen regarding phone, e-mail, and SMS text messaging contacts).*
>
> PRESENTER: Well our guest today is Terry Waite, who knows more about negotiating on behalf of hostages and being a hostage than most people do....
>
> We've had many thousands of emails already from people who are concerned about the situation and have got a lot of people who want to talk to us on the telephone as well....
>
> CALLER: Sajida Bandukwala, Karachi, Pakistan. With all due respect to your guest and for those others who have been kidnapped, while I totally condemn these types of kidnappings ... I feel that the Americans are waging an unfair war against people who are not as developed or as sophisticated, and they cannot fight this war the way the West fights this war. And I suppose that is one of the reasons that they fight it the way they know best.

While the BBC World satellite program above has managed to involve geographically dispersed and politically divergent views, other national-based programs have deliberately sought to reflect on the regional implications and responses of the war on terror. Consider this excerpt from South Africa's *African Journal*:

> HOST: On the third anniversary of the terrorist attacks in the U.S., response to the attacks has been an American-led global war on terrorism. Experts say the global threat of terrorism demands a global response and shortly after the attacks some African countries overwhelmingly expressed their support for the efforts on the war against terrorism. The opponents to the counter-terrorism approach in Africa say that some African governments are using tactics designed to fight terror to also silence domestic opponents and critiques. In just a moment my guests and I will discuss the following: Where does Africa stand in the war on terrorism three years later? What is the African view of the war on terrorism? *(African Journal, SABC [South Africa], September 16, 2004)*

Lest we assume that all current affairs and documentary programs depart from dominant political agendas, however—which many certainly do not— we can also acknowledge the ideologically powered use of filmic codes and impact of visual dramatization in certain program forms, and how these add emotional intensity to the events depicted.

HOST *(visuals: host dressed in fatigues, helmet in hand leaning against a tank; footage of battles)*: I'm Oliver North. This is *War Stories* coming to you from a Marine base in Iraq. We're here with the Second Battalion, Fourth Marines, the unit that has inflicted more damage on the enemies of democracy and taken more casualties than any other in Operation Iraqi Freedom. Tonight we'll take you along on the dangerous missions the one thousand marines of 2-4 run every day. We're there when they're ambushed by the enemy and you'll see firsthand how our troops respond to these deadly attacks. From IEDs [improvised explosive devices] that detonate without warning, to hours-long gunfights in enemy-held buildings at a hundred and twenty degrees. It's the anatomy of battle in the war on terror. . . .

HOST *(visuals: ongoing battle, Marine captain limping with bloodied cheek staying in charge)*: Though badly wounded with shrapnel in his face, arms and leg, Carton refused to leave his men.

MARINE CAPTAIN: He didn't want to go and I wasn't going to ask him to go. That's something that you just don't do, you don't ask the commander to leave his command. And the Captain stayed in the fight until the end. . . .

HOST: Mark, when you think about that moment when you almost got killed, does that make you rethink what you're doing out here?

MARINE CAPTAIN: Not at all. If for nothing else, I'm out there because those boys are out there. So there's no other place for me. (*War Stories: Under Fire in Iraq*, Fox News, September 20, 2004)

While Oliver North's brand of close-up-and-personal patriotism may, for some, be considered to be a peculiarly myopic public eye on the war on terror, and one seemingly blinded to the wider politics that drive such military adventures, it nonetheless exhibits a different and possibly revealing insight into the nature of military thinking played out on the ground in Iraq and in the Fox News program presentations.

Finally, an example of a celebrated British current affairs genre in which audiences pose preselected questions to a studio audience of invited guests and, occasionally, respond and intervene to express their own, often, divergent viewpoints. The United Kingdom's *Question Time*, broadcast in prime time to a large national audience, is modeled on a parliamentary agora or deliberative forum that remains firmly under the control of the program host, Sir David Dimbleby, and program production team. Nonetheless, notwithstanding a widespread professional TV "agoraphobia" or dread of wide-open TV spaces by program producers (Cottle 2002), this format also permits meaningful encounters and sometimes electrifying political exchanges. The precariousness of live unscripted speech, the opportunities for agenda-shifting, the challenging of dominant political and program presuppositions, and the engaged opposition and public airing of dissenting views *all* occasionally break through the professional and normative constraints inscribed into this established TV agora and produce meaningful public discussion. Consider the following:

PRESENTER: Good evening. Welcome to this the first edition of a new series of *Question Time.* . . . The rules are the same as ever: the audience will ask straight questions and the panel will give answers. And, um, the panel don't know, needless to say, what questions are going to be put to them. So let's have the first question tonight. It comes from Kay Amona. . . .

KAY AMONA: Is it too much to ask for the release of two female scientists in exchange for an innocent British life?

SIMON HUGHES, PRESIDENT OF THE LIBERAL DEMOCRATIC PARTY: . . . No government, no prime minister of any party could say we're going to give into demands from people who are clearly warped individuals who are claiming divine authority for something that cannot be right in the eyes of God. And I think we have to be very clear about that. Just one other thing. Behind the scenes I am sure there is all the work that anybody can manage being done to try to identify where this person is being held, where Ken is being held, and to try to release him, as you expect to be done by intelligence services and the secret services. But the answer is, although of course any saved life might be a price worth paying—even if we have to let other people go free who've done terrible things—it isn't something you can judge tonight on its own, and if you do it once, then the people who took this man and are holding him and have beheaded two people horribly, are likely to think that they can get away with it again. *(Audience applause)*

RICHARD DREYFUSS, HOLLYWOOD ACTOR: . . . This is all from the consequence of this war which has made ourselves all the more secure and relaxed in that region. We're all much more secure because of this war and we haven't ignited anything provocative or anything terrible because we've done this war, this good war thing. *(Audience mirth)*. . .

PRESENTER: Let's not get away from the question. There's a number of you wanted to speak. I would like to bring in several but if you could keep your remarks fairly succinct I think it would be good because we have a lot of questions tonight. I'll go to the man in the front row first.

MAN IN FRONT ROW: The people of Iraq were attacked by what the UN General Secretary called an illegal war. They say you cannot negotiate with terrorists. What about the terrorists who tortured the people in Abu Ghraib? What about the terrorists who held thousands upon thousands of Iraqi men, women and children held without trial, without any due process, in their jails? They're murdering them, they're devastating them left, right and center. The people of Iraq are turning around and saying we cannot, we cannot negotiate with the terrorist George Bush, so therefore we are going to use our way of getting back at him.

PETER HAIN *(interrupting)*: But are you saying that that is the equivalent of people beheading somebody on live television, are you saying, are you saying, are you saying that the abuses, are you saying that the abuses at Abu Ghraib, which were unacceptable . . .

MAN IN FRONT ROW: Where is the difference between beheading someone and shooting them in the head, shooting them in the back, hitting a crowd, hitting a crowd of people who are standing on the pavement with helicopter gun ships or using depleted uranium shells on them, or blanket bombing Baghdad. What is the terrorism; tell me what is the terrorism, what is the terrorism?

PETER HAIN: What is your conclusion? Sorry, what is your conclusion from this about this particular case?

MAN IN FRONT ROW: My solution is that they should not have been there in the first place. Tony Blair and George Bush illegally went to war and it is a consequence of their illegal acts that this poor man is now facing death. *(Audience applause)*

PRESENTER: All right, I don't want this discussion to become about democracy in Iraq or the future of Iraq, because it is specifically about the events surrounding Kenneth Bigley. That's what the question is about and that's what I'd like to stick with. . . . The woman next to you, on your left there, in the red shirt.

WOMAN IN RED SHIRT: We keep on about Ken Bigley and if we do nothing it will happen again. It's going to happen again anyway because the Americans are still bombing civilians and they are dying and we don't care about them. *(Audience applause)* *(Question Time*, BBC1 [UK], September 23, 2004)

This contrived forum for public speech and engaged debate, then, though controlled and generally contained by the producers and program host, nonetheless can produce useful exchanges and necessary encounters between opposing views and values and, arguably, begins to provide vital resources for deepening understanding of the unfolding war on terror and some of the contending political perspectives that surround it.

CONCLUSIONS

The research findings presented above have served to document how television as a medium necessarily makes use of an established communicative architecture. It is in and through the established communicative forms of television journalism that conflicts and dissent become mediatized and publicly known. This architecture, as we have seen, is internally variegated, complexly structured, and, importantly, consequential in terms of its delimiting impacts as well as democratizing possibilities. Though researchers are beginning to empirically pursue and theorize the complex interactions between political elites, the media, and the public in times of war and insurgency and how these inform the inevitable accompanying "propaganda war," insufficient attention has been paid to exactly how mediatization is enacted in and through the media's available communicative forms. In its established repertoire of communicative frames of "display" and "deliberation," television journalism has powerfully conditioned the mediatized war on terror.

It needs to be said that, whatever their communicative architecture, the media alone cannot deter hubristic states, aggrieved insurgents, and the violently self-righteous from committing acts of terror, and inevitably news journalism will remain a prime site for "propaganda war" in times of conflict, terror, and insurgency. Nonetheless, by examining its communicative architecture, we can better understand television's Janus-faced relation to systems of domination *and* democracy. The findings presented here invite us to reconsider the democratizing possibilities that inhere within television journalism's existing communicative architecture, which is now routinely deployed in countries and by satellites around the world, as well as the systematic use of communicative structures that permit dominant views to go unchallenged. Though less frequent and under enormous commercial and cultural pressures, current affairs and documentary programs can, and sometimes do, manage to meaningfully expand the public eye of television. They do so principally by widening television's field of vision, offering different perspectives, engaging dominant and dissenting views, and providing deeper analysis and insights into the war on terror as well as its human and geopolitical consequences around the globe. Television's communicative architecture, necessarily, is an integral part of the mediatized war on terror. It is also an indispensable part of the struggle for the democratization of violence.

NOTES

1. This chapter draws on findings from a wider research study funded by the Australian Research Council entitled "Television Journalism and Deliberative Democracy: A Comparative International Study of Communicative Architecture and Democratic Deepening" (DP0449505). I would like to thank Mugdha Rai and Lynn Fahselt for their help in preparing some of the data on this project. Further discussion and elaboration of the theoretical underpinning to this wider project in respect of positions of contemporary social, political, and journalism theory can be found in Cottle and Rai 2006.

2. The two-week sample period (September 13–26, 2004) was a period when Coalition forces continued to battle against the forces of insurgency in Iraq prior to the democratic elections held in early 2005, when hostage taking and bombings continued, and when regionally based insurgency related to the war on terror in other countries

attracted considerable news interest. This sample period, then, is not "representative" of the changing dynamics and major events characterizing the war on terror over an expanded period of time, but it does set out to capture the systematic deployment of communicative frames by television news and illuminate how these have conditioned and impacted on this coverage. The sample of countries, networks, and news programs included in this study comprised the following:

Country	Network	News Programs
Australia	ABC	ABC News, 7.30 Report, Lateline
Australia	Channel 9	Today, Nine News, A Current Affair, Nightline
Australia	Channel 7	Sunrise, Seven News, Today Tonight
Australia	Channel 10	Ten News, Late News
Australia	SBS	World News
India	DD National	The News
India	DD News	Metro Scan, The News
India	NDTV 24×7	Evening News, 9 O'Clock News, The X-Factor
South Africa	SABC3	News
South Africa	SABC Africa	Today in Africa, 60 Minutes Africa
South Africa	eTV	News@7
Singapore	Channel 5	News 5 Tonight
Singapore	Channel i	Channel i News
Singapore	Channel NewsAsia	World Today, Asia Tonight, Prime Time News, Singapore Tonight
Satellite TV	BBC World	BBC News, Asia Today, Asia Business Report
Satellite TV	CNN International	World Report, Newsnight, World News, World News Asia
Satellite TV	Fox News	Fox Report, O'Reilly Factor, On the Record with Greta
Satellite TV	Sky News Australia	Five Live, Sky News UK, News on the Hour
United Kingdom	BBC1	BBC News, BBC Regional News
United Kingdom	BBC2	Newsnight
United Kingdom	ITV	ITV News, ITV Local News
United Kingdom	Channel 4	Channel 4 News
United Kingdom	Channel 5	Channel 5 News
United States	ABC	ABC News, ABC World News Tonight, Nightline
United States	CBS	CBS Evening News
United States	NBC	NBC Nightly News
United States	PBS	NJN News, Newshour with Jim Lehrer

3. Future research will pursue further the possible differences between different television news programs within particular countries and across satellite providers, and also attend to possible regional inflections and national differences of reporting the war on terror. The findings presented here simply serve to document that a common communicative architecture exists within and across television news provision, that this routinely structures television news output in countries around the world, and that this impacts in consequential ways on the mediatized war on terror.

REFERENCES

Allan, S., and B. Zelizer, eds. 2004. *Reporting war: Journalism in wartime.* London: Routledge.

Altheide, D. 1987. Format and symbols in TV coverage of terrorism in the United States and Great Britain. *International Studies Quarterly* 31:161–76.

Bennett, L. 1990. Towards a theory of press-state relations in the United States. *Journal of Communication* 40 (2): 103–25.

Butler, D. 1995. *The trouble with reporting Northern Ireland.* Aldershot, U.K.: Avebury.

Carruthers, S. L. 2000. *The media at war: Communication and conflict in the 20th century.* Basingstoke, U.K.: Macmillan.

Cottle, S. 1997. Reporting the Troubles in Northern Ireland: Paradigms and media propaganda. *Critical Studies in Media Communication* 14 (3): 282–96.

———. 2002. TV agora and agoraphobia post September 11. In *Journalism after September 11,* ed. B. Zelizer and S. Allan, 178–98. London: Routledge.

———. 2005. In defence of "thick" journalism; or, How television journalism can be good for us. In *Journalism: Critical Issues,* ed. S. Allan, 109–24. Maidenhead, U.K.: Open University Press.

Cottle, S., and M. Rai. 2006. Between display and deliberation: Analyzing TV news as communicative architecture. *Media, Culture and Society* 28 (2) (in press).

Curtis, L. 1986. *Ireland, the propaganda war: The British media and the battle for hearts and minds.* London: Pluto Press.

Elliott, P. 1980. Press performance as political ritual. In *The sociology of journalism and the press,* ed. H. Christian, 141–77. Sociological Review Monograph no. 29. Keele, U.K.: University of Keele.

Elliott, P., G. Murdock, and P. Schlesinger. 1986. Terrorism and the state: A case study of the discourses of television. In *Media, culture and society—A critical reader,* ed. R. Collins, J. Curran, N. Garnham, P. Scannell, P. Schlesinger, and C. Sparks. London: Sage.

Entman, R. E. 2004. *Projections of power: Framing news, public opinion and U.S. foreign policy.* Chicago: University of Chicago Press.

Geertz, C. 1973. *The interpretation of cultures.* New York: Basic Books.

Glasgow University Media Group. 1985. *War and Peace News.* Glasgow, Scotland: Open University Press.

Hall, S., C. Critcher, T. Jefferson, J. Clarke, and B. Roberts. 1978. *Policing the crisis: Mugging, the state and law and order.* London: Macmillan.

Hallin, D. 1986. *The "uncensored" war? The media and Vietnam.* Oxford: Oxford University Press.

———. 1994. *We keep America on top of the world.* London: Routledge.

———. 1997. The media and war. In *International media research*, ed. J. Corner, P. Schlesinger, and R. Silverstone. London: Routledge.

Harris, R. 1994. *The media trilogy.* London: Faber and Faber.

Herman, E., and N. Chomsky. 1988. *Manufacturing consent.* New York: Pantheon.

Hoskins, A. 2004. *Televising war: From Vietnam to Iraq.* London: Continuum.

Kamalipour, Y. R., and N. Snow, eds. 2004. *War, media, and propaganda: A global perspective.* Oxford, U.K.: Rowman and Littlefield.

Keane, J. 2004. *Violence and democracy.* Cambridge: Cambridge University Press.

Kellner, D. 1992. *The Persian Gulf TV War.* Oxford, U.K.: Westview Press.

Knightley, P. 2003. *The first casualty: The war correspondent as hero and myth-maker.* London: André Deutsche.

Liebes, T. 1997. *Reporting the Arab-Israeli Conflict: How hegemony works.* London: Routledge.

Miller, D. 1994. *Don't Mention the War: Northern Ireland, propaganda, and the media.* London: Pluto Press.

———, ed. 2004. *Tell me lies: Propaganda and media distortion in the attack on Iraq.* London: Pluto Press.

Morrison, D. E., and H. Tumber. 1988. *Journalists at War: The dynamics of news reporting during the Falklands conflict.* London: Sage.

Nassar, J. R. 2005. *Globalization and terrorism: The migration of dreams and nightmares.* Oxford, U.K.: Rowman and Littlefield.

Nichols, B. 1991. *Representing reality: Issues and concepts in documentary.* Bloomington: Indiana University Press.

Paletz, D. L., and A. P. Schmid, eds. 1992. *Terrorism and the media.* London: Sage.

Pedelty, M. 1995. *War stories: The culture of foreign correspondents.* London: Routledge.

Philo, G., and M. Berry. 2004. *Bad news from Israel.* London: Pluto.

Robinson, P. 2002. *The CNN effect: The myth of news, foreign policy and intervention.* London: Routledge.

Rolston, B., and D. Miller, eds. 1996. *War and words: The Northern Ireland media reader.* Belfast: Beyond the Pale Publications.

Schlesinger, P. 1991. *Media, state and nation: Political violence and collective identities.* London: Sage.

Sonwalker, P. 2004. Out of sight, out of mind? The non-reporting of small wars and insurgencies. *Reporting War: Journalism in Wartime*, ed. S. Allan and B. Zelizer, 206–23. London: Routledge.

Taylor, P. M. 1992. *War and the media: Propaganda and persuasion in the Gulf War.* Manchester: Manchester University Press.

Thussu, D. K., and D. Freedman, eds. 2003. *War and the media.* London: Sage.

Tuman, J. S. 2003. *Communicating terror: The rhetorical dimension of terrorism.*
    London: Sage.
Tumber, H., and P. Palmer. 2004. *Media at war: The Iraq crisis.* London: Sage.
Van Der Veer, P., and S. Munshi, eds. 2004. *Media, war, and terrorism: Responses
    from the Middle East and Asia.* London: Routledge.
Wolfsfeld, G. 1997. *Media and political conflict.* Cambridge: Cambridge University
    Press.
Zelizer, B., and S. Allan, eds. 2002. *Journalism after September 11.* London: Routledge.

Discussion Questions for Part 1

1. What are myths? In what ways does television news perpetuate myths?
2. How are Western media myths different from those in the non-Western world?
3. What is the link between the *reality* of Islamic terrorism and the *myth* of Islamic terrorism?
4. In chapter one, Thussu says: "The most important myth being televised around the world is about the U.S. crusade to spread democracy." Do you agree with this statement?
5. In chapter two, Cottle says: "When democracies are challenged by transnational 'apocalyptic' terror . . . public deliberation and debate . . . is vitally necessary." How have the U.S. media helped or hindered such a debate around the events of 9/11?
6. Consider a recent terrorist media event (e.g., a suicide car bomb) and, using Cottle's framework, outline the communicative architecture of television news coverage of that event.

Part 2

Genres and Contexts

3

Prime Time Terror: The Case of *La Jetée* and *12 Monkeys*

Marion Herz

"The producers of catastrophe films are of course terrorists, simply in a milder form," Klaus Theweleit makes clear in his study of media commentaries of 9/11.

> They destroy and film this; this is their work. In such a way the Earth was destroyed long ago, in atomic and/or cosmic catastrophes, via killer viruses from space or from illegal laboratories, mankind dies away; we all know that. The question is, how long can the Earth itself hold out? The question is, when someone, somewhere decides to direct the Earth's destruction in the form of cinematic reality onto the Earth itself, and, if he so decides, whether he has access to sufficient potential—logistics!—in order to carry it out. (Theweleit 2002, 75)

Theweleit's *Der Knall: 11. September, das Verschwinden der Realität und ein Kriegsmodell* is not only a book about the big bang of September 11, but also about the bang on the head that Theweleit demonstrates to all those who, in view of the TV-repetition-replay of the collapsing World Trade Center, no longer know what is real.

> It could be heard and seen everywhere, how the word-fabrication machinery of the expert-perceivers, culture administrators, print and image-media makers were getting into trouble from the real arrival of an occurrence, that everyone had not only previously known, but had apparently seen . . . apparently . . . "at the cinema" . . . on monitors . . . in Shéhérazade's thousand and one billion transgressive little pictures on MTV . . . "prominent in film and television" . . . in comics . . . in elevated narrative literature. . . . Words began to whirr: The monstrosity of our "collective subconsciousness" . . . phantasm . . . nightmare . . . vision . . . trauma. The inability to keep apart "the real and the symbolic" was

stated as; we are victims of a "tremendous delusion," a "virtual versus physical world" was evoked. . . . Along these lines are more or less the main points. (Theweleit 2002, 68)

For Theweleit, the hastily compiled corpus of catastrophe films, which was believed to *anticipate* this event, stands for the epidemically spreading impression that reality had become unreal and unreality had become real. Theweleit points out here that *the* reality does not exist in any case. More so—by the attacks of September 11, "the various reality-segments of an event of global significance were to be seen for the first time at their best in a TV image" (265). The real location on this occasion "was not only New York and the World Trade Center's twin towers, Washington and the Pentagon," but also "the TV screen with which we were linked up via live-transmissions. The perpetrators, with their timing and the whole setting of this massive coup had achieved this live link with us, the minds of a worldwide TV audience" (266–67). This attack occurred not only in our homes but also in the heads of the TV audience, which was forced to aim for the potential targets of the four skyjacked airplanes as if they were in the position of the terrorists themselves. No one had ever seen all these images combined in a TV image.

The new quality of such terrorism exists then not so much in the extremely competent use of media, to facilitate the broadcasting of messages or images *of* terrorist acts, but mainly in the ability to turn the TV image into a *medium of terror*, which unites the extradiegetic reality of the spectators with the intradiegetic reality of the incident, and which suspends the distinction between fictionality and factuality. The *terror of the medium* targets the media sciences, and their unsuccessful attempts to conceptionalize *the* reality as well as to distinguish between the spectators' reality and that of the media, between subject and object of observation. The resulting states of confusion or even delusion, which also manifest themselves in all kinds of déjà-vu experiences, have been exactly recorded by Theweleit in his meticulous evaluation of the medial processing of the events. Not so much in order to see again the supposed seen-it-once-already but more to find an answer to the formation of this effect and the terror of the medium, it is now necessary to examine not only a film about a terror attack, but also to revisualize an important branch of film theory and to examine the connections between phantasm and fantasy, dream and trauma. This approach also means to switch from TV to cinema.

The first strike, the first sign. Decades after the attack, which handed the planet over to the animals, a first clue is found to answer the first question, "Who did it?" From a persistently recurrent nightmare—an airport, a man shot dead, and a terrified woman—James Cole wakes up in the year 2035 and climbs out from underground, where the remains of humanity just manage to stay alive after a bioterrorist attack. The trail he finds, a trail of confessions, grows into the epidemic's epicenter, Philadelphia at the turn of the year 1997, because it is he himself who will in future lay the signs for "We did it" all around this *ground zero*.

James Cole is once again sent up not only to the surface, but to the year 1996, to gather information on the perpetrators. The disorientated Cole (Bruce Willis) finds himself, however, in April 1990 in a psychiatric center. To his psychiatrist Dr. Kathryn Railly (Madeleine Stowe), her patient strangely seems familiar, and to her staff, Cole's reports of foreboding doom and destruction and his rescue mission, are the classical discourse of paranoia. At the same time, Cole's fellow patient and animal-rights activist Jeffrey Goines (Brad Pitt), thinks that founding an underground organization called the "12 Monkeys" and releasing a virus to wipe mankind from the planet would be a really excellent idea. On his second trip through time, Cole must now obtain a primal form of the virus. With the kidnapped Dr. Railly, and the police on their heels, he encounters Goines once again and finds out that he is the son of the Nobel–Prize–winning virologist, Dr. Leland Goines. Confronted by Cole, his former asylum companion, Jeffrey Goines replies that the idea for the 12 Monkeys organization, and the releasing of a mankind-deadly virus stolen from his father's laboratory, originates from no one other than Cole himself.

The time–machine—cinema—transfers the past of the film-shooting and the absence of the photographed object into the here and now of the moving projection. The science fiction film *12 Monkeys* (1995) tells, for its part, of time travel from the future into the past, as well as into the future of this film from 1995, to make present to the film's spectators the cinematic space that is in itself split in time.[1]

On the one hand, the question of the epidemic's starting point spatializes time into a chronology of *before* and *after* the bioterrorist attack. On the other hand, the time-travel paradox once again breaks down this dissection of time into zones—as also here performed by Dr. Railly with the aid of photographs that show Cole and a time-traveling colleague in the World War I trenches. At least up to this point in the narrative, Cole must have *always* been living in a post-apocalyptical world, in order to travel back in time and to have been able to set off the catastrophic event.

As every child knows, when using the medium of time travel, meddling with events in the past is strictly forbidden, since that can have unforeseen consequences and even endanger the future existence of the time traveler. Cole breaks not only this law of fiction, but also breaks that law of science, which Dr. Railly's theory of a "Cassandra complex" formulates as "the torment of knowing the future, but with the impossibility to influence it." The ban on any such intervention is the prerequisite for the fiction of scientific discourse, which adheres to the neutrality of standpoint and a viewpoint removed from the event, in order to discriminate between fantasy and reality and to give science an external referentiality. In the case of *12 Monkeys*, this also forms a specific discourse about cinema, which haunts this great production in Cole's continually recurring nightmares, and which comes from the avant-garde film *La Jetée* (1962).

La Jetée is a stills movie from the early 1960s that recounts in roughly twenty-seven minutes the story of a man who is chosen, due to his especially vivacious fixation to an inner vision, for an experiment for the salvation of mankind. His last scene of recall of the time before the great catastrophe shows a woman on the runway at Orly and a running, falling, dying man. Shortly after, Paris collapses into the debris of the Third World War. The survivors in the catacombs are lab material for an elite group of scientists, which exhibits fascistic features with its cold-blooded rationality and bioscientific fanaticism. The scientists infuse this imaginatively gifted man with a serum in order to transport him first into the past and later also into the future. As a dreamlike sedated medium, the guinea pig evokes images from the prewar period. As a side effect, by each visit he is drawn emotionally ever closer to a woman, for her part with neither a past nor a destiny, but—how could it be otherwise?—desirable. The success of these months-long operations culminates in a meeting with scientists in the future, who provide the time traveler with knowledge of energy technology to regain possession of the Earth's surface and free the planet from radioactive fallout. The scientists, also time travelers, promise to give the man a life in the prewar period with the desired woman. But when he is sent into the past and to the woman waiting for him, he also encounters his other childhood self at Orly. While being led by his parents he, as a child, becomes a witness to his own death as an adult, as the scientists break their promise and have him shot.

Like hardly any other film, *La Jetée* has subsequently offered to bring together an Oedipal concept of the primal scene with an Oedipal theory of spectatorship. In the very concept of the primal scene, nothing about a forbidden, incestuous desire for the mother—or father—is asserted. However, Constance Penley (1991, 77) interprets *La Jetée* as a reminiscence and compulsive repetition of the Oedipal drama.

> The woman he is searching for is at the end of the jetty, but so is the man whose job is to prevent him from possessing her, the man and the woman on the jetty mirroring the parental (Oedipal) couple that brought the little boy to the airport.

For Penley, *La Jetée* is based on the logic that one cannot be in the same place at the same time as adult and child. The movie reproves this incestuous desire not simply with a symbolic castration but with death. Thus *La Jetée* purports to show that the fantasy of time travel is no more and no less than compulsive repetition, which manifests itself in the fantasy of the primal scene. Furthermore, the film puts forward the idea that each film-viewing is an infantile sexual investigation. Also, compulsive repetition and regression lead to a dissolution of the subject.

This infantile sexual research, Penley claims, is judged to direct the very same phallogocentric gaze at the woman that Freud's little boy aspires to, in order to see nothing other than the lack of the self-same penis. Penley sends exactly the same genuinely male and Oedipal spectator as conceptualized by Christian Metz (1986) and Jean-Louis Baudry (1986) into the cinema. There, he regresses into an infantile, passive, sleeplike motionlessness, which makes any reality check impossible. In a moment of psychosis, he misinterprets representations as perception (Baudry) or allows himself to be lulled by the imaginary signifier (Metz).

Synchronized with the psychic apparatus, the time-machine cinema conveys not only the absent, filmed object into the here and now of the projection but also the spectator into infancy. In his comparison between Plato's cavern and the cinema—"Plato constructs an apparatus very much like sound cinema" (1986, 305)—Baudry allows the spectator become "intrinsically part of the apparatus." The intrauterine film theater is, according to Baudry, the "maternal womb . . . the matrix into which we are supposed to wish to return" (306). The desire for a return to pre-Oedipal desires and feelings is the moving force behind all (audio-) visual media.

> But if cinema was really the answer to a desire inherent in our psychical structure, how can we date its first beginnings? Would it be too risky to propose that painting, like theatre, for lack of suitable technological and economic conditions, were dry runs in the approximation not only of the world of representation but of what might result from a certain aspect of its functioning and which only the cinema is in a position to implement? These attempts have obviously produced their own specificity and their own history, but their existence has at its origin a psychical source equivalent to the one which is stimulated the invention of cinema.
>
> It is very possible that there was never a first invention of the cinema. (Baudry 1986, 307)

Accumulatively to these thoughts of the cinema as a machine fulfilling Oedipal desires, Metz proposes a cinematographic signification process, which is of course not pre- but post-Oedipal.

> For its spectator the film unfolds in that simultaneously very close and definitively inaccessible "elsewhere" in which the child *sees* the amorous play of the parental couple, who are similarly ignorant of it and leave it alone, a pure onlooker whose participation is inconceivable. In this respect the cinematic signifier is not only "psychoanalytic": it is more precisely Oedipal in type. (Metz 1986, 264)

In a Lacanian turn, the imaginary signifier signifies solely because the filmed object as well as the spectator are not present in the film. In oft-flagrant disregard of the audative, the spectator is connected with the film only via a disembodied view. Although Metz takes into account sociocultural factors during the formation of the cinema, he also deals with cinema from an idealist tradition, namely the separation between the observed and the observer given by the camera obscura and Renaissance perspective, which, as Metz puts it, is even stronger in the cinema than in the theater. On the basis of this separation between image and spectator and also between presence and absence of the filmed object—which makes signification at all possible—the spectator identifies himself with the transcendental all-seeing, and thereby itself unseen, divine eye of the camera.

Whereas, according to Baudry, the time-machine cinema is driven by the desire for a pre-Oedipal fusion with the maternal womb of the film, the incest prohibition alone maintains the cinematographic signification process, which according to Metz belongs to the symbolic and the secondary process. In the Apparatus Theory, the time-travel paradox—two versions of one and the same person find themselves at the same place at the same time—is a problem of incest. The prohibited meddling with the events on the screen is the same as the incest taboo, which guarantees that the primal scene of the parents' coition is simply observed, and the spectator does not appear in the scene as a participant. The Apparatus Theory tends toward channeling its tension relationship between psychoanalysis and idealism into products of the film industry, which uncritically fulfill Oedipal desires, and into the arty avant-garde film, which fully utilizes the critical and subvertive potential of psychoanalysis. The cinematographic, representational economy conveys a bourgeois, antimaterialist consciousness, which the avant-garde film alone is able to surpass, or at least to portray in critical self-reflection. As a consequence, with Penley, the incestuous desire of a protagonist watching his own movie and which is under penalty of death, is the illusion-breaking self-reflexive element. This ennobles *La Jetée* alongside its ingenious photographic composition into a unique and in itself an unrepeatable avant-garde film.

If *La Jetée* applies the violence of the Oedipal drama to itself, then the death of its protagonist more than anything guarantees the separation between a passive spectator and the screen and prevents a potential participative involvement in the events—as in *12 Monkeys*—from taking place. If the scene on the runway reflects the spectators' Oedipal viewing position, then the incest taboo ensures that the spectator does not commit illicit autoerotic, masturbatory, or incestuous acts with either his other self or with his parents, and that he remains restricted to a viewing position separated from events, in order to acquire neutral and objective knowledge of future technologies or of the cinema, as does the Apparatus Theory itself. *La Jetée* and its theorizing encounter the Oedipal cinema, and the ideology of a neutral and transcendental standpoint built into it, as a given fact, which every film is condemned to reproduce and which the avant-garde film can only expose.[2]

Although Penley's model of an Oedipal primal scene in the movies does not prevail without Jean Laplanche and J.-B. Potalis's concept (produced two years after *La Jetée*) of the primal scene, it misses the crucial point. In their effort *not* to follow Jacques Lacan's structuralist and anthropological reworking of Freud, Laplanche and Pontalis conceive in their essay "Fantasy and the Origins of Sexuality" the primal fantasy aside from the Oedipal drama. The structure they found in Freud's texts—of an insoluble, constitutive subsequence between a second and a first time, from which fantasizing and sexuality originates—is sustainable without the kinship-generating and incest-prohibiting law, the Name-of-the-Father principle, and in this way allows the subject a place in a less verbal but much more visual scene, in all its positions at the same time and even in its syntax itself.

> In fantasy the subject does not pursue the object or its sign: he appears caught up himself in the sequence of images. He forms no representation of the desired object, but is himself represented as participating in the scene although, in the earliest forms of fantasy, he cannot be assigned any fixed place in it. (Laplanche and Pontalis 1986, 58)

Without even thinking about devising a scenario in which the presence of two versions of one person at the same time and at the same place is a paradox, Laplanche and Pontalis conceive the time travel of the primal scene as constitutive for a subjectivity that is able not only to develop beyond the incest taboo and the Oedipal phallogocentric heterosexuality but also to actively participate in the sequence of images. Although Laplanche and Pontalis localize the source of fantasy in the undatable reflexivity of autoeroticism, which however is placed after the loss of the original object, and where preconscious daydreams equate with unconscious fantasies, they refuse to accept the reproach of regression and therefore make the orthodox connection between incest taboo, threat of castration, and masturbation ban become even more apparent. Moreover, for Laplanche and Pontalis, fantasy is not in contrast to material reality—rather, it makes up a psychic reality, which is simply the psychoanalytical object and is of independent value.

Due to their abstinence from the Oedipus complex and their historicized redrawing of the Freudian discovery, Laplanche and Pontalis are also able to present the question of the origin of psychoanalysis itself, which, like that of the fantasy, lies in the constitutive subsequence between a second and a first time—thus Freud "was able to use fantasy as a scientific theory" (Laplanche and Pontalis 1986, 32n38). With his "fantasy of origin" in *Totem and Taboo*—the primal horde, with a natural revulsion to incest, rejects having intercourse with the women made use of until now by the murdered "urvater"—Freud creates a real first time in order to find the principle that establishes the universal law of the incest taboo and structures the psychic apparatus and bestows a final meaning to the fantasies analyzed by him for the second time in the talking cure.[3]

In the phylogenetic explanation, the straight chronological line of evolution bends into a time-travel loop, in which beginning and end join up into a paradox of an always-has-been. Although a parental or phylogenetic past and a childlike or ontogenetic present very incestuously bite each other's tails, psychoanalysis receives a reference point by resorting to a real, ever-existing first time of the incest taboo, which apparently lies beyond its own discourse and imparts scientific meaning as well as an objective possibility to describe the psychogenesis. The incest taboo should not only assure that the second and the first time do not impregnate each other but also conceal that psychoanalysis instituted this law and originated itself with it. Thus, the origin of psychoanalysis as well as its very own object (which is fantasy or psychic reality) is caught in this irresolvable time loop of constitutive subsequence between a second and a first time.

When Freud writes that every child uses fantasies in order to veil the history of his or her childhood "just as every nation disguises its forgotten prehistory by constructing legends" (1989, 368), the question is, what has psychoanalysis for its part—and the Apparatus Theory it supports—forgotten in order to legitimate its discourse? While Michel Foucault answers this question in *The Will to Knowledge* (1978) concerning psychoanalysis, Jonathan Crary in *Techniques of the Observer* (1990) is able, by means of Foucault's concept of bio-power, to reply to the apparatus-theoretical fantasy of origin.

Foucault differentiates between two diverse power forms—juridical and biological—that belong to two diverse societal forms, an aristocratic-sovereign form with the power to *make* its subjects die and a bourgeois biomedical form with the power to *make* its own biological species live. Foucault allows both power forms to interoperate as dispositives, so that at node points new strategic setups can evolve just as with psychoanalysis. In consequence of Foucault, the juridical discourse of psychoanalysis intervenes in the racisms and degeneration-theories powered by bio-power. While bio-power cultivates perversions and biologically specified bodies without any adherence to an inner juridical logic, psychoanalysis codifies these wild proliferations once again back into a juridical framework so as to impart to all humankind an ever existing universally valid, egalitarian, psychic, fundamental condition.

In contrast to psychoanalysis, bio-power conceives incest not as a cultural and juridical but as a biological problem. If Freud's diachronic formulation of the incest taboo was hitherto a reaction to state racism, then, after fascism it receives a synchronic reformulation via Levi Strauss and Lacan, in which the "ever existing" also turns into a "ubiquitous." As Lacan raises Freud's lawgiving intervention into the generative Name-of-the-Father principle that initializes the transition between nature and culture as well as the entry into the symbolic order, then all historicity, including that of psychoanalysis itself, becomes suspended in a purely juridical time loop that closes itself up around the historical trauma or Ground Zero of a bio-forced, racist barbarism, which is not affected by this law.

Lacan's formula for psychosis is "that which has not been admitted to symbolic expression...reappears in reality in the form of hallucination" (Laplanche and Pontalis 1986, 30n28) and precisely asserts that this is concerned with the fundamental signifier of the Name-of-the-Father. Insofar as the Name-of-the-Father establishes the symbolic and thereby also the psychoanalytical discourse, psychosis is the penalty for the nonrecognition of the psychoanalytical law, and that's why it is not curable by the psychoanalytical cure; while in counterpoint, psychoanalysis itself is phantasmagorically haunted by bio-power as the element, which psychoanalysis had to bury within itself or abject in its sense and which constitutes, so to speak, its real. The biological/physical is not only the place where, in the form of hallucinations and phantasms, there is a reappearance of what psychoanalysis had to abject in order to establish itself as a juridical form of power and its juridical time loop but also certain elements of the biological and physical can appear as the abjected, which comes back in form of a terrorizing phantasm.

However, the Apparatus Theory, in order to develop its primal fantasy of the ever-existing cinema and its Oedipal economy of desire, must also abject the influence of the bio-power on the creation of the cinema. Whereas the *entry of life into history* around 1800 marks for Foucault the break—repatched by hybrids in his model of origin—between the juridical and the biological power-regime, for Crary this represents the breakdown of the *camera obscura* as the theoretical model of perception and the appearance of the body as an intrinsic part of the image-producing ensemble. Just as the body is combined with the capitalist production apparatus, it follows that in the optical apparatus of the nineteenth century, which is based on the newly conceived physiology of seeing, it is no longer possible to differentiate between the observer and the observed.

Although Crary understands the development of the photographic camera as an attempt to return to the neutral standpoint of the camera obscura and to its observer-position separated from the events, then at least the cinema remains dependent upon the *sluggishness of the eye*, and precisely this corporeality of seeing must indeed abject the Apparatus Theory, in order to retain an idealistic view, bound only via identification with the projection.

> Spectator-fish taking in everything with their eyes, nothing with their bodies: the institution of the cinema requires a silent, motionless spectator, a *vacant* spectator at once alienated and happy, acrobatically hooked up to himself by the invisible thread of sight. (Metz 1986, 97)

La Jetée presents its time-traveling protagonist as essentially calm, motion-less, and hooked on the line; however, despite this theory one cannot easily presume that his task, receiving images from the future or the past and me-diating them, is a purely spiritual or psychic one. Physically connected to the apparatus, his body remains in the laboratory during the time-trip, on the one hand; on the other hand, though, he walks through the movie-projected and -produced past to finally appear there in double-existence and, in accor-dance with the psychoanalytic-cinematographic incest prohibition, to be shot. Alongside the binary splitting-up into female and male, homo- and heterosex-ual, parent and child, the introduction of the Oedipal incest taboo serves in the film and its theory, which is a means of viewing in itself, to bring the cinema back to a safe and secure viewer-position, based on a division between the ob-server and the observed that apparently always existed—"it is very possible, that there was never a first invention of the cinema" (Baudry 1986, 307)—and thus also with an apparatus-theoretical, media-pessimistic Socrates, who es-capes from the incarceration of the cinematic cave and receives the truth that the shadowy realm is falsehood and deceit.

Psychoanalytic Apparatus Theory cannot grasp—and even forbids—the bodily intersection of the observer with the observed. For Apparatus The-ory, this very capacity of cinema to connect its filmic body with the body of the observer, not only means that cinema breaks the law that is claimed to be the founding principle of Western civilization but also that this is a form of terror, which can only be answered with an act of counterterror—the threat of castration or even death.

In the extremely psychotic monkey business of *12 Monkeys* meanwhile, bio-power and psychoanalysis are found on a confrontation course. On the one hand, they come together disciplinarily correctly in the figure of the psychiatrist Dr. Railly, but on the other hand, they miss each other's grip in the airport scene toward which Cole and Dr. Railly are heading. *12 Monkeys*, like *La Jetée*, also employs a primal-fantastic time loop around a catastrophe of global scale. In *La Jetée* the center of this loop, the outbreak of World War III, remains untouched. In *12 Monkeys*, however, one must not only close in on the origin of the pandemic but maybe even forestall it.

In order not to have to reproach himself for having the death of five billion people on his conscience, Cole begins to believe Dr. Railly's explanation about his paranoid mental state. In the catacombs of his nightmarelike unconsciousness, he meets the scientists of 2035 and tells them that they are not real, but simply his mental illness. Following the advice of one of the voices speaking to him, Cole decides to play this mad game once more, so as to return to the reality of 1996 and seek a salvation of love from Dr. Railly. However, Dr. Railly, looking at the photographs that prove to her the reality-content of Cole's account of events, meanwhile loses her belief in her own Cassandra complex. The paranoid discourse of the global-ruin madmen examined by Dr. Railly—such as the warning announced by Cole's colleague in World War I of an apocalypse at the turn of the year 1997—now no longer tells her of delusional mania but from a forthcoming reality. Dr. Railly is not only convinced that Cole's disappearance is due to him being taken back into the future, but she now also becomes active herself in order to reverse Cole's time-traveling intervention into the course of the world's events. She warns Dr. Goines of his son's plans and is just describing the 12 Monkeys' headquarters, with the graffiti that Cole was shown in the postapocalyptic underworld as a proof of the organization's perpetration, when he meets her once again. As Dr. Railly, whose patient always seemed so strangely familiar to her, for her part now participates in the time loop, so Cole counters by convincing his doctor that they are both mad.

After they decide to fly to Key West the following morning and wait out the course of events, Cole and Dr. Railly spend the evening in a movie theater. As Cole falls asleep during *Vertigo* (1963)—whose time-travel motif was also visited by *La Jetée*—then *The Birds* (1963) pluck him out of his dream of cinema as a dream and announce the coming takeover of the world by animals. As have already often been seen, Cole's dreams are about a man being shot at the airport and a woman mourning him. To conceal themselves from the police, he and Dr. Railly dress up exactly as the man and woman in Cole's dreams. Insofar as *12 Monkeys* plays out this disguising-scene in a movie theater that, of all things, is presenting a retrospective of the director most admired by psychoanalytical film theorists, this film displays the conceptualization of cinema as an infantilizing and dream-soporific time machine.

12 Monkeys configures time travel more clearly than *La Jetée* already had—as something that actively involves bodily participation. Cole, wired up to every imaginable medical apparatus, is transported in time via images of a staircase whose quick playback has the effect of the flickering black-and-white of an empty filmstrip. Now the film also shows that Cole and Dr. Railly, who are spreading the signs for the 12 Monkeys' perpetration in order to pick up the trail of the name "Goines," have been following a false chain of signifiers from the beginning.

The 12 Monkeys organization frees the zoo animals in a night action and locks up virologist Dr. Leland Goines (the father of leader Jeffrey Goines) in the monkey house. Certainly they do not release the virus, but they anticipate its effect. On the following sunny morning, these wild animals cross Dr. Railly and Cole's path. Not only the division between nature and culture but also that between beginning and end, future and present, becomes ever more permeable. At Philadelphia Airport, the events catch up with each other. The adult Cole recognizes the scene of his dreams, with himself and Dr. Railly as their protagonists. He can remember, "shortly before the dying started," having been at this location once before—and the child Cole enters the airport holding his parents' hands. On the answering machine that serves as a means of communication between time phases, Cole leaves the message that the 12 Monkeys had nothing to do with the virus. Immediately after leaving this message, he meets his time-traveling colleague, who is also in the service of epidemiology, and who confirms that the future has already received the message. He requests that Cole seize the virus at the gate for the flight to San Francisco and therefore on a second narrative path becoming only now clear at this point.

It's not the name Goines but the much less important name Railly that stands for the bioterrorist attack. Dr. Railly once signed a copy of her book about the Cassandra complex for none other than the assistant in Dr. Leland Goines's laboratory who was trusted with the security measures after her alarming call. And now this laboratory assistant, nominally unknown by the film, is about to give Dr. Railly the "torment to know about the future, without the ability to influence it."

At the gate for the San Francisco flight, as he finally agrees to the demands of the security agent to open the test tube he is carrying, this employee of Goines releases the virus. Precisely this bio-power narrative thread quite obviously does not know the Name-of-the-Father law and implements for its part, going back in time, a fantasy of origin of the virus, which breaks down the division between nature and culture marked by psychoanalytical law.[4] The bio-power narrative path follows an evolutionary, straight-line trail of a pathogenic agent back to the moment of its emergence, in order to attain at the same time predictions of its further spreading. The laboratory assistant leaves an infectious trail, which epidemiology follows back from Beijing via Bangkok, Karachi, Kinshasa, Rome, Rio de Janeiro, New Orleans, and San Francisco to finally Philadelphia. This and a search back along genealogical divisions of mutations result in determination of the origin of the epidemic and the original form of the virus in Philadelphia—or more exactly, in the research laboratory of Jeffrey Goines's father, who carries out experiments on monkeys there, although neither he nor his son have anything to do with the bioterrorist attack. Bred by humans in animals, the virus is only virulent among humans and transforms the civilized world into a wilderness and the last refuge of man into a place in which despotism and the survival of the fittest is the only law. "The law pronouncing a permanent state of emergency" is a rule for the permanent suspension of law and permits the retention of Cole and of other prisoners as animal laboratory material, in order to once again achieve for the human species, which is no longer human, a lebensraum.

At Philadelphia Airport, Cole's time-traveling colleague and Dr. Railly set Cole on the straight escape path of the lab assistant. Cole breaks out of the enclosed spaces in which he has until now been shown and his circular movement. He runs through the security lock, in order to shoot the attacker. But finally it is Cole who is shot by the very police officers from whom he thought he was disguised, and he witnesses his own death with his own child-eyes. These eyes of the Cole-child are not only the first and the last few frames in this movie, but in the airport sequence they also insert a scene that shows the female leader of the bioscientific ruling elite of 2023 sitting next to the attacker in the airplane.

Whereas Cole is just as unable to avoid the time loop as the protagonists in *La Jetée*, it now appears that the scientist will get her hands on the initial form of the virus, necessary for the development of an inoculation drug, and escape on the straight-line trail of a pandemic which has now become unstoppable. If one day the antidote really should free all humankind from their catacombs, this antidote is still dependent on Cole's incarceration in the eternal repetition of his death. Although the setting is not Oedipal and does not even equate to that comparative one in *La Jetée*—Cole is not even running toward a man and a woman who could represent the parental couple that brought the young Cole to the airport—*12 Monkeys* also does not allow its protagonist to be in a young and an adult version at the same time at the same place. If the death of Cole nevertheless should denote an incest ban and the cinematographic ban of involvement in this scene, then exactly this has the effect that the plague will be spread worldwide.

At the very location of the mythical origins of the United States' constitution, Philadelphia, *12 Monkeys* shows how the biological and the juridical collide, in the form of two models of origin and two primal scenes of the cinema, but cannot grasp each other. Not only the TV images of 9/11 but also the cinema as a medium in itself is able to generate a live-effect—which is in the service of bio-power also a life-effect—and furthermore, to physiologically connect the observer with the observed. This ability of the cinema to interweave our reality with its own is surrounded by a technology of safety. But this construction is nothing more than one of the inner charges that was detonated on 9/11 from the outside and which exploded in a collective psychosis.

NOTES

1. Built in 1820, Eastern State Penitentiary in Philadelphia was specifically renovated and used as the psychiatric asylum of 1990. The subterranean prison town from 2035 was spread across the industrial ruins of Westport Power Plant, built in 1906 in Baltimore.

2. As to the Oedipus complex as given fact, compare: "Freud's concept of the Oedipus complex is, in fact, remarkable for its realism: whether it is represented as an inner conflict (nuclear complex) or as a social institution, the complex remains a given fact; the subject is *confronted* by it. . . . Perhaps it was the realism of the concept which lead Freud to allow the notion of original fantasy to coexist alongside the Oedipus complex without being concerned to articulate them: here the subject does not encounter the structure, but is carried along with it" (Laplanche and Pontalis 1986, 31n34).

3. Laplanche and Pontalis cite Freud's Introductory Lectures: "It seems to me quite possible that all the things that are told to us in analysis as fantasy . . . were once real occurrences in the primaeval times of the human family . . . and that children in their fantasies are simply filling in the gaps in individual truth with prehistoric truths" (Laplanche and Pontalis 1986, 17).

4. See Herz 2002 and Waldby 1996.

REFERENCES

Baudry, Jean-Louis. 1986. The apparatus. In *Narrative, apparatus, ideology: A film theory reader*, ed. Philip Rosen, 299–318. New York: Columbia University Press.

Crary, Jonathan. 1990. *Techniques of the observer: On vision and modernity in the nineteenth century*. Cambridge, Mass.: MIT Press.

Freud, Sigmund. 1989. *Introductory lectures on psychoanalysis*. Trans. and ed. by James Strachey. New York: Norton.

Foucault, Michel. 1978. *The will to knowledge*. Vol. 1 of *The history of sexuality*. New York: Pantheon.

Herz, Marion. 2002. Die wunderbare Zwischenwelt des Virus. In *Krankheit und Geschlecht: Diskursive Affären zwischen Literatur und Medizin*, ed. Tanja Nusser and Elisabeth Strowick, 23–33. Würzburg: Königshausen & Neumann.

The Birds. 1963. Film. Directed by Alfred Hitchcock. USA.

L'age-Stehr, J., and M. G. Koch. 1991. AIDS. In *Immunologie: Grundlagen Klinik Praxis*, ed. Diethard Gemsa, Joachim Robert Kulden, and Klaus Resch, 564–94. Stuttgart: Thieme.

La Jetée. 1962. Film. Directed by Chris Marker. France.

Laplanche, Jean, and J.-B. Pontalis. 1986. Fantasy and the origins of sexuality. In *Formations of fantasy*, ed. Victor Burgin, James Donald, and Cora Kaplan, 5–34. London: Methuen.

Metz, Christian. 1986. The imaginary signifier. In *Narrative, apparatus, ideology: A film theory reader*, ed. Philip Rosen, 244–78. New York: Columbia University Press.

Penley, Constance. 1991. Time travel, primal scene, critical dystopia. In *Close encounters: Film, feminism, and science fiction*, ed. Constance Penley, 62–81. Minneapolis: University of Minnesota Press.

Theweleit, Klaus. 2002. *Der Knall: 11. September, das Verschwinden der Realität und ein Kriegsmodell*. Frankfurt am Main: Stroemfeld/Roter Stern. Citations translated by Marion Herz.

12 Monkeys. 1995. Film. Directed by Terry Gilliam. USA.

Vertigo. 1958. Film. Directed by Alfred Hitchcock. USA.

Waldby, Catherine. 1996. *AIDS and the body politic: Biomedicine and sexual difference*. New York: Routledge.

Williams, Linda. 1997. Introduction to *Viewing positions: Ways of seeing film*, ed. Linda Williams, 1–20. New Brunswick: Rutgers University Press.

4

Mediated Terrorism in Comparative Perspective: Spanish Press Coverage of 9/11 vs. Coverage of Basque Terrorism

Teresa Sádaba and Teresa La Porte

Hours after the terrorist attacks on the World Trade Center in New York and the Pentagon in Washington, President Bush delivered his first speech and established the nature and the scope of the conflict: "The deliberate and deadly attacks which were carried out yesterday against our country were more than acts of terror, they were acts of war"—a declaration of war that required an equal response. However, this was not just any war. As early as then, albeit against an enemy still faceless and nameless, the president already anticipated the nature of the struggle in store for the United States, and maybe even the rest of the world: "This will be a monumental struggle of good versus evil. But good will prevail."[1]

"Acts of war" and "struggle of good versus evil"—with these two expressions, the terrorist attacks of 9/11 and the framework the ensuing foreign policy of the United States were defined. The succeeding rhetoric and campaigns did nothing more than to develop these two key ideas in one way or another.

On this new stage, ushered in by the actions of al-Qaeda, political discourse is just as decisive as designing an efficacious security policy. We do not live solely in a world of arms but one of symbols as well (Richmond 2003) calling for appropriate, persuasive, and convincing political argumentation.

The president's words were directed at his nation, but also at the international community as a whole, which, without being the terrorists' target, should feel just as implicated and threatened by the turn of events. "Freedom and democracy are under attack. . . . This enemy attacked not just our people, but all freedom-loving people everywhere in the world."[2] In the days to follow, the president would underline that repercussion: "Civilized people around the world denounce the evildoers who devised and executed these terrible attacks. . . . We will use all the resources of the United States and our cooperating friends and allies to pursue those responsible for this evil, until justice is done."[3]

This political speech was delivered with the intention of being a global message. First, it was global because of the range of audience it reached, as the entire international community was waiting to see the president's reaction. Second, it was global for its content, inasmuch as the circumstances affected every nation worldwide. Finally, it was global for its end, since it established a principle and a course of action. It would not only determine the foreign policy of the United States for years to come but, in a certain measure, form a new world order wherein the different players must define where they stand (Rhodes 2003).

Critics and detractors of this policy have questioned its aims and procedures but not its global dimension. It is precisely these accusations that have helped spread it with that far-reaching effect.

Nevertheless, it seems evident that the way to process and comprehend 9/11, and the subsequent response, varies greatly among the different coverage and public opinions (Chakravartty 2002; Baiocchi 2002; Buonano 2002; Yinbo 2002). The supporting arguments for or counterarguments against the American proposal are many, and they bring to light diverse cultural experiences. The way in which the media present the message especially shows these divergences in the process of assimilation.

The following is a description of the cultural filters that modify and adapt what is in principle a global message for a local audience through a study of the coverage of 9/11 and the terrorist attack perpetrated in Madrid on March 11, 2004, as received in the main Spanish newspapers. In so doing, this chapter will examine the news paradigm used by the Spanish press in its coverage of 9/11 as compared to that used in the ongoing issue of Basque separatism. The focus of the chapter will be on how issues of nationalism and terrorism intersect at these different points, and the specific roles of nation-states in the discourses of these mediated terrorism. Finally, coverage of the events of March 11, 2004, in Spain will be cited as it sheds new light on the way terrorism is covered by the media.

THE PROCESS OF "GLOCALIZATION": THEORETICAL FRAMEWORK

Ever since Marjorie Ferguson (1992) divulged the fallacy of some myths of surrounding globalization, criticism of these supposed processes of this phenomenon have multiplied. Most of them can be grouped according to two tendencies. The first group comprises the ones that are situated at the source of the message and disclose the presence of specific interest transmitted with the appearance of world interest. The second is made up of those situated at the receiving end of the message, indicating the different interpretations with what is assimilated by different audiences.

Ferguson admits that the media can develop an indubitable international influence, "globalizing" the demand for democratic reforms, for example. In this sense, she acknowledges the merit of the support given to the nations that abandoned communism in favor of a democratic system. However, with respect to the messages about an intended "new world order," she considers the resort to the "global message" as nothing more than part of the rhetoric of public diplomacy of the American government. The "Pax Global" that would derive from the new world order would be one "Pax Americana" wherein the United States reserves the right to act as regulator. "Therefore, we may usefully distinguish between 'world order' as the creation of the order in the world and as an ordering of the world (according to a particular set of ideological conditions or economic practices)" (Ferguson 1992, 85).

Other authors describe the difference in the processes of assimilation among peoples. Implicitly, they share a definition of globalization as an intensification of reciprocal dependencies (Beck 1998; Giddens 1990), where the globalizing currents interact with the local currents (Giddens 1990). Referring in particular to the reception of the global message, Ronald Robertson coined the term "glocalization" (1995) in order to explain the adaptation global content suffers in each of the communities where it is received. According to Robertson, the local and the global are not mutually exclusive. Global messages are processed in a different way in each local community and the theoretical "fabricators" of local content—such as CNN—try to adapt their products to the local markets. In accordance with this affirmation, the risk of homogenization of content, which can be present in communication media, balances the very heterogeneity of each audience's culture.

Following this theoretical current, Rico Lie centers his attention on the process of cultural globalization of the media and, according to this theoretical trend, formulates the key question: "How do people in a local setting deal with global mass media content and do they counteract, in an interpretative sense, the increase in a foreign (global) cultural flow?" (2003, 78). Having some bearing on the same idea as Robertson, Lie suggests that the relationship between communication and global culture generates two opposite but complementary and simultaneous processes. Together with a phenomenon of homogenization, synchronization, integration, unity, and universalism—manifestations proper to the dissemination of a global message—an inverse phenomenon of heterogeneity, differentiation, disintegration, diversity, and particularism occurs, produced by the different local assimilation.

For Lie, globalization and *localization* (as opposed to glocalization) are two ways of interpreting the same content. That is why neither of the two is objective and unique and why they depend on the subjects that receive the message, which are at the same time differentiated by the community they belong to, by time, and by space. In this way, globalization and localization are two sides of the same coin, the same process with the same origin that lends itself to as much a local as a global interpretation (Lie 2003).

Following this theory, the study aims to observe how this process of local interpretation of global content develops in the media. That is to say, what filters are present in the Spanish press that modify and reformulate the generalized focus of the nature of international terrorism, and the appropriate way to fight against it.

First, the most salient characteristics of the American administration's policy after 9/11 will be revisited. Next, the processes of localization that act in the transmission of these contents in Spain will be determined.

THE BUSH ADMINISTRATION ON INTERNATIONAL TERRORISM: A GLOBAL MESSAGE

Some difficulties exist in admitting, indisputably, that the American response to the terrorist attack on the Twin Towers of New York can be taken as a global message. There are those who would claim it is exclusively about specific foreign policy that, like all action undertaken outside its borders, has international consequences. That view notwithstanding, in this study we understand that the ideas of the American administration could be understood as global by the same measure or with the same limitations as other messages (e.g., preserving the environment and upholding human rights) that have indeed been considered as such. To the arguments regarding range of audience, content, end, and the manner its detractors have of conceiving it, one more aspect is added, perhaps the most interesting: the intention of the terrorists themselves in making their message acquire a global dimension by attacking buildings as symbolic as the World Trade Center and Pentagon and perpetrating their attacks at a time of maximum television audience (Richmond 2003).

With the scope of the message established, the essential ideas gathered by foreign media, highlighting those with major impact on Spain, must be dealt with. First of all, the focus used to interpret the terrorist attack is insisted on—that it is a declaration of war on the United States of America. Reference to Pearl Harbor is constant. Some TV news programs are even allowed to begin their broadcasts by airing images from the recent movie of that title. Acknowledging this approach, the reaction of unanimous support for the government by the North American people as well as the country's media is understandable (Hutcheson et al. 2004). Together with these ideas, the image of an unwavering president assuming the responsibility of defending his country and ready to face a threat of such caliber is aired. Bush regains his leadership and polishes his image as leader.

As stated earlier, the second important idea in the message of the American government is the peculiar character that the war acquires. It is about not merely a military or political struggle but a war understood as having a moral nature—the struggle of good versus evil. This view prospers from the beginning, when the audience was still reeling from the impact of the magnitude of the attack. It is rejected, however, when it is invoked with the use of words such as "crusade" or when the enemy is identified as a vertex in an "axis of evil." These words provoke negative cultural resonance, and the historical European references make these expressions seem disproportionate and undermine confidence in the American perspective.

Nonetheless, it is coherent with the rest of the message. The struggle, thought of in this way, is closely linked to the clash of civilizations. Huntington's theory has been assimilated by social imagery, and the intention of the terrorists attacking the enclave of international capitalist commerce and the center of world democracy is read in this context. Liberalism and democracy are two characteristic features of Western culture; therefore it is a confrontation, or clash, of civilizations.

The sheer dimension of the terrorist attack, in its real as well as its virtual aspect, demands international collaboration. It is a threat that affects the world's society as a whole and calls for a proportionate response. It is the time for solidarity, not only in condemning the attack but also in the enforcement of punishment and prevention measures. Effective alliances are necessary, removed from traditional organisms if these do not prove efficacious enough (Chesterman 2004). And this criterion reestablishes differences between those who are "friends" and those who are not, depending on the disposition in accepting the policy and the effective collaboration with troops.

Lastly, this global message gives off a perception of vulnerability. The same sentiment of insecurity of the American people extends to the whole international population. Traditional methods are useless in guaranteeing citizen security, governments are not prepared to face these new dangers, and technology becomes a dangerous weapon.

All these affirmations are presented as conclusions drawn from one premise: The world changed on September 11, 2001. European media in general, but specifically Spanish media, have adopted a certain distance with respect to that perspective and set previous content in a more skeptical context—that what changed was the American perception of the world and the way they understood terrorism.

The relationship of the ideas presented does not intend to exhaust the content included in the message of the American government. It simply points out those the media gather persistently and which significantly contribute to forming the global orientation of the American position.

THE PROCESS OF GLOCALIZATION: CULTURAL FILTERS THAT MODIFY A GLOBAL MESSAGE

News of the 9/11 terrorist attacks turned the world upside down. Mass media of the entire planet collected what happened, and in many places, coverage of the events was continuous. However, as studies done on the coverage of 9/11 have shown (Baiocchi 2002; Buonano 2002; Yinbo 2002), the perspectives from which the events were narrated were as diverse as the places from where they were being narrated, the media used, and the focus.

The case of the coverage available in Spain lends itself to an interesting analysis, since terrorism has been ever-present in the young democratic life of this country. Because of this, terrorism always appears as one of the most important problems in the public agenda.[4] It is also an issue that takes up the most time and pages in the media. The brand of terrorism Spain has suffered has some unique characteristics due to its origin and modus operandi, which in great part, have defined the stand of society and the media.

It is for these reasons that, as the events of 9/11 unfolded, Spanish media reacted by covering the news in the standard way it has done over the years. The global message is interpreted within local parameters. In order to know what these are, how the Spanish media has understood the phenomenon of terrorism and specifically what the evolution of the coverage of Basque separatist terrorism has been since its inception has to be explained in some detail first.

Evolution of the Coverage of ETA Attacks since 1959

Euskadi Ta Askatasuna—or ETA, as the Basque separatist and terrorist group is more commonly known—means "Basque Homeland and Freedom" in the Basque language. It was founded in 1959 to wage an armed struggle for national liberation in the Basque Country, a northern region of Spain bordering France. It was an offshoot group of youths of the Partido Nacionalista Vasco (PNV, or Basque National Party).[5] After a beginning marked by ideological debate, ETA defined itself on nationalist and Marxist theses.[6] In 1968, it began its activities, resulting in the first victims of terrorist-related violence. To date, the number of deaths ETA has caused exceeds eight hundred.

For the purposes of this project, a detailed history of the terrorist organization is not of interest; rather, the ways with which the media has treated it are.

Taken from this perspective, it is significant to point out that the position has not always been the same, and that different stages in the ways terrorism has been dealt with can be discovered.

A first stage corresponds to the time of the group's origins, when there was an obvious lack of information, confusion with other types of terrorism, and ideas of international conspiracy. It must be noted that the first apparitions of ETA took place during the dictatorship of Franco, a time when freedom of the press was still nonexistent. For this reason, the reaction of the Franquist media was quite uniform. Censorship filtered information and commentaries, presenting only the version and slant that interested the government. ETA's actions were lumped together with other elements destabilizing to the regime, with the idea of an external enemy or a conspiracy against the regime.

It is in this sense that some members of the group made declarations to the effect that there existed exaggerated information regarding its activity: "Long before ETA began to carry out any kind of action that could be considered violent, in the year 1964, a feature appeared in the weekly *El Español* talking about ETA as a terrorist organization. . . . In the four pages of the feature there was exaggerated publicity of what ETA actually was up to that moment. It was as if they wanted to foster the strengthening of an enemy" (Uriarte 1997), so indicating that the media actually urged the group on in a way. "That the clandestine group could have at its disposal a history offered by a newspaper constituted a very important psychological boost" (Uriarte 1997).

A second stage took place after the Press and Print Law of 1966 (the so-called Fraga Law) with which there was a breakthrough, in a political sense. It can be said that until a certain point, ETA targeted only those "oppressive elements of the regime," and with this policy it found some sort of support. "It was believed that terrorism was an extreme and paroxysmal reaction against the dictatorship and once gone, terrorism would vanish with it." (Muñoz Alonso 1982).

In this context, an event that would help propagate a good image of ETA happened in 1970, the Prosecution at Burgos. This was a military trial in which sixteen terrorists were condemned—six sentenced to death and 752 years of prison terms in total were passed on to the others. From there, the press rallied a measure of support for the group. ETA is forgiven because of its fight against the dictatorship, said the press, pleading for clemency from its pages.[7] What is certain is that the press drummed up social mobilization in favor of the condemned—universities took to the streets, there was a demonstration in Paris led by Sartre, three hundred Catalan intellectuals signed the Manifesto of Montserrat, and so on. The result of the image of Burgos was one where the armed group was in tune with demands of democracy of the Spanish and international society, an image that has endured for many years in many countries. The condemned were seen not as terrorists but as heroic fighters against a dictatorship that tortured them. Eventually, General Franco exercised the right to pardon them.

With the coming of democracy, a third stage in the information about the terrorist organization took place in the Spanish press, in which the media realized that the terrorism of ETA would not disappear.[8]

After the promulgation of the Political Reform Law of 1976, the liberalizing mood of the press increased with the changes that occurred in the legal framework. That way, the decree of April 1, 1977, put an end to the Article II of the Fraga Law, source of so many disciplinary proceedings and sanctions. The Ministry of Information and Tourism was also scrapped. The Press of the Movement became the "Media of Social Communication of the State." The news services of the radio stations were liberalized, and finally, with the new Constitution of 1978, Article XX was promulgated, in which freedom of information was encapsulated. Two more years would have to pass until television had its Statute of Renewal, which in the end was not all that it was chalked up to be, since it continued to assert the character of "public service" and "state ownership." Politically, the 1978 Constitution contained an article (XV) abolishing the death penalty, aside from proclaiming amnesty for all prisoners through Law 46/1977 in 1977. On the other hand, Euskadi elected its own autonomous regime, ratified by a majority of 90.27 percent of votes in a popular referendum on October 25, 1979.

As for terrorism, however, the bloodiest years of the group were to be witnessed as the group broadened the scope of its targets to another type of civilian target, contrary to what everyone thought. This is how it was expressed in an interview of a member of ETA by *Cambio 16*: "Deep down, things have not changed," because they had not yet achieved either the amnesty nor the self-determination they demanded. Because of this, even with the dawn of democracy, the media noticed that ETA was not about to change. An editorial house came out with an interesting publication on January 25, 1977, by all the press entitled *Por la unidad de todos* ("For the Unity of All"), wherein a call was made for unity to save democracy. However, it was not until 1981 with the kidnapping and killing of José Mª Ryan, that media such as the nationalist daily *Deia* use the word "murder" for the first time with reference to a terrorist attack.[9]

The eighties marked a fourth stage, characterized by confusion in the media and a certain news silence. Justification for this attitude can be found in that the legitimacy of the terrorist cause was questioned—on the one hand, because of the veritable popular support enjoyed by Herri Batasuna (HB), the political arm of ETA, which reached its electoral peak in 1987,[10] and on the other, because of the appearance of the first news about the Antiterrorist Liberation Groups (GAL), which promoted armed confrontation with ETA.[11]

After a few years of indiscriminate and bloody terrorist attacks (such as the attacks on the Hipercor supermarket in Barcelona and the military barracks in Zaragoza), January 28, 1988, marked the first time ETA offered a conditional truce (subject to the creation of a table for dialogue). The kidnapping of Emiliano Revilla in February for 249 days forced the government's hand in announcing that there will be no contact. Nevertheless, on January 8, 1989, ETA declared a fifteen-day truce together with the state. Thus began the so-called Algiers Conversations. The newspapers *Egin* on one side and *El País* on the other were the authentic speakers, more than those seated at the table in Algiers, since both were used to issue press releases. The newspapers had the last word. In Algiers it was evident that ETA's dictionary got through to the media and that, at least according to governmental sources, ETA won the "communications battle."[12]

It was during this time that the Basque government, as well as the Spanish, tried a global news strategy to deal with the issue of news of terrorism. In the Basque Country, ten points of the Legislation Pact were published, and one of the points was to solicit an *ad hoc* news policy of the media.

The fifth stage in the media's treatment of terrorism was set in the nineties, the moment in which a strong social impetus was felt through the movements against terrorism by pacifist groups and a political thrust promoted via the Peace Pacts of Ajuria Enea (signed toward the end of the previous decade). But, the armed group stepped up its terrorist activity and political targets increased, even to the point of attempts on José MaríaAznar and the king. Moreover, there was a reinforcement of the strategy of kidnapping Basque businessmen.

July 1, 1997, is a historic date given that the armed group released two kidnap victims. One of them, Ortega Lara, had suffered 532 days in captivity. The images of the place where he was held and his haggard face and blank stare appeared in the media. Even some famous radio presenters broadcast directly from the place where he had been retained in a communication strategy of the Ministry of Interior to let what had happened to this man be known. In this euphoric climate of the liberations, a mere ten days later, Miguel Angel Blanco, councilor of the Popular Party (PP) of Ermua was abducted. ETA demanded that its political detainees be brought closer to the Basque Country within twenty-four hours; otherwise, it would execute the councilor (Iglesias 1997).

This time, the media assumed a more belligerent stance, and a climate of political and social unity against terrorism saturated the intense coverage that called for the mobilization of the citizenry (Sádaba 2004). In what was called the "Spirit of Ermua," the media came to define ETA as a "mafia" organization. There were historic media behaviors to convey one single image; for example, every television channel blacked out transmissions for one minute, the minute of hope, before the ultimatum expired. One headline in those days read "The

Killers Do Not Watch Television," unequivocally expressing the widespread coverage the media made of the innumerable mass actions. The media distanced themselves from the vocabulary of the group, retrieving the words "liberty," "unity," and "democracy" and calling the terrorists "fascists." Strong parallels were made with the times of the Transition; even songs and personalities of that era were revived. In the international media arena, this event was widely covered, although there was hesitation to call the armed group "terrorists." In any case, the coverage in Spain seemed to turn radically and decisively position itself on the side of the victims of the terrorist attacks. From then on, this interest in respecting and supporting victims has been present in the media as never before. Ever since the nineties, it can be seen that the Spanish media act in unison with the government's position, crying out with one voice against terrorism.

This age of media, social, and political unity was followed by a sixth stage that could be called a stage of "fronts." Owing to the creation of the Forum of Ireland and the signing of the Pact of Lizarra by the nationalist parties,[13] two fronts were consolidated: the constitutionalist front,[14] formed by the majority parties in Spain (the Spanish Socialist Worker's Party or PSOE, and the Popular Party or PP), and the nationalist front formed by the nationalist majority of the Basque Country (the Basque Nationalist Party or PNV, and the former HB, renamed Basque Citizens or EH).[15] When on September 17, 1998, ETA declared an indefinite cease-fire one month before the Basque elections in the region, there was no more unity, in the media or in society. However, each front tried to claim democratic values as its own.

In this manner, before 9/11, the media found themselves divided by their political preferences and according to the strategy they considered most effective in dealing with terrorism. Pro-independence parties and media favored establishing a dialogue prior to a cease-fire. Centralists or "pro-constitutionalists" refused to consider any kind of negotiation unless there preceded by a complete surrender of arms.

The evolution of the coverage of terrorism before 9/11 in the Spanish media has gone from ignorance to support, from confusion to silence, from belligerence to fronts. Nevertheless, with any of these attitudes, the values the media associate with the coverage of terrorism remain the same, though treated with different approaches:

1. It is a problem political in nature, with significant effects on society
2. A connection is established between terrorism and democracy, first to justify it, later as a destabilizing agent of it
3. It is inserted into a particular history, the history of Basque nationalism that thrives in a centralist state first, then in a state, that of a highly decentralized autonomous regime

4. Social unity can be spoken of as an instrument of support for the terrorists or for the fight against terrorism and helping the victims depending on the respective cases
5. Culpability of terrorist acts goes beyond the terrorists themselves; not only are the perpetrators guilty, but so are the ones who protect them in some cases, or those who have fostered political conditions conducive to the manifestation of terrorism in other cases.

The events of 9/11, very different in nature from local terrorism, in a way are nothing new neither to the public nor the media in Spain. The internationalization and globalization of the message about terrorism after 9/11 will do nothing but reinforce the positions of the media in a phenomenon of the localization of what is global or globalization, just as has been defined earlier.

Spanish Press Routines Covering Terrorism

Having described the historic evolution of press coverage of ETA's terrorist activity, the habitual practices of Spanish newspapers that determine a specific approach of treatment are briefly summarized below.

The Spanish people have direct experience with terrorism. This is the first determining factor that favors a local interpretation of the terrorist attacks committed on September 11, 2001, in New York and Washington. In this sense, as can be observed, many routines are developed and resources similar to those used by the editorial staff in the coverage of ETA's crimes, this terrorist group that operates in Spain under the banner of nationalism. Furthermore, possibly it is this experience with terrorism that numbs the media somewhat to attacks like those that occurred in the United States.

The first reaction is unanimous support for the government. In the face of a terrorist attack, the Spanish media and press generally react by condemning the act. At this moment, there are no political or ideological differences, and support for the government has hardly any flaws. The official interpretation that qualifies the killing and the reactions the armed forces consider convenient are respected and backed.

Condemnation is based on the principles of the defense of democracy and freedom. Although the harm or damage caused to the victims and the families are the priority and are considered before anything else, this does not exclude the affront to the entire nation considered from the very first moment. Resorting to violence is considered an attack against social dialogue and freedom of expression. In this sense, the national press highlights the outrage that the law of terror supposes for the entire Spanish people and does not even think twice in calling the imposition of one's will using force a totalitarian practice.

Different acts of terrorism are not distinguished from one another—they are all equally reprehensible. There is no differentiation according to the number of victims in a terrorist attack nor the condition or qualification of the same. The difference lies precisely in the ways with which they are handled by the very media, for example.

After the first hours after the commission of the terrorist attack had passed, newspapers revert back to their habitual ideologies and from that standpoint, evaluate the government's actions, the politicians' reactions, and the Security Armed Forces' effectiveness. The position each one adopts in relation to the government appears in this second moment, along with more critical postures with regard to the political yield or advantage the different parliamentary groups want to get out of the event.

Basque regional media, directly affected by the terrorist attacks and directly involved in the nationalization process of the community, have maintained a particular protocol from the very beginning. Organs especially in favor of the nationalist project keep a distance with respect to the government in Madrid but join in condemning attacks and in exploring different solutions, sometimes even in contraposition to Madrid, other than the official ones from the start of their coverage.

EFFECTS OF POLITICAL DISCOURSE AND SPANISH MEDIA ON THE COVERAGE OF 9/11

Despite the characteristics of what happened, 9/11 presents completely different features from those of the terrorism in Spain. Without a doubt, all of the political and social players tended to project Basque problems onto the 9/11 attacks (Sádaba 2002).

The Spanish government did it at first instance, establishing a parallel between international terrorism and Basque terrorism. Not many days after the events, the Spanish prime minister at the time, José María Aznar, related the two situations on various occasions: "Unfortunately, we in Spain have too much experience in that area. We know what all terrorists want, and we know it is impossible to distinguish between different types of terrorists."[16] Aznar said that in Spain, "we know that kind of suffering" and "we know how to react."

The Spanish government's discourse arguably influences four issues: that the perversion and destructive capacity of terrorism reaches unimaginable extremes; that terrorism is justifiable under no circumstance whatsoever; that every brand of terrorism is the same as the next—they are indistinguishable from one another; and that ETA's terrorism is just as bad and reprehensible as what was suffered in those grim days in the United States.

With this line of argument, the government sought to make its 9/11 message fit the general framework of its fight against its own terrorism, a framework that has ruled its agenda for years. Indeed, the Spanish government had insisted that in order to end terrorism, the collaboration of other countries was necessary and the struggle should be aimed at not only the terrorists but also those who support them (in relation to the social and political surroundings of ETA).

The media in Spain followed this discourse, although with slight differences proper to the political approach in which the framework of terrorism is found. For the analysis at hand, the sample selected was gleaned from the main national and regional newspapers representing the different ideologies and editorial lines closely linked to political options. As a matter of fact, among all the communication media, for its origins and subsequent evolution, it is the press that presents a high degree of diversity of options and a distinct political character.[17] *El País* stands out from the rest of Spanish newspapers for its political alignment with the PSOE and for enjoying the widest readership. *ABC* is a conservative newspaper; is a defender of Spanish tradition; is monarchist, liberal, and independent; advocates Spanish unity; is Catholic; and favors a free-market economy. *El Mundo* defines itself as antiimperialistic and antimilitary, a radical defender of human rights and public liberties. It tends to favor the PP and to lean toward the conservative, although the newspaper itself has claimed that its ideological space is center-left. In the regional press of the Basque Country, there are three main organs; *El Correo*, with a more centrist ideology; *Deia*, representing democratic nationalism; and *Gara*, a substitute for the closed *Egin* that has not condemned ETA's violence outright and is supportive to ETA's thesis.

The analysis uses qualitative methodology, where the guidelines of Bush's and Aznar's speeches are applied to the analytical categories and a high degree of coincidence can be seen.

In order to analyze 9/11 coverage by the Spanish press, one has to take into account the wide coverage these events had. Even though in Spain it took place at around three in the afternoon local time, the main newspapers came out with special editions published mid-afternoon and television stations devoted their whole airtime without interruption to cover what was happening. In other words, the media considered 9/11 to be news of the first order, as only on few occasions they have done in the past with ETA terrorism. In the pages of the newspapers, news alluding or related to 9/11 could be found in practically any section (Opinion, Economy, Culture and Television, International, and even Domestic News).

Following the guidelines of covering the terrorism at home, the characteristics of the message the media conveyed were the following. On the one hand, and differently from the Americans, the Spanish press normally did not talk as much about war as it did about terrorism, following what was happening in the United States (Kellner 2002; Entman 2003) and its own government's discourse. The September 12 front page of *El Mundo* is a clear example of this, but the most important cases are found in the newspaper *ABC*, which assumed the same stance as the PP. Its editorial pages are replete with allusions to ETA terrorism. Some comparisons were quite explicit: "World Trade Center and the Terrorism of ETA," "The Dynamite of Zarauz [a Basque village] and the Suicide Planes of Manhattan." The attack in New York was compared to the ETA attack on Hipercor (a popular Spanish supermarket). Others raised arguments that the Spanish readership was already familiar with, such as the call for dialogue to put an end to terrorism, which was a futile endeavor. It was repeated that Spain is already a veteran in this area.

The editorial "Las democracias contra el terror" (Democracies against terror) deals with the fight against terrorism, which is the biggest threat to freedom and democracy of the century. This is how the framework wherein ETA terrorism was traditionally arranged appears. The references kept reappearing in this daily; on September 23, the editorial's title read "ETA and 9/11."

This localization tendency manifests itself even in the very use of language that uses Basque to make puns, plays on words, and punch lines. For instance, that very day a column entitled "Bin Ladentxo" appeared, and next to it the "News in Brief" section carried a picture of Arnaldo Otegui with the caption: "Tal-Ibán para cual."[18]

El País, generally opposed to the politics of the incumbent government then, also echoed the message of terrorist experience launched by Aznar—"In Spain we know that the fight against terrorism requires tenacity"—even if at times it criticized the Spanish government for being electoral opportunists when it comes to making comparisons that are too explicit. In any case, it is surprising how this newspaper made these comparisons in the same tone with which they were made in *ABC*. The article "ETA, Globalized," where the "Taliban Arzalluz" is spoken of, also bears significance.

This posture is also observed in Basque regional newspapers, for example, *El Correo*, which gathered antiterrorist discourse of the Spanish government in its first editorial: "We are all threatened by terrorism. . . . They assault our freedom." Immediately they recalled the framework of the ETA case: "Attack against politics and democracy."

Apart from the focus on terrorism, the Spanish media, aware of the efforts of the antiterrorist struggle to gain support from other countries, unflinchingly seconded the involvement of the government. For example, *El País* would highlight, "Many years of having to endure ETA's violence and that of other terrorist groups means that Spain has developed more than just a special sensitivity for this terrible menace. For years it has sought greater international collaboration to combat it. And in this case, the Spanish secret services . . . must have special knowledge of the networks that may have been set up by Islamic terrorists in Spain." It continued, "This will also be an opportunity to concentrate every effort on something that Spain has been seeking since 1995, the creation of a common security space with the removal of EU borders." For this newspaper, the attack was not committed only in the United States but also in our political civilization, and it could very well be repeated in Europe. The newspaper made a call for international cooperation between democracies to ward off the threat. This need for cooperation was also underlined in *El Mundo*: "In favor of a concerted response and under parliamentary control," "Unconditional solidarity but not blind involvement."

ABC, in its editorial "Without Fissures," showed its satisfaction at the posture the European Union took to actively pursue these crimes of terrorism, an issue which also redounds to the fight against ETA. With regard to this, it was said that Islamic terrorism had dragged the world into a crisis similar to what the Japanese achieved when they bombed Pearl Harbor, which demanded an international response, above all from those permissive countries that harbor, take in, facilitate the financing of terrorist activity, or allow the training of terrorists within their borders. In the article "Spain in Its Role," the newspaper viewed Spain's support for the Americans' response as logical, combining the concept of a justified war with the argument that Spain had suffered this same evil and that all terrorism was aggression, and a war initiated against terrorism was a just one.

El Correo agreed: "Terrorism is a universal problem that attacks cruelly in Spain." A leading article called for "international justice" and "a new international order to fight terrorism." What is more, days later, it published an interview with the Spanish minister of justice, who took advantage of the context of international reaction against terrorism to speak about the Basque problem: "ETA has to know," he said, "that all Europe is against terrorism."

In this fashion, and as a peculiar characteristic of the media in Spain, does the theme of terrorism acquire its political aspect. It is not a cultural, moral, or religious question as it is in the United States. When it comes to terrorism in Spain, political stances appear precisely because the problem is politically framed. For instance, as opposed to the earlier remarks, the media of the Basque Country seem closer to the nationalist position. Democratic nationalism, best represented by *Deia*, is an example of this. *Deia* alluded to the fact that Bush's speech was translated erroneously to favor the position of the Spanish government. It is said that the words "people who allow [terrorists] to escape" were changed to "people who support them." Moreover, *Deia* wrote that 9/11 demonstrates that the solution to terrorism is "to dialogue," "to negotiate," and "to prepare conditions for pacific and mutual tolerance" more than provoking open confrontation or the arms race: "More effective than an anti-missile shield for eliminating the excuses of violent people, building better and more equitable conditions."

Finally, the daily *Gara*, which upholds the theses of ETA, put forward the idea that the 9/11 attacks were an answer to American foreign policy. According to the newspaper, from the United States and its imperialism derive "horrible crimes like the ones they are now suffering in their own territory." For *Gara*, the United States was reaping what it has sowed for years.

Another point to be made here is that, unlike the United States, not much surprise was felt from the Spanish media toward what happened. It may be for political motives, which leads *Gara* to speak of consequential logic of a determined policy, or the view of terrorism, as it seems the media digest events and find meaning. Such is the case of *El Mundo*, which, in the first editorial on the topic, "An Infamy That Will Change Our World and Mark Our Lives," tried to give an explanation for 9/11 in the setting of the Arab-Israeli conflict, inasmuch as their economic consequences. The subject of economics always raises questions on other occasions more than in any other medium: "Benefits for Spain," "Cheaper Money to Prevent the Collapse of Wall Street," "Wall Street Collapses,"are just some examples.

To end the analysis of 9/11, it has to be pointed out that the difference between the coverage of the Spanish and the Americans is precisely what Spanish newspapers allude to. In this way, it has to be stressed how the American media do not publish images that are too bloody—neither excessive blood nor corpses, as is sometimes the case with Spanish media. This fact, presented by *ABC*, is seen as hypocritical by *Deia*, which came out with "Images of Tragedy: Not Over There, But Here Yes," while another article noted that "in the Spanish State, bodies destroyed by car bombs are always first page photos in all media."

ABC assumes yet another media posture: the image of ETB (the public television channel of the Basque Country) denying the victims of the United States its solidarity when the rest of the television channels dedicated three minutes of silence. Within the text, the denunciation made of "Ekaitza," upon publishing an illustration of the Twin Towers crashing down and the caption: "We all dreamed of it. . . . Hamas did it."

The localization tendency of the media is not only checked by the continuity of guidelines and approaches to events—there are also significant images and formats that seek to bring messages closer. For an example of this, the front page of *El Mundo* on September 16 is very significant, as the five-column front-page story is titled "Bush Targets Bin Laden and the Taliban Threaten Whoever Assists in an Attack against Them," but the accompanying photograph portrays Aznar signing the book of condolences in the American embassy in Madrid.

SOME VARIATIONS IN THE COVERAGE OF 3/11

The terrorist attacks in Madrid on March 11, 2004, put the specter of terrorism right back on the front pages of the Spanish press and the rest of the world. This time, with almost two hundred fatalities three days shy of the national elections, these events surpassed any previous event—first of all because of its dimensions, second the date in which it occurred, and third the appearance of a new band of terrorists in national territory.

The first social, political, and media reactions following the established SOPs tended to give a logical priority to the victims and appeal for unity in the face of terror. In fact, the pages of the newspapers overflowed with testimonies, personal stories, lists of casualties, and so forth.

Notwithstanding, the proximity of the election date and the dominant focus of responsibility for terrorist attacks made the media take political postures, each defending a certain position. For this reason, it is impossible to speak of the government's position being supported with unanimity or that discourses got through to the media. It could have happened in the first hours after the terrorist attacks, when every sector was reactionary and pinning the blame on ETA.[19] The special editions of the three main newspapers were headlined: "Massacre in Madrid: ETA Murders More Than 130 People," "Murder by ETA in Madrid," and "Murderers: Profound Shock in Spain after the Savage Attacks by ETA in Madrid." *El País* went so far as to compare Madrid to New York: "Madrid is symbol of all that ETA defeats, like the Twin Towers were the symbol of capitalism and the American way of life for the radical Islamite."

However, other messages soon appeared that pointed the finger of blame to al-Qaeda, such as claims of authorship in a British newspaper or the discovery of a cassette tape of the Koran that began to raise suspicion. By then, the message of the government began to blur as other sources attributed the violence to al-Qaeda. The media behavior of taking up fronts reared its head again, as some took the government's side while others accused it of lying and withholding information (Artal 2004; García-Abadillo 2004). *ABC*, for example, insisted that "the attack could be the result of the imposition of the most radical wing of ETA," or that the government's strength was necessary "to keep in the vanguard in defeating terrorism" under whatever banner it may be. *El País*, however, insinuated that the government's intervention in Iraq has caused the ire of Islamic terrorism to fall upon Madrid. Another question was derived that appeared in the guidelines of the coverage of the terrorism of ETA—that culpability for the terrorist acts does not fall solely on those who perpetrate them but also on the political situation that engenders them.

Finally, it can be said that, as had happened in the past, terrorism was interpreted as the most grave attack against democracy, and because of this, in all the media, it was said that the response of the citizenry had to be that of going out and voting. What happened was that on this occasion there was also talk of a breach of rules of democracy (some speak of lies, others of manipulation).

In any case, and in the absence of investigations that would explain in depth the role of the media during those days of March, it can be stated without a doubt that the media once again took fronts, this time driven by the imminent general elections.

CONCLUSIONS

The coverage of 9/11 in Spain is a clear example of the localization of a global message.

In the same manner that President Bush's speech got through to the North American media, President Aznar's speech dominated the media agenda in those days. His arguments, wherein he tried to draw parallels with the situation of terrorism in Spain, were amply gathered by the press. In other words, the governmental agenda dominated the agenda of the press. Nevertheless, it must be pointed out that this dominion happened not so much because of the media's support of the government's stance, but because of the fact that the very speech of the Spanish president was a directed discourse on terrorism with roots deep in the public opinion of the country. Therefore, both political and media discourse were appealing to a way to comprehend terrorism experienced by many over the years. The value of democracy and unity, being at the victims' side, the absolute condemnation not only of the terrorists but also of their supporters, just as the need for international collaboration, were some of the issues that shifted from one agenda to the next.

Following the attacks on the World Trade Center and the Pentagon, the Spanish press gathered events by looking for analogies with the situation of ETA terrorism in Spain. It is in this way that the message was localized in form and in function, according to the examples analyzed, appealing to the political experience of the country. The terrorist nature of the events was underscored and there was less talk of war. The political aspect of terrorism was discussed more than moral, cultural, or religious aspects. Arguments for the internationalization of the attacks proposed by Bush were also taken advantage of to demand world recognition of ETA as a terrorist group. Finally, there was an appeal to unity and democracy as indisputable values threatened by terrorism as had happened in the stages of the coverage of terrorism in Spain.

The terrorist attacks of 3/11 brought together some of these same tendencies, but introduced greater politicization due to the proximity of the date of elections. Whether these differences were due to the government's inability to affix its agenda on the media owing to a lack of communication and synchronization with the citizenry is something that has to be considered.

NOTES

1. Remarks by President George W. Bush during a photo opportunity with the National Security Team, Washington, D.C., September 12, 2001.

2. Ibid.

3. Remarks by the President Bush during the National Day of Prayer and Remembrance for the Victims of the Terrorist Attacks on September 11, Washington, D.C.

4. This is confirmed by surveys conducted by the Center for Sociological Studies over the last twenty years.

5. ETA is born as an offshoot of a group related to the youth chapter of the PNV. Its ideological framework can be found in Federico Krutwig's book *Vasconia: Estudio dialéctico de una nacionalidad* (Buenos Aires: Norbait, s.d., 1963).

6. With the spread of the "KAS alternative" in 1975, total and perpetual amnesty and self-determination for the Basque Country, including Navarra, were demanded.

7. The posture of *El Correo* is significant: "La hora de la clemencia."

8. In 1974, the definition of the post-Franco strategy leads to two branches: military (which advocates military separation from the political for HB, the political arm of ETA, to be legal and they do not accept democracy) and politico-military (the political and the military in the same organization, makes the democracy more legitimate). Politico-military ETA calls a truce on February 28, 1981, and in 1982 celebrates its VIII Assembly in which a fourth of those present decided to abandon arms.

9. The day President Adolfo Suárez resigns José M Ryan is kidnapped. The groups allow for seven days in which Iberduero has to dismantle the power plant in Lemoniz. In spite of the massive popular reaction, the engineer appears dead.

10. HB was formed on April 27, 1978, as a political coalition that sought to unify the left-wing nationalists. It advocates the KAS program and justifies the struggle of ETA. It is opposed to the Constitution, the Statute of Guernica, and the Improvement. HB ran for elections in 1979.

11. On October 15, 1983, two members of ETA, José Ignacio Zabala and José Antonio Lasa, disappeared in the vicinity of Bayona (their bodies appeared in Alicante in 1995). Almost at the same time, news got out that members of the special police unit were arrested in France by the Gendarmes after a traffic incident near Hendaya involving the ETA member Larrechea. Shortly after, on December 4, Segundo Marey, a French Basque resident, was kidnapped, but he was freed days later as his abduction was a result of confusing him with the terrorist leader Mikel Lujua. The GAL made themselves known by owning up to the kidnapping, and according to *El País*, the Ministry of Interior as well as the government "express a total lack of knowledge to the police about the GAL." In 1987 the first investigations of the GAL case were made

public, where it was discovered that they were an instrument used by the Ministry of Interior to combat ETA. Together with other minor cases of corruption, this news begin to corrode the image of the socialist government (De Miguel and González 1989).

12. The terminology the terrorist group uses in its communiqués represents their constant war: commando, guerrillas, *gudaris*, executions, seizures, and so forth.

13. Through the Pact of Lizarra, application of the sponsoring factors of the Peace Agreements in Ireland are tried in relation to the Basque case, internationalizing the issue since it involves France as well as Spain. The negotiations had to take place first among the nationalist forces then go to the state.

14. This faction is described as "constitutionalist" because they justify their position by arguing that they follow the political principles of nationalism and independence contained in the Spanish Constitution.

15. The closing down in July 1998 of *Egin* was a warning sign that led to the creation of EH before any possibility of HB being outlawed. The change of initials also supposes a change of image within the other nationalist groups.

16. Statement by Prime Minister José Ma Aznar to the Congreso de los Diputados, September 26, 2001.

17. The Spanish press is highly politicized. Cf. Sádaba and Vara 2003.

18. These two titles are plays on words. The former turns bin Laden's surname into a Basque-sounding name, and the latter plays with the expression "tal para cual" meaning "two of a kind/meant for each other," referring here to the Taliban and the leader of the recently outlawed Batasuna, the political arm of the ETA terrorist organization.

19. The first politician to address ETA publicly was the president of the Basque government, Juan José Ibarretxe.

REFERENCES

Artal, R. 2004. *11-m–14-m: Onda expansiva*. Madrid: Espejo de Tinta.

Baiocchi, G. 2002. Media coverage of 9-11 in Brazil. *Television and New Media* 3 (2): 183–90.

Beck, U. 1998.*¿Qué es la globalización?* Barcelona: Paidós.

Buonano, M. 2002. Italian ambivalence. *Television and New Media* 3 (2): 177–82.

Chakravartty, P. 2002. Translating error in India. *Television and New Media* 3 (2): 205–12.

Chesterman, S. 2004. Bush, the United Nations and nation-building. *Survival* 46 (1): 101–16.

De Miguel, A., and J. L. González. 1989. *La ambición del César*. Madrid: Temas de Hoy.

Entman, R. M. 2003. Cascading activation: Contesting the White House's frame after 9/11. *Political Communication* 20:415–32.

Ferguson, M. 1992. The mythology about globalization. *European Journal of Communication* 7:69–93.

García-Abadillo, C. 2004. *11-m: La venganza*. Madrid: Esfera de los Libros.

Giddens, A. 1990. *The consequences of modernity*. Stanford, Calif.: Stanford University Press.

Hutcheson, J., D. Domke, A. Billeaudeaux, and P. Garland. 2004. U.S. national identity, political elites and a patriotic press following September 11. *Political Communication* 21:27–50.

Iglesias, Maria Antonia. 1997. *Ermua: Cuatro días de julio, el país*. Madrid: Aguilar.

Kellner, D. 2002. September 11, the media, and war fever. *Television and New Media* 3 (2): 143–51.

Lie, R. 2003. *Spaces of intercultural communication: An interdisciplinary introduction to communication, culture, and globalizing/localizing identities*. Cresskill, N.J.: Hampton Press.

Muñoz Alonso, A. 1982. *El terrorismo en España*. Barcelona: Planeta.

Rhodes, E. 2003. The imperial logic of Bush's liberal agenda. *Survival* 45 (1): 131–54.

Richmond, O. 2003. Realizing hegemony? Symbolic terrorism and the roots of conflict. *Studies in Conflict and Terrorism* 26:289–309.

Robertson, R. 1992. *Globalization: Social theory and global culture*. London: Sage.

———. 1995. Globalization. In *Global modernities*, ed. M. Featherstone, S. Lash, and R. Robertson, 25–44. London: Sage.

Sádaba, T. 2002. Each to his own: September 11 in Basque media. *Television and New Media* 3 (2): 219–22.

———. 2004. Enfoques periodísticos y marcos de participación política: Una aproximación conjunta a la teoría del encuadre. *Política y Sociedad* 41 (1): 65–76.

Sádaba, T., and A. Vara. 2003. Elecciones 2000: Carrera de caballos y partidismo mediático. *Revista ZER* 14, May, 59–74.

Sinclair, J. 2000. *Televisión: Communication global y regionalización*. Barcelona: Gedisa.

Uriarte, E. 1997. El tratamiento periodístico de ETA desde 1964 a 1975. Doctoral diss., Universidad del País Vasco, Bilbao.

Yinbo, L. 2002. How Chinese television and new media presented the US 9-11 tragedy: A comparative study of SINA, CCTV and Phoenix TV. *Television and New Media* 3 (2): 223–30.

5

National Politics of Belonging and Conflicting Masculinities: Race and the Representation of Recent Wars

Antje Schuhmann

In these days, war and terrorism seem to be intrinsically linked: Terrorist attacks, torture acted out by American and British soldiers against Iraqi prisoners, the "War against Terrorism"—called a "human intervention" with "collateral damage" against the civil society. In a perverted way, all of this goes hand in hand, and furthermore, in media reports, both text and visuals, the representations of terror and war are inevitably linked with gender, race, and certain notions of culture and civilization. In the West, culturalized and ethnicized violence mingles with national identity processes and their highly gendered phantasms of modernity and antimodernity.

The discourses of progressiveness and atavism are often symbolized in the icon of the Western white emancipated woman and the gender-sensitive white man.[1] The assumedly natural-born chauvinistic non-Western man and his victimized Other woman serve as contrast foils for white phantasms of their own advanced civilization. Women's liberation, serving as guarantor for the construction of a superior national identity, is always of high interest when it suits certain domestic or international interests. It might be to fight immigration, to challenge the fact of multicultural societies, to legitimate "national security measures" such as video monitoring of public spheres, or to justify so-called humanitarian interventions, formerly named war. The role of the media in mediating these alliances of human rights as women's rights in the name of civilization is manifold and informs dominant notions of Western white masculinity as essentially enlightened.

This chapter will exemplify discourses organized along the axes of race, gender, and modernity/civilization within three political fields highly discussed in the media. An analysis of the torture scandal in the context of the Iraq war will explore the linkages of gendered and ethnicized notions of perpetrators and victims. A short excursion into the German leading culture debate will provide the ground to unfold the basic discursive elements of national identity processes in the light of Western superiority phantasms and certain notions of masculinity and femininity. Having prepared the analytical ground for the manifold intersections of Western notions of superior civilization, nation-building processes, gender, and violence, I will explore the production and reproduction of these discourses in German media reports about the German participation in the Kosovo war.

Deeply rooted in the assumedly universal values of Western culture, white men are pictured theses days as tolerant, responsible, and fair partners, husbands, politicians, and—last but not least—soldiers. The discourse of women's emancipation in the context of the Afghanistan war was easily functionalized by human interest stories of unveiling Afghani women and liberating them according to Western feminist standards. I am not focusing right now on whether this is in the interest of Afghani women or not. I am more interested in the contradictions of these seemingly altruistic legitimizations of war based on an elegant amnesia about whose money and interests brought into power those forces the Western troops pretended to liberate the victimized women from. Was the occidental self-image as messianic women's paradise during the Afghanistan war a still relatively unbroken one? The metropolitan discourse of women's liberation seemed to have been changed in the context of the Iraq war.

WOMEN'S LIBERATION TO BE REVISED IN THE LIGHT OF TORTURE?

The torture scandal involving the U.S. occupying forces shocked the world daily with new pictures of the Baghdad prison Abu Ghraib. The weekly supplement of the *New York Times* in the German newspaper *Süddeutsche Zeitung*, in "The Manufacturing of Heroes and Villains," covered a story about two special pinup girls: Jessica Lynch and Lynndie England. On the one side we see the blonde, brave soldier and teacher-to-be, who was captured in spite of her heroic fight with Iraqi soldiers. Only through the even more heroic action of her male comrades was Lynch freed out of the hands of the Iraqi enemies—at least according to the official and later completely revised version of the embedded media. As her mirror image the article presented a woman who "is dark, a smoker, divorced" (Rich 2004) and who found her way into the headlines as the "torture witch" and a perverted example of falsely understood women's liberation: Lynndie England.

It is not necessary to discuss at length the iconic pictures—one showing England standing next to a naked man, who is lying on the floor with a leash around his neck held by England as she grins into the camera, another in which we see her face and her erected thumb and finger, imitating a pistol aiming at the penis of an Iraqi prisoner. Still another document of her perverted women's liberation, in the sense of doing as one pleases, shows her standing next to a male soldier behind a human pyramid arranged of naked human bodies. The media discussed the series of daily-surfacing torture pictures widely as pornographic and sadomasochistic-inspired documents of torture. In the highly heated debate, many questions were asked, but some crucial aspects remained untouched, indicating the limits of dominant discourses around violence, gender, and race: What happened to the female prisoners in Abu Ghraib? The fact that most torture acts were carried out by men was not considered debate-worthy. At least in the German media, possible structural linkages of sadism with masculinity and military structures were not discussed. Hence, the question of why England "as a woman" was doing such a thing was the main focus of public debates. Was she under the spell of her fiancée—and in this reading a semi-innocent victim herself—or did this "evil" come out of herself? Did this woman even enjoy her actions?

Antifeminists felt as much confirmed—"this whole thing with women's emancipation was completely out of control"—as feminists were shocked. Barbara Ehrenreich wrote in her article "A Uterus Is Not a Substitute for a Conscience: What Abu Ghraib Taught Me" in the *Los Angeles Times:*

> A certain kind of feminism, or perhaps I should say a certain kind of feminist naiveté, died in Abu Ghraib. It was a feminism that saw men as the perpetual perpetrators, women as the perpetual victims and male sexual violence against women as the root of all injustice. Rape has repeatedly been an instrument of war and, to some feminists, it was beginning to look as if war was an extension of rape. There seemed to be at least some evidence that male sexual sadism was connected to our species' tragic propensity for violence. That was before we had seen female sexual sadism in action. (Ehrenreich 2004)

Did we really see female cruelty's first time in action in Abu Ghraib? In Germany, since the 1980s one can observe a shifting focus of the feminist debate. From the universal female victim of patriarchy to the "Mittäterin" (a kind of helper of the perpetrators), the debate finally has acknowledged the fact of fully responsible female perpetrators during German fascism.[2] In the United States, the critique of the universalistic attitudes of white middle-class feminism and the fading out of historically and current privileges and racisms are even older. Considering these contexts, the now widely formulated shock— the astonishment that the concept of femaleness is no longer and never was innocent—can only be read as another expression of ignorance.

So why this sudden outcry? Maybe because the notion of a universal female powerlessness is sometimes so much more comfortable than acknowledging one's own situated and ambivalent relations to power? How is it possible that in today's advertisements from light food to the cosmetics industry, female empowerment seems to be the interest of everybody, but nobody seems to ask anymore for the price of participating in dominant power structures? Commodifying the motto of the women's movement "Good Girls go to Heaven, Bad Girls go everywhere," everyone seems to agree: Women must take their life in their own hands and finally do what men always did. There is nothing wrong with this demand, isn't it?

> What is particularly interesting in these photographs of abuse coming out of Iraq is the prominent role played by Lynndie England. A particular strand of feminist theory—popularised by Sheila Brownmiller and Andrea Dworkin—attempts to argue that the male body is inherently primed to rape. Their claim that only men are rapists, rape fantasists or beneficiaries of the rape culture cannot be sustained in the face of blatant examples of female perpetrators of sexual violence. In these photographs the penis itself becomes a trophy. Women can also use sex as power, to humiliate and torture. (Bourke 2004)

Often negotiated like a natural law, the dominant analogy woman = victim, man = perpetrator reaffirms a notion of male (sexual) invulnerability. The German media described the acts of torture often as forms of "sexual abuse"—the word "rape" was never used. Acknowledging that men can be raped and especially that men can be raped by women seems impossible. Still, female perpetrators are more shocking than men doing the same, even if cruel women participating in systems of power-dominant structures of violence are nothing new. In light of two very different historical examples, and without intending any comparisons—female wards in Nazi German concentration camps and the cruelties of white slaveholding women in the United States—it is astonishing that feminists and the general public are so astonished about a female torture perpetrator.

"How can a woman do such a thing?" This inquiry was not accompanied by any form of interest in the question: how can men do such things? It seems that the participation of a woman was leading to the assumption of a loss of Western values. Is this to be read as an acknowledgment that Western men never cared for these proclaimed values anyway? Unfortunately not. Still, women are supposed to symbolize these values and men are expected to fight for them. It is interesting and scary that even such a significant incident does not at all destabilize notions of superior Western white masculinities. On the contrary, after the first waves of shock, counterdiscourses took over—accusing the critiques of being unpatriotic, destabilizing, and endangering the troop's morality.

In public discussions, an act of torture carried out by a woman becomes directly linked to her gender, while an act of cruelty by a white man will not necessarily produce questions around male identities and their roots in patriarchal structures of Western society. Contrary to that, violence acted out by nonwhite/non-Western men will immediately lead to discussions about what I name ethnicized gendered violence. Without hesitating, linkages are made between masculinity concepts and the particular culture (these days often Islamic) the perpetrator is said to be related with. That means, as long as nonwhite men are concerned, their violent actions will be immediately interpreted in a wider framework of gender stereotypes mixed with essentialized notions of ethnicity and culture. In other contexts as well as the Iraq war, torture or any other form of violence perpetrated by white Western men or women does not cause the necessary questions to be asked. For example, how are these acts intrinsically linked with a praxis and theory of (racist) and gendered violence inscribed deeply in Western cultures, shaped by diverse systems of suppression, exploitation, or extermination—such as slavery, colonialism, and the Holocaust? Following that, how are these legacies reproduced and modernized in national discourses and international politics of the West?

The shock created by the negative image of an empowered but cruel phallic woman is only the flip side of a coin whose other side presents the positive image of the white Western woman doing a man's job, being fully equally with men, having all citizens' rights, and being sexually freed and economically independent. The emancipated Western woman became a powerful discursive icon for Western national identity processes, symbolizing social progress of advanced civilizations. As the dominant gender system is a relational one, certain notions of femaleness influence specific ideas about masculinity. Especially in the context of gendered national boundary managements, the reflexivity of gender constructs becomes obvious: the more progressive "our" women are, the more progressive are "our" men. The more progressive "we" are, the more atavistic must be those Others we have to enlighten—if necessary, by humanitarian interventions or a just war in the name of women's rights, human rights, democracy, and freedom. In short: Western civilization.

Informed by colonial legacies, German national identity politics are shaped by more or less underlying racist discourses that include the notion of so-called progressive, secularized Western and atavistic non-Western masculinities. In the following section, new forms of masculinity and their intersection with the notion of civilization and whiteness in the current processes of German nation building will be analyzed in a twofold way.

The notion of a new German masculinity constructed as opposed to an atavistic, fundamentalist, juvenile, Islamic, suppressive, and so forth Other masculinity can be exemplified in a twofold way: in domestic and international contexts. I will introduce the German media coverage of the Kosovo war in 1999 and its construction of a superior German masculinity with a short analysis of the domestic German leading culture debate—a discourse that contextualizes current processes of creating a positive male German identity, as opposed to an ethnicized male Other, stereotypes with national and international political relevance.

NATIONAL BOUNDARY MANAGEMENT, THE POLITICS OF OTHERNESS, AND NEW GERMAN MASCULINITIES

The national politics of Otherness are an interesting starting point to explore how images of so-called Others are functionalized for the construction of a collective "We" for the ongoing process of German "nation building." This little example is helpful to describe some crucial elements of ethnicized and gendered forms of actual nation building in Germany, whose central elements will be identified later again in the context of German media reports about the Kosovo war.

What was a "German leading culture" meant to be? This debate came up first time in November 2000 after a summer of violent pogroms against immigrants and was defined by Member of Parliament Friedrich Merz as grounded in three basic elements: German language, constitution, and the position of women.[3] In Merz's eyes, "*the* position of women" is granted by the enlightened way that German men treat women. Of course, this self-idealization must exclude questions like, How they treat *which* women? Do they treat with respect women generally or only "their own"? Besides the fact that Germany is no feminist heaven, not even for white German women, one should explore how German men treat immigrant women in Germany or foreign wives they order by catalog. Is anyone asking how respectfully German men treat sex workers in Thailand, Poland, and other countries with women fantasized as still genuinely feminine and submissive?

The proclamation of an advanced "position of women" in Germany leads to the phantasm of modern forms of German masculinity that contradict other more atavistic forms—all of them non-German, of course. To explore this male national vanity, I want to discuss "the position of women," conceptualized as a basic element of German national culture, or let's put it this way: gender equality understood as a central ground for the construction of ethnicized sameness and Otherness. Is women's liberation a newfound cultural value of the German "Kulturnation der Dichter und Denker"?

For the Christian Social Union (CSU) minister of the interior in Bavaria, Günther Beckstein, the case is very simple: "For me leading culture is that there won't be a minaret in a Bavarian village and that Turkish women in Germany have at least as much say as their husbands."[4] The CSU, a party that exists only in Bavaria in southern Germany, has been in power since the end of World War II and supplied the federal conservative opposition with the right-wing chancellor candidate Edmund Stoiber in the autumn 2002 federal elections. Naming the CSU and feminism in the same sentence seems oxymoronic. Stoiber's family pattern has been described by his wife as "Wherever you go, I will follow you," and summarized in the *Berliner Morgenpost*: "She is watching the cave and he is hunting."[5]

For those unfamiliar with the CSU, the political party claims a serious interest in supporting women's emancipation, presented in strong sentences like "Those who have resentments against women's equality are not welcome here," but this policy is contradicted in all of their politics. In spite of its proclaimed women's liberation attitudes, the CSU has no problems with deporting migrant women whose residence permission depends on the maintenance of their marriage, but who have fled into a women's shelter to be safe from domestic violence enacted by their German or non-German husbands. Also, until 1996, the CSU blamed the participation of women in the labor market for the generally high unemployment rate.[6]

In the above quote, Beckstein is not demanding that his boss's wife should adjust right now to the obviously essential German practice and theory of feminism. Beckstein is talking about oppressed Turkish women; the Other woman functions here as the antithesis of one form of newly idealized German femininity. In this rhetoric, the Other woman is used for the self-definition of German national culture, stigmatized as a gendered and ethnicized boundary marker that is not and never will, due to her static mentality/culture, be part of the national German collective.

But it is not only the image of the Other women that is used in the self-inventing process of male German identity. The Other woman is used to define the specifics of the German woman; the German woman is needed to finally provide German masculinity the point of reference for its own modernity. The male Other is also part and parcel of the reinvention of German masculinity. The non-German, and of course non-Western, Other man—and this is a slippery slope as Eastern European men are "Othered" constantly as well—is constructed as uncivilized, constantly partaking in sexist behavior, and placed in opposition to real German men, who need no extra enlightening about how to deal with the "modern European women in the twenty-first century." This is exactly what the CSU demanded in the Munich city hall after nine rapes in two weeks took place during the Oktoberfest (Munich's big annual beer festival); they voted for "enlightening courses in migrant and refugee quarters." Even though nearly all offenders were identified by the victims as Germans,[7] the ruling party of Bavaria announced, "The increasing assaults against women—especially acted out by foreign citizens, give evidence to the fact that the multicultural society suffers from a sick image of women."[8]

Beckstein's definition of a German "leading culture" includes new and old aspects of what Floya Anthias and Nira Yuval-Davis (1992, 33) named gendered "border management." The tendency to use women as symbolic "border guards" is not new at all. Yuval-Davis (1997, 46) adds:

> Women, in their "proper" behavior . . . embody the line which signifies the collectivity's boundaries . . . Women usually have an ambivalent position within the collectivity. On the one hand, as mentioned above, they symbolize the collectivity, unity, honour and the *raison d'être*, . . . on the other hand, however, they are often excluded from the collective "we."

Surprisingly enough, feminism seems nowadays defined as proper behavior for German white women, at least as long it is comfortable and doesn't hurt. This typical form of gendered national boundary management, dressed up in the new clothes of gender equality, has a direct impact on how so-called new and progressive masculinities are constructed as typically German. By doing so, the "leading culture" debate as part of the German nation-building process swallows women's emancipation, a historical and ongoing social and political struggle against dominant patriarchal structures. This political struggle is now included in national rhetoric as an ahistorical boundary signifier of the German national narration.

In this process, we can identify two mechanisms that are essential for national discourses and the dominant politics of Otherness. One goal is the production of unity, the production of an imagined homogeneous collective without inner tensions and contradictions. This is very important for the construction of an "imagined community" (Anderson 1993)—in the German case, a collective of German men and women living peacefully together without gendered conflicts—an illusion achieved simply by outsourcing the conflict and by shifting the frame of problem analysis from gender asymmetries to conflicts grounded in fundamental and universal differences informed by mentality, culture, or nationality. Sexual assault is no longer understood as a patriarchal act but as a clash of civilizations.

This problematic (non)understanding of sociohistorical power relations and struggles, or shifting of a framework of interpretation, is based on what Yuval-Davis (1997, 12) calls the ongoing "colonization of the social by the cultural." We have to keep in mind that all arguments on civilization are grounded on a strong belief in dualistic concepts: nature versus culture, progress versus atavism, evolution and development versus stagnation and being out of history. All this plays into a certain conception of nation-time that Ann McClintock calls a "temporary anomaly" (McClintock 1997)—preserving one's own culture and traditions that are perceived as valuable, while at the same time protecting one's own progress from all other traditions that are perceived as backward oriented, "uncivilized," and alien. Moving the analysis of gendered nation-building processes from a domestic to an international framework makes it obvious that foreign politics and the representation of the participation in war are also heavily engaged in the construction of a superior white Western masculinity as an element of a dominant national German identity—a masculinity constructed in opposition to atavistic, childlike, and threatening forms of non-German/non-Western manhood.

WAR AS A NATIONAL DISCOURSE MACHINE FOR A POSITIVE GERMAN MASCULINITY

In 1999 German military forces entered Yugoslavian territory as part of the NATO Kosovo Peacekeeping Force (KFOR) and participated in an, according to international law, illegitimate warfare. This was covered by German media in text and visualization. As highly gendered representations, the media reports of the first German participation in warfare since 1945 were shaped by several frames such as nationalism, violence, and racial stereotyping. The ideological arrangement could be described as following: On the one side, we find the primitive-nationalistic Serbs, driven by an irrational southern Slavic mentality. On the other side, we find the German soldier, a member of a collective that considered itself to be dealing with its history in the best way possible: We have learned how to do nationalism in a healthy and civilized form, so now finally we can educate Others how to do it.

Analyzing the media coverage of the war we find analogies and tropes borrowed from different discourses. Some of them can be identified as racist-colonial legacies, others as referring directly to traditional rituals of male bonding or as classics in the canon of gendered national representations.

Journalists compare the Kosovo war with a sporting event like the Tour de France: "The withdrawal of Milosevic's soldiers doesn't appear as an army which has just lost the war but they act as if the Yugoslavian basketball team has won the championship." Connections were made with novels and films: "The refugee drama in and around Kosovo is transferred into Hollywood-style visuals of the historical humanitarian intervention of the West" or "The first western convoy got stuck before the bridge of Kacanik. A village like in a Hemingway novel." Cities are compared with women: "Pristina was never a beauty among the cities but now it appears like a whore."[9]

The topos of the child also comes up again and again: Children are a threat standing at the sides of the streets when Western convoys pass by; the non-Western soldiers are perceived as immature youngsters rather than as an army one is fighting. The Serbs are not referred to as soldiers at all and their actions are described as irrational and in an infantilized way. Mostly they seem to be just crazy—mad in a scary way, like marauding bandits. "Rotten uniforms gaze and faces like in a horror film, aggressive, threatening...." or "They were like animals. Often they used drugs, we found lots of needles and they were always drunk."[10] Described either as terrorists or immature youngsters the political motivation of Serbian soldiers and their government was no point of interest in the media coverage, at least not one engaged in a serious manner. I am far from defending either the Serbian or the Kosovo nationalism, but it remains interesting to explore the double standards in the debates on separatist conflicts. Maybe we should remember the early Weimar Republic in Germany and the attempts to create a socialist anarchist inspired Räterepublik in Bavaria and how the Prussian government reacted to that. I wonder what would happen if Bavaria started to separate again from the federal state of Germany. In the public perception, the violent reaction of the Serbian state to the ongoing separation of the country was mainly pictured as motivated by an insane and irrational Serbian nationalism.

In the context of national separation and conflict, we continually find representations of the scary, irrational, and brutal Serbian nationalism, as opposed to the partisans of the Kosovo Liberation Army (KLA). Visualized by tracks of fleeing women, or as desperate but brave fighting men with no other interest than to protect their soil and their women, people from Kosovo are constructed exclusively as victims, as feminized victims in relation to the brutal masculinity of the Serbs. The description of a KLA fighter in a plundered mosque, saying with tears in his eyes, "They don't have a heart, they must be crazy, aggressive people,"[11] fits in with Western politics: Rape, plunder, and killing no longer appear part of war and the military as institutionalized forms of male bonding and patriarchy but as an expression of a specific national culture understood as based on mentality. In the media coverage, "misbehaving" is much more linked to nonnormative mentalities embodied in specific national masculinities. The imperial interests of the various Western governments, hidden in the language of humanitarian intervention, become invisible as the rapes and war crimes committed by the Western KFOR troops remain unspeakable. Similar to the torture debates, theses acts of violence were labeled as collateral damage or were, if mentioned at all, explained as nonstructural but individual faults of men whose white, Western origin was in this context of no interest.

The way the former Yugoslavian combatants—the Serbs versus the KLA—were portrayed had a direct influence on the hierarchical positioning and reinvention of the good German soldier, a soldier who is considered by the international community as being mature enough to participate in international warfare, for the first time since World War II. A new modern form of white, Western masculinity was publicly created and can be linked to the discourses I identified in the leading culture debate. Facing the two squabbling kids, the German soldier appears at the last minute and sorts it all out. In the tradition of the racialized hierarchical family of humankind of the nineteenth century, with the enlightened Northern races and nations on top guarding the colonial children of the South toward the light of civilization, Western troops now protect the East from itself.

A well-known German newspaper carried an article in June 1999 describing how a German general heroically prevented a massacre: "He disarmed a group of young Serbian soldiers threatening civilians—and so he stopped a bloody incident."[12] *Focus*, a weekly political magazine, wrote about the same incident in "A German Hero Was Born."[13] The accompanying pictures show a kind of father–son constellation. The German general, much older than the Serbian soldier, took the "boy's" gun bravely with bare hands and with a gesture expressing his natural authority. This metaphorical castration could be summarized: "Give it to me. You'll only make nonsense with that thing anyway!" The various reports on this incident dwelled on the fact that the general knew how to disarm his opponents as he unfolded a kind of natural authority the immature Serbs had to obey. "Suddenly they seemed to be smaller, youngsters only and not killers any longer."[14] Considering this and other similar incidents, the summary could be an analog to the *Tagesspiegel* article "German Soldiers Are Good Soldiers."[15] They are mature and reflective, not in spite of but especially because of German history. The bestiality of Nazi German warfare, especially in the region of former Yugoslavia, was never directly referred to but was a constant underlying foil in the construction of a new mature German soldier. German history was used as an invisible but present experience that forced Germans to grow up and entitled German soldiers of today to act out a historical and quasi-natural authority over the irrational, childlike Serbian soldiers.

Throughout history, it is well known that the topos of a hierarchical, patriarchal family helps to essentialize and naturalize political conflict and violent situations of change. Described as liberation, the fact of an (according to international law) illegitimate occupation of Yugoslavian national territory was rhetorically erased. At the same time, the German military could finally recover from its own past by linking it to the necessity of current political developments as proof the lesson has been learned. In the twisted sense of "Because of Auschwitz, the Germans have to participate in that war," the German foreign minister argued against critiques from the peace movement. The Yugoslavian partisan army fighting Nazi German troops and occupation nearly half a century ago was completely veiled with the new image of the wise, reflective, and civilized good German soldier. A father grown out of puberty, he can now show the rest of the world how to deal with conflict, and he provides the reason for national pride, so badly needed at home.

CONCLUSIONS

Similar discussions on whiteness, civilization, and superior Western masculinities are countless in the diverse media coverage of international war. One analysis I want to point out is that of Dominique Malaquais (2004), who looked at the media coverage of the U.S. military intervention in Somalia with a special focus on the construction of U.S. masculinity and African femininity. Also, Katja Diefenbach had a closer look at the politics of representation and Othering in the context of Somalia. In her article on the Hollywood film *Black Hawk Down*, a pop-cultural representation of the Somalia conflict from an American point of view, she argues:

> The image of the southern warlord is one of the strongest stereotypes of bourgeoisie discourses on warfare. The warlords of the North, international weapon dealers and security corporations like MPRi, Defence Systems, Limited, Executive Outcomes, DynCorp12 and others, who sell weapons from Croatia to Colombia, remain relatively invisible. (Diefenbach 2001, 27)

Invisible in their ties, suits, and conference venues and in their normative whiteness, I would add. Meanwhile, the young warlord of southern Somalia is constructed as a juvenile form of corrupted masculinity.

> Out of control, with no discipline, corrupted by money and popular culture—Rap [gangster style] and Ray-Ban sunglasses, he is the embodiment of a monstrous, illegitimate killing and raping machine. (Diefenbach 2001, 27)

In earlier times, warfare in Europe was a business not monopolized by the state. It included burning down villages, raping, plundering, robbing, and killing. When the business of lawless killing was transferred to the colonies, the massacres of the Middle Ages were tamed in Europe. State-supported and written rules of warfare aimed to protect civil society. This was and is still considered an accomplishment of European civilization, opposed to the so-called atavistic forms of warfare and resistance in non-European countries. The image of the out-of-control and selfish warlord of today serves as a contrast to the bastions of institutionalized masculinity in the form of disciplined, state-organized military forces, lobbyists of the weapons industries, politicians, and all those others pretending to act according to the law of international warfare Western nations have subjected themselves to.

This is the theory, but not the reality. The new forms of war we currently have to face are considered a kind of police intervention, often breaking international agreements and fought by hired combatants, by outsourced private companies. Since Afghanistan and especially since the Iraq war, we encounter daily new realties of warfare, brutality, and torture.

It seems as if the dominant notions of Western/white superior masculinities are not at all destabilized by these developments. The uncovering of acts of torture committed by U.S. soldiers against Iraqis could have been a moment of at least starting to question the dominant discourses of Western superior masculinity—it could have been, but it was not. Maybe due to the normativity of white masculinity, the acts of torture were not interpreted in the same frameworks as violence acted out by discursively ethnicized men. Culture and mentality were never made an issue; the brutal perversion of enjoying torture was neither interpreted in a gendered way, at least not with a focus on masculinity nor in a framework of Western culture/mentality. The acts were not understood as structural but as individual failures, individuals who left the common ground of Western values. But why were these acts even considered to be a loss of Western values and not as forms of brutality, notions of entitlement, racism, and chauvinism that are historically deeply rooted in Western culture and patriarchy.

Especially with reference to racialized discourses of civilization, progress, and development in the context of war, one wonders if we even can observe an ongoing reaffirmation of whiteness. A notion of whiteness that is specifically grounded within the imagination of progressive masculinity developed in the context of ethnicized and gendered violence and within new forms warfare, including the war on terror and its anti-Islamic outcomes.

NOTES

1. The usage of terms such as "whiteness"/"Western" subjectivities, as opposed to "Blackness"/"Otherness" in this chapter, refers neither to a physical appearance in form of black or white skin color nor necessarily to a geographical origin. I rather understand categories of whiteness/Western subjectivities as historically developed social constructs that grant and legitimize privileges and different notions of entitlement and superiority toward all those "Others" subjected to racism. In the German context, these can be, for example, immigrants of Southern or Eastern European origin as well as Black people. I use Black or Other with a capital letter, referring to antiracist struggles and concepts of self-identification and to distinguish these terms from dominant phenomenological or essentializing usage and to stress the constructedness of these concepts.

2. For a survey of the debate, see Walterspiel 1993.

3. Friedrich Merz, following the advice of the Allensbacher Institute. Petra Bornhöft, Christoph Leinemann, and Christoph Mestmacher, "Stolze schwarze Deutsche," *Der Spiegel* 44/2000, 30–32.

4. Annette Ramelsberger, "CSU Parteitag in München: Stoiber und Merkel verteidigen 'Leitkultur,'" *Süddeutsche Zeitung*, November 18/19, 2000.

5. Daniel, Hans. "Aus der Höhle. Was heißt hier Küche, Kinder, Kirche? Edmund Stoiber pflegt noch andere Traditionen" in *Konkret* 2/2002, 17.

6. Martin Zips, "CSU gibt Frauen und Zuwanderern die Schuld," *Süddeutsche Zeitung*, February 17/18, 1996.

7. Most were described as wearing traditional Bavarian clothes.

8. "CSU klagt über 'krankes Frauenbild,'" *Süddeutsche Zeitung*, October 6, 2000.

9. Rolf Pasch, "Streunende Hunde und die Michael Jackson Show," *Frankfurter Rundschau*, June 14, 1999.

10. Annette Blettner and Hans Borchert, "Kosovo: Gnadenloser Machtwechsel; Die Rebellen der albanischen Befreiungsarmee," *Focus* 25 (June 21, 1999), 240, 244.

11. *Spiegel TV*, RTL (Germany), June 12, 1999.

12. Peter Michalski, "Deutscher Major verhindert Massaker: Er entwaffnete eine Gruppe junger serbischer Soldaten die mehrere Zivilisten bedrohten und stoppte so ein Blutbad" *Die Welt*, June 15, 1999.

13. Blettner and Borchert, "Kosovo," 242.

14. Michalski, "Deutscher Major verhindert Massaker."

15. Stephan-Andreas Casdorff, "German Soldiers Are Good Soldiers," *Der Tagesspiegel*, June 14, 1999.

REFERENCES

Anderson, Benedict. 1993. *Imagined communities: Reflections on the origin and spread of nationalism*. London: Verso.

Anthias, Floya, and Nira Yuval-Davis. 1992. Racialized boundaries: Race, nation, gender, colour and class and the anti-racist struggle. London: Routledge.

Bourke, Joanna. 2004. Torture as pornography: For some of these Americans, creating a spectacle of suffering was part of a bonding ritual. *Guardian* (Manchester), May 7, 2004.

Diefenbach, Katja. 2001. Just war: Neue Formen des Krieges; Polizeirecht, Lager, Ausnahmezustand. In *Alaska: Materialien World War Militarisierung, Kolonialismus, Neue Kriege*, ed. Alaska Redaktion, 24–32. Bremen: Alaska Redaktion.

Ehrenreich, Barbara. 2004. A uterus is not a substitute for a conscience: What Abu Ghraib taught me. *Los Angeles Times*, May 16, 2004.

Malaquais, Dominique. 2004. Sexing Africa, again pop as politics: Watch it tonight on HBO. *Chimurenga* 5 (April). Available at http://www.chimurenga.co.za/modules.php?name=Content&pa=showpage&pid=66.

McClintock, Anne. 1997. "No longer in a future heaven": Gender, race, and nationalism. In *Dangerous liaisons: Gender, nation and postcolonial perspectives,* ed. Anne McClintock, Aamir Mufti, and Ellen Shohat, 89–113. Minneapolis: University of Minnesota Press.

Rich, Frank. 2004. The manufacturing of heroes and villains. In the *New York Times* supplement to the *Süddeutschen Zeitung*, May 24, 2004.

Walterspiel, Gabriela. 1993. Das "zweite" Geschlecht und das "dritte Reich": Über "Rasse" und "Geschlecht" im Feminismus. Ed. Initiative Sozialistisches Forum Freiburg. *Krise und Kritik* 6: 23–30.

Yuval-Davis, Nira. 1997. Gender and nation. London: Sage.

6

Terrorism and the Exploitation of New Media

Bruce Klopfenstein

As indicated elsewhere in this book, there are many definitions of terrorism. The U.S. Federal Bureau of Investigation defines it as "the unlawful use of force or violence against persons or property to intimidate or coerce a government, the civilian population, or any segment thereof, in furtherance of political or social objectives." What is lacking but crucial in this definition of terrorism is the necessity of communicating the intentions behind a terrorist act. In addition, the mere threat of terrorist acts can serve the same purpose as an actual terrorist event if it creates fear in the minds of the target audience. One cannot divorce communication from terrorism. Without communication of the terrorists' messages (whether, for example, violent atrocities or demands for, usually, revolutionary change), the corresponding impact would be greatly reduced. This chapter discusses how new and emerging media have, in many ways, empowered today's terrorists' abilities—from planning to financing, recruiting for, executing, and publicizing their activities.

While contemporary terrorist activities may seem to be a phenomenon launched in the Middle East, particularly in Israel where Palestinian groups have employed terrorist tactics since the late 1960s,[1] there are many examples throughout history. Perhaps most notable in the modern era is the role that turn-of-the-20th-century "anarchists" played as, among other things, a catalyst to World War I. Historically parallel to the war in Vietnam, terrorists relied on the traditional news media, particularly television, to broadcast images of their terrorist acts throughout the world. To punctuate this point, global media in the twenty-first century are capable of reporting terrorist acts shortly after, if not during, the actual event.[2] Revolutionary movements from post–World War II until the early 1990s (coinciding with the collapse of the Soviet Union) did what they could to further their causes. One can only ponder what radicalized

Marxist, other leftist, and reactionary groups might have done had the tools of the Internet been available to them ten to twenty-five years ago.

Historically, terrorism was limited in its ability to spread its messages in two key ways that differ from our contemporary world. First, they could not control whether their images of violence and intended messages would be captured by news media at the time. There were no guarantees of film (i.e., not video, but film) crews being there to capture the spectacle. Even if there were, film has to be edited, and the standards for what was, for example, broadcast in the United States at that time was more conservative (sanitized) than today. Second, terrorists could not control the two-step flow of mediated communication. That is, they had no guarantee that old news media (broadcast or print) would cover their story. Even if the story were covered, editors would choose the angle by which the story was presented to mainstream news audiences.

New and emerging media absolutely have changed this picture. Through small, simple-to-use video cameras, for example, terrorists can easily create their own messages regardless of their professional production values. Second, they can publish whatever they want on Internet websites. Thus, for the first time in history, terrorists can take whatever message and images they decide to straight to the online world, and that world is global in reach. Clearly, new and emerging media have made it possible for terrorists to publicize their messages (including graphic images of violence) to the world via websites at their own discretion. This is a dramatic change in the context of terrorism that has accelerated only in the last five years.

The role of the mass media vis-à-vis terrorism is covered throughout this anthology. The present chapter focuses specifically on the role of new and emerging media by terrorists. Generally speaking, "new media" are those mediated forms of communication that have diffused throughout society more recently than the traditional media of newspapers, magazines, radio, and television. Mass communication is a child of technology, with new media being the most recent additions to the family. New and emerging media offer terrorists many new vehicles through which they may communicate between and among themselves as well as present messages directly to various audiences, whether locally or globally.

DEFINING NEW AND EMERGING MEDIA

Defining new media is, perhaps, almost as difficult as defining terrorism. While we might "know it when we see it," we must constrain the definition of new and emerging media in order to focus our attention on the new media and their use by terrorists. In this chapter, we define new and emerging media as *electronic technologies that enable the creation, storage, and transmission of digital media content from point to point or point to multipoint.*[3] Examples of new and emerging media, which are by definition digital media, include any Internet-based communication medium (e.g., websites, streaming media, e-mail, Internet telephony, chat rooms, Usenet groups, etc.), satellite telephony, and any other form of computer-mediated communication. Clearly, the Internet provides the fertile field in which today's new and emerging media take root.

Another way of looking at new and emerging media is to note the ubiquity of the Internet Protocol (IP) which is being applied to a variety of digital communication media well beyond the Internet itself. IP is being applied to the use of the telephone as of this writing, and preparations are being made to apply IP to the distribution of video up to high-definition television (HDTV) in resolution even through traditional telephone lines. So it is reasonable to suggest that as new and emerging media are born and grow, many are or will be using IP. For the purposes of this chapter, electronic communication via IP is not a bad definition for the acquisition, storage, transmission, and reception of new and emerging media and their content.

Emerging media include convergence technologies such as IMS (IP multimedia system), which allows users to share video and images and launch data collaboration services with other mobile phone users while having ongoing conversations. WiMAX is a recent standard, also known as WirelessMAN (metropolitan area network). This standard deals with fixed wireless data networking over the range of miles (a metropolitan area), as opposed to the more well-known and shorter range 802.11 WiFi standards, which operate over the range of hundreds of feet. The trend in emerging media is for more bandwidth and storage at lower costs, allowing increased varieties of digital content to be stored and transmitted globally. How terrorists will use these media in the future is the subject of speculation, but it is not difficult to believe that a higher-definition image of a beheading than the current low resolution versions might be a very attractive alternative to those who believe these grotesque images further their aims.

Clearly the Internet and its ancillary technologies are the foci of new and emerging media as exploited by contemporary terrorists. Ironically, the strengths inherent in the creation and establishment of the Internet and its ubiquity make it ideal for use by terrorists for both point-to-point and point-to-multipoint communication. An individual associated with a terrorist organization need not necessarily even have his or her own computer. Regardless of the home penetration of the Internet in various locations, including especially the Middle East itself, access to the Internet is available in many "anonymous" spots both private (e.g., Internet cafés) and public (schools, universities, and libraries).

TERRORIST ORGANIZATIONS AND USE OF NEW MEDIA

Although the digital new media do allow counterterrorism experts new means for tracking terrorists, the overall advantage might go to terrorist groups. New media were defined above as electronic technologies that enable the creation, storage, and transmission of digital media content from point to point or point to multipoint. This definition goes a long way in making clear the ways in which terrorist groups can use new and emerging media. As is discussed below, individuals and terrorist organizations can and do use new media to create, store (even archive), and transmit information from point to point (e.g., e-mail or one-on-one live chat sessions) or multipoint (e.g., a website designed for various audiences from other members of the terrorist organization to the various intended audiences for their messages).

There are a number of trends in new media that are predictable, even if the response to them is not. Bandwidth continues to be available in larger and larger channels, even as the cost for transmission declines. My interpretation of Stewart Brand's notion that "information wants to be free" (1983, 202) is that new and emerging media are making it possible. That is, the cost of storage, transmission, and reception continues to decline with "free" being the only end point.

Interestingly, digital media may one day work against terrorism. As new and emerging media proliferate, those who are interested in protecting commercial content are pursuing ways to track content to be sure that it is paid for as appropriate. It seems reasonable to believe that some of the antipiracy technologies might make it more difficult for users, including terrorists, to use new media anonymously. The antipiracy technologies and debate are, however, outside the purview of this chapter.

CYBERTERRORISM

Dr. Gabriel Weimann is a communication scholar who has devoted much of the past seven years to studying terrorism. As a recent fellow at the U.S. Institute for Peace in Washington, D.C.,[4] he prepared two detailed reports on terrorism. In one, he argues that the threats of "cyberterrorism" (attacks on key infrastructure, including the U.S. electric power grid and a myriad of other possible hacks of critical computer networks) are overemphasized by counterterrorism experts, the media, and, perhaps, the general population (Weimann 2004a). Readers are encouraged to seek these documents (Weimann 2004a, 2004c) for their complete analyses, only a sampling of which is discussed here.

As research was conducted for this chapter, one discovery was the relative lack of emphasis on—if not even evidence of—cyberterrorism in the most recent literature. There is a large, multibillion-dollar private computer security industry in the United States alone, and it is in their interest to emphasize the possibility of cyberterrorism. In truth, there are few, if any, public reports of acts of cyberterrorism. This is not to say there is no threat. Instead, however, the focus of terrorists continues to be defiant acts of violence, perhaps graduating to negotiations at some point. We focus here on terrorism and new media, acknowledging the real threats possible in cyberterrorism but leaving that topic to others (see Verton 2003). Cyberterrorism is beyond the scope of this chapter.

APPLICATION OF NEW MEDIA BY TERRORISM

The use of new media by terrorists is limited only by the capabilities of the channels. Law enforcement agencies do have countermeasures to various uses of the Internet, but whenever an activity is shut down (e.g., a terrorist-sponsored website), it can reemerge in a manner of hours—*or less.* In addition, cutting off terrorist means of communication via new media is not always in the best interests of law enforcement. Counterterrorism experts may prefer to track communications by known terrorists on known web and other sites such as those discussed below.

Terrorist Websites

Terrorist websites have come into widespread use only in recent years. They serve several purposes: (1) they offer the news from their perspective, (2) they attempt to justify their actions, (3) they spread their view of the world and how it should be, (4) they attempt to gain recruits, and (5) they may also raise funds. The number of terrorist-related websites has rocketed to 4,350 from just a dozen in 1997 (Swartz 2005).

In a second research document prepared by Gabriel Weimann while at the U.S. Institute of Peace, he examined the exploitation of the Internet by terrorists. In July 2004, Weimann summarized some of his research findings (Kumler 2004). Among his conclusions at that time:

- The Internet has become the new Afghanistan for terrorist training, recruitment, and fund-raising.
- Terrorist groups are exploiting the accessibility, vast audience, and anonymity of the Internet to raise money and recruit new members.
- The number of terrorists' websites has increased by 571 percent in the past seven years.
- Al-Qaeda doesn't operate like a terrorist organization anymore. They don't live together, train together, and sometimes they don't even meet interpersonally as long as they can communicate.

- Al-Qaeda's publication *The Sword* is an online training camp for its network around the world. A recent edition included instructions on kidnapping methods, potential targets, negotiating tactics, and even directions on
  how to videotape the beheading of victims and post the video on the Web
  (that issue was posted before a round of kidnappings and beheadings in
  Iraq).
- Some websites target their messages to audiences by, for example, language. Hezbollah has Arabic and English versions that look alike visually
  but carry different messages.
- At the time of Weimann's (2004b) presentation and of this writing, the
  Hezbollah site provided links to downloadable children's videogames that
  train children to play the role of terrorists, to be suicide bombers, and to
  shoot actual political leaders.
- Hamas had a section that features cartoon-like stories meant to recruit
  young people.
- Other terrorists' sites display doctored pictures of Tony Blair and George
  W. Bush shot or lying in caskets.
- Sites provide detailed instructions on how to make a detonation device out
  of a cell phone, how to make a bomb, or how to deliver poison through
  the mail.

In a related presentation at the Peace Institute in May 2004, Weimann
(2004b) expanded on the various ways terrorist groups use the Internet. The
attention was paid disproportionately, if not inevitably, to al-Qaeda, but there
are some commonalities between terrorist groups and their use of the Internet.
For example, when a terrorist act is committed, it can be transmitted virtually instantaneously over the web to anyone with access. This phenomenon is
made far more important because various news media search the web to see
who may claim responsibility for a terrorist act. This also can lead to instant
communication of information with little context, a problem that has grown
with increased competition for electronic news media (television and online)
(Zuckerman 2005).

Weimann and Winn 1994 discusses terrorism as "theater" at a time before
the Internet was in widespread use. In this context, terrorism is not actually
aimed at its direct victims, but instead to the audience of the "staged" act.
Weimann 2004c compares "old" terrorism to "post-modern" terrorism. For
example, al-Qaeda is not one group of terrorists such as the Black September
Palestinian movement. Instead, it is a network of networks practicing psychological warfare. The desired outcome of 9/11 was to frighten and intimidate
audiences through the media, Weimann (2004b) says, more so than the actual
killing of innocent people. Since that one monumental attack, much smaller

actions have been propagated via the Internet where tracking the source can be difficult.

Terrorist websites now are used to show violent acts in the hope that they will be picked up by old media. They also publish manifestos of the terrorists' views, allow users to print posters that bolster those views, and even sell items such as T-shirts. Weimann (2004b) notes that terrorists take advantage of the very attributes that the creators of the Internet envisioned: a medium that allows unbridled global access for the free and open sharing of ideas. In his view, "extremist" views being exchanged on the Internet might not be inappropriate if they are done in a spirit of nonviolence. Clearly this does not apply to al-Qaeda and a variety of other groups wishing to encourage the outbreak of violence and display the results soon after (one wonders when the first "live" terrorist act will be carried on the Worldwide Web).

Weimann has noted the irony of the anti-Western Muslim extremists using the West's own technologies against it. The paradox is that many extremists wish to purge their territories of Western influence, media, and related technology (i.e., the Internet). The same paradox has been noted related to 9/11, as hijackers took on the look of Westerners and used commercial airliners as their vehicles of destruction.

The Internet remains largely unregulated and allows for messaging services that can be difficult to trace; these messages can be read around the world. A user can send a message from the public sphere (e.g., an Internet café or public library) that can contain plain text or even multimedia (graphics, audio, and/or video). Setting up a website simply does not compare in any way to the cost and expense of setting up an "old media" facility such as a newspaper or broadcast facility. Even when a website is shut down, it can reappear at another site literally within minutes (Weimann 2004c). The ability to instantaneously depict graphic images and/or video on the Internet cannot be duplicated by old media (Project for Excellence in Journalism 2005). Even for satellite channel al-Jazeera, time passes before material is delivered, producers and editors review it, and it is possibly scheduled for airing.

Terrorists have posted some of the most gruesome videos on their websites, and those images have been picked up in their raw form by news outlets. Standards in the Middle East are not the same as in the West, so young satellite news networks such as al-Jazeera have broadcast raw material from websites, whether it be messages from terrorist leaders or images of injured and dead human bodies. Ironically, al-Jazeera ran a story explaining how effective the web video decapitations are for the terrorist groups for (1) raising their own morale, (2) harming the morale of the terrorist opposition, and (3) demoralizing the antiterrorist fighting troops who may believe their capture will lead to the same end (Bodi 2004).

The amplification of messages originating via new and emerging media by established media has raised eyebrows. As noted by Oberg (2004):

> Television certainly needs to show the cruel face of war—whether in Iraq or the war on terrorism—for the sake of truth and accuracy. But TV's hunger for shocking pictures ["If it bleeds, it leads"] is distorting Americans' view of this war, and its excessive use of terrorist video is spreading propaganda of an even more damaging sort. TV outlets run the risk of becoming mindless, amoral communications tools by which terrorists advertise their brutality, enlarge their reputations and belittle those who would protect us.

It is safe to say the new media are changing the structure of the old media.

The Pew Charitable Trusts' Project for Excellence in Journalism's report on the state of the U.S. media in 2004 also notes the trend of news outlets "disseminating" news from other sources rather than collecting it themselves. The end video product often becomes repetitive, chaotic, and incoherent "raw news." The report concludes that news decisions were surrendered to those who would manipulate it for their own ends, resulting in nonstop images of hostages, street fighting, and gun-waving insurgents. With virtually each new kidnapping or slaughter, a video emerges and is dutifully aired. The source of the footage frequently is not identified (Project for Excellence in Journalism 2005).

Use of the Internet as a Communication System

Stealth is one of the key attributes of the terrorist. At the same time, independent terrorist or terrorist cells must have some way to communicate. Once again, the Internet provides a means for them to do this with a great deal of anonymity.

The *Wall Street Journal* (Johnson 2005) reported what is believed to be a typical method for trying to elude authorities while also communicating with other members of the terrorist community. This passage refers to the terrorist bombing of trains in Madrid on March 11, 2004:

> Spanish investigators say [Mr. Haski] was using new techniques to communicate from his distant hideout in the Canary Islands resort of Lanzarote. According to interrogations of fellow cell members in France and Belgium, Mr. Haski and his associates stopped sending e-mails over the Internet because police had become adept at snooping on even anonymous e-mail accounts. Instead, he shared passwords for the accounts with cell members, enabling them to log on to the accounts and read messages left in the "drafts" box, leaving no trace for police to follow.

Terrorist Use of Chat Rooms and Boards

Chat rooms are synchronous ("live") places on the Internet where strangers and friends can "meet" to talk about anything from dog grooming to sources on the Internet that detail how to construct a fertilizer bomb. Some chat rooms are limited to text; others allow voice and even webcams. The number of open chat rooms on the Internet is easily in the thousands, and a participant can be anywhere in the world where there is an Internet connection.

It has been reported that individual terrorists have used these chat rooms to communicate with one another and have even used "adult" (pornographic) chat rooms.[5] For example, Carey Goodman (2005) suggests the following:

> Does al-Qaeda recruit its members in Internet chat rooms? Several captured terrorists are known to be frequent visitors to particular chat rooms and message boards. Perhaps the preferred "code" for attack planning is the language of sexual contact? Since pornography and Islam are two very incompatible ideals, porn sites are the last place investigators would expect terrorists to conduct their business, but often the place that seems the least likely is the most likely because it seems so unlikely.

It appears, however, that this story is an example of an urban legend. There are no known public examples of 9/11 or other terrorists using adult chat rooms for meeting places, although they do use chat rooms and static forums to communicate (Weimann, personal communication, March 7, 2005). Law enforcement officials, however, reportedly have found it difficult to track use of chat rooms by terrorists (see Kladko 2004 and Zeller 2004).

A search on March 7, 2005, of Yahoo groups using the word "jihad" found 179 groups. A brief review of these groups showed that they appear to be serious groups and not spoofs by detractors. Weimann (2004c) found even more groups than this when he did a similar search, and both searches found postings in which arguments are made to try to justify the taking of innocent human lives in the pursuit of the terrorists' goals. Perhaps moderate students of Islam will be willing and able to engage these groups and challenge their approaches to violence.

The general use of chat rooms has been studied by academics for some time now (e.g., Beisswenger 2005), and some research has suggested that terrorist use of chat rooms may be more easily identified than one might think. A group of researchers at Rensselaer Polytechnic Institute already know that a secretive minority of chat room users engage in more closed communication. That is, while most chat room users participate in this mode of communication quite openly and with the intent of meeting new people online, more nefarious users of the chat rooms limit their contacts to only one another. In so doing, their identification is made far simpler. In fact, the content of their messages does not necessarily need to be known, just the connection between the same users (Kladko 2004; Weimann 2004b).

In late 2004, an Internet privacy watchdog group commented on the National Science Foundation project and how it was funding the writing of software that would create an automated surveillance system to monitor conversations on Internet chat rooms. The chat room project assumes that terrorists communicate through crowded public chat channels, where the flurry of odd usernames and disconnected, scrolling messages make it difficult to know who is talking to whom. The automated software would monitor both the content and timing of messages to help isolate and identify conversations. Critics point out the inherent privacy issues and note that even if successful, chat rooms are only a small piece of a large puzzle. From free e-mail accounts and unsecured wireless networks to online programs that can shield Internet addresses, terrorists have many other ways to communicate virtually anonymously on the Internet (Zeller 2004).

Satellite Telephones

Satellite telephones allow users around the globe to communicate with or without a local telephone infrastructure (landlines or cellular), assuming the parties each have a satellite phone. Before 9/11, and especially afterward, intelligence services were able to locate satellite telephones and tap into the conversations. This is a seemingly monumental task. According to Michael Wertheimer (2004), the

> numbers are staggering. In 2002 there were about 180 billion minutes of international phone calls representing the communications of roughly 2.8 billion cellular and 1.2 billion fixed-line subscribers worldwide. Excluding North America, the bulk of these communications is made possible by several hundred satellites orbiting the globe.

While it is unclear in the public sphere (as opposed to the inner intelligence circles) to what extent satellite phones are being used by terrorists today, it seems reasonable to believe they are in use in areas where their being targeted for attack is less likely (e.g., in an urban or other more densely populated area, especially where civilians are at risk as potential casualties in a military attack). It was reported that terrorist users in Afghanistan learned that the phones could be pinpointed geographically, allowing for military attacks and/or eavesdropping (see, e.g., Rohde and Khan 2004, for a recent example).

WHAT CAN WE EXPECT FROM HERE?

New and emerging communication technologies will continue to make it easier and less costly to promote terrorist causes, allow point-to-point and point-to-multipoint communication, and even deliver stunningly graphic multimedia messages to various audiences, both internal and external. This will exacerbate the already growing debate about censoring information that is distributed via the Internet and other future media. This issue will create a great challenge to free and open democracies, and it would seem that the threat to citizens' privacy is likely to increase dramatically in the near term. It will be necessary for political leaders to listen to privacy advocates and learn from areas around the globe where governments have more experience historically in dealing with direct domestic terrorist threats. The United States has suffered the worst terrorist act in modern history, and yet it has not had one known incident since then.

There are additional issues related to new media and terrorism that are not covered in this chapter. One very notable example is the possible issuance of national security IDs (Guterl and Underhill 2004). In Great Britain, for example, as of this writing, a bill was being debated in Parliament that would require British citizens to carry an ID card that would use face recognition, fingerprints, and iris identification theoretically to insure that only citizens would be able to access government entitlement programs such as health care. Clearly, this initiative is not unrelated to the fight against terrorism. A similar debate is going on in the United States (see, for example, Clement et al. 2005).

In addition, the Middle East has seen a virtual explosion in the number of new media outlets, led by satellite television news channel al-Jazeera in Qatar. There are many others who are broadcasting via satellite and/or the Internet. The relevance of these new media is that they not only give a very different perspective on the news than Western news organizations do but also have different standards of what's acceptable and what is not. While U.S. television and cable news networks mull over such things as the latest message purportedly from Osama bin Laden, new networks like al-Jazeera are far more likely to broadcast the entire message unedited. In addition, their willingness to broadcast raw video of scenes of violence and human casualties may result in Western (especially U.S.) online and broadcast media changing their historically far more stringent standards as to what is permissible. In any case, websites can be expected to pick up the raw content, given the wide variety of websites and webmasters who have their own often apolitical reasons for exposing such material. It seems reasonable to assume that we will be exposed to more, not less, brutal images of terrorist acts now and into the future.

Since 9/11, there has been a great intensification of the debate over privacy and government surveillance of communication. The Patriot Act is set to expire as this book goes to press. Politicians and citizens in the United States have quite a dilemma on their hands as they try to balance genuine national security threats with individuals' rights to privacy as well as freedom of speech (see, e.g., Kearsley 2005). The law, it must be noted, usually has a difficult time keeping up with the pace of technology.

There seem to be no limits on the possibilities for new and emerging media in the near and more distant future. For example, the U.S. military is refining a handheld voice-translation device, which will also be used by police and emergency-room doctors back home. The palm-size, PDA-like "Phraselator" lets users speak or select from a screen of English phrases and matches them to equivalent prerecorded phrases in other languages. The device then broadcasts the foreign-language MP3 file and records reply dialog for later translation (Harrison 2005).

New and emerging communication technologies, like all technologies, are merely tools. Just as an automobile can be an affordable means of independent transportation, it can also be made into a vehicle for the transport and detonation of high explosives. Just as unthinkable as it would be to eliminate the use of automobiles or roads, there are times when it may be prudent to limit their use. For better or worse, this would seem to be the fate of electronic media both now and in the future. Now is the time for all great minds to address the issues of freedom and control of communication media in the age of terrorism. The arguments for restrictions are simple to make, but light must also be shown on the reasons to keep the communication channels open.

NOTES

1. As the saying goes, "One man's terrorist is another man's freedom fighter." Certainly the Palestinians have accused the Israeli government of acts of state-sponsored terrorism against the Palestinian people.

2. For three days in October 2002, the world watched as Chechen rebels held a crowded theater in Moscow demanding the withdrawal of Russian troops from Chechnya. The same live coverage was seen as more Chechen rebels held the students and staff hostage in an elementary school in Beslan in a southern Russian state.

3. December (1996) includes additional descriptors such as "point to server narrowcast" which implies an audience limited, for example, by password access to the narrowcast.

4. The U.S. Institute of Peace in Washington is a nonpartisan think tank funded by the U.S. Congress, studying, among many other things, terrorism and new media.

5. In the case of Islamic terrorists, the assumption is that because their beliefs exclude the use of pornographic materials, counterterrorism officials would have been less likely to search for them in adult chat rooms.

REFERENCES

Beisswenger, Michael. 2005. *Bibliography on chat communication.* Available at http://www.chat-bibliography.de/ (accessed March 3, 2005).

Bodi, Faisal. 2004. Decapitation: Execrable, but effective. September 11. Available at http://english.al-Jazeera.net/NR/exeres/3567453C-FD1D-4FAC-A185-A2637E2 B61BB.htm (accessed March 5, 2005).

Brand, Stewart. 1983. The Media Lab: Inventing the future at MIT. New York: Viking Press.

Clement, Andrew, Felix Stalder, Jeff Johnson, and Robert Guerra. 2005. National identification schemes (NIDS) and the fight against terrorism: Frequently asked questions. Palo Alto, Calif.: Computer Professionals for Social Responsibility. February 14. Available at https://www.cpsr.org/issues/privacy/natIdentity/natidfaq/ (accessed March 3, 2005).

December, J. 1996. Units of analysis for Internet communication. *Journal of Communication* 46 (1): 14–38.

Goodman, Carey. 2005. International trade and politics: Terrorism and pornography. January 24. Available at http://www.suite101.com/article.cfm/international _trade_politics/113526 (accessed March 7, 2005).

Guterl, Fred, and William Underhill. 2004. Taking a closer look: Governments the world over are watching citizens like never before, but are we any safer for it? *Newsweek*, March 8: 42.

Harrison, Ann. 2005. Machines not lost in translation. *Wired news*, March 9. Available at http: // www.wired.com/news/technology/0,1282,66816,00.html?tw=wn_tophead_1 (accessed March 9, 2005).

Johnson, Keith. 2005. Terrorist threat shifts as groups mutate and merge: Disparate radicals united to bomb Madrid trains, court documents reveal. *Wall Street Journal*, February 14.

Kearsley, Kelly. 2005. Some state lawmakers want Congress to rein in Patriot Act. *Seattle Post-Intelligencer*, March 1.

Kladko, Brian. 2004. Chat rooms may be meeting places for terrorists, researchers believe. *Knight-Ridder Tribune Business News*, October 12: 1.

Kumler, Emily. 2004. Terrorists rely on tech tools, researcher finds. *Computerworld*, July 8. Available at http://www.computerworld.com/securitytopics/security/ story/0,10801,94390,00.html (accessed March 5, 2005).

Oberg, Alcestis. 2004. Terrorists have their way on TV: Network news' mentality of 'if it bleeds, it leads' fails us; lives are at stake. *USA Today*, September 15.

Project for Excellence in Journalism. 2005. *The state of the news media, 2004: An annual report on American journalism.* Washington, D.C.: Project for Excellence in Journalism. Available at http://www.stateofthenewsmedia.org/2005/index.asp (accessed March 3, 2005).

Rohde, David, and Mohammed Khan. 2004. Ex-fighter for Taliban dies in strike in Pakistan. *New York Times*, June 19.

Swartz, Jon. 2005. Terrorists' use of Internet spreads. *USA Today*, February 26. Available at http://www.usatoday.com/money/industries/technology/2005-02-20 -cyber-terror-usat_x.htm (accessed March 3, 2005).

Verton, Dan. 2003. Black ice: The invisible threat of cyber-terrorism. New York: McGraw-Hill/Osborne.

Weimann, Gabriel. 2004a. Cyberterrorism: How real is the threat? Special Report 119. Washington, D.C.: United States Institute of Peace. December. Available at from http://www.usip.org/pubs/specialreports/sr116.html (accessed February 28, 2005).

———. 2004b. Terror on the Internet: The new arena, the new challenges. Washington, D.C.: United States Institute of Peace. May 13. Available at from http://www.usip.org/fellows/reports/2004/0513_weimann.html (accessed March 5, 2005).

———. 2004c. www.terror.net: How modern terrorism uses the Internet. Special Report 116. Washington, D.C.: United States Institute of Peace. March. Available at http://www.usip.org/pubs/specialreports/sr116.html (accessed February 28, 2005).

Weimann, Gabriel, and Conrad Winn. 1994. The theater of terror: Mass media and international terrorism. New York: Longman.

Wertheimer, Michael A. 2004. Crippling innovation—and intelligence. *Washington Post*, July 21.

Zeller, Tom. 2004. On the open Internet, a web of dark alleys. *New York Times*, December 20.

Zuckerman, Mortimer B. 2005. *U.S. News & World Report*, February 28: 76.

SELECTED ADDITIONAL RESOURCES AVAILABLE FOR RESEARCH ON TERRORISM AND EMERGING MEDIA

Au, Melanie. "Terrorism Online: A Brief Look at Terrorists' Use of the Internet and the Issues of Surveillance, Security, and Liberty." December 10, 2004. Available at http://www.slais.ubc.ca/courses/libr500/04-05-wt1/www/m_au/index.htm (accessed March 7, 2005).

Branscomb, Lewis M. "Counterterrorism, in AccessScience@McGraw-Hill." March 4, 2004. Available at http://www.accessscience.com, DOI 10.1036/1097-8542. YB041000 (accessed March 5, 2005).

Çamtepe, Ahmet, Mukkai S. Krishnamoorthy, and Bulent Yener. "A Tool for Internet Chatroom Surveillance." Troy, N.Y.: Department of Computer Science, Rensselaer Polytechnic Institute, n.d. Available at http://www.cs.rpi.edu/~yener/PAPERS/35.pdf (accessed March 3, 2005).

U.S. Congress. Senate. Committee on the Judiciary. Subcommittee on Terrorism, Technology, and Homeland Security. *Virtual Threat, Real Terror: Cyberterrorism in the 21st Century*. S. Hrg. 108–516. 108th Cong., 2nd sess., February 24, 2004.

Verton, Dan. "Web Sites Seen as Terrorist Aids." *Computerworld*, February 11, 2002. Available at http://www.computerworld.com/printthis/2002/0,4814,68181,00.html (accessed February 28, 2005).

Discussion Questions for Part 2

1. Based on your reading of chapter three, critique a Hollywood-inspired movie on war such as *Black Hawk Down*.
2. Write a concept for a "catastrophe film" that draws on some of the tensions identified in chapter three.
3. In what ways is the Spanish public different from the American one? Will the American audience reflect concerns similar to the Spanish one in the future? Discuss these questions with reference to chapter four.
4. What models of masculinity dominate German culture and media coverage? How are they similar to and different from American models of masculinity? Discuss these questions with reference to chapter five.
5. Based on your reading of chapter six, identify the similarities and differences between the mainstream media's use of the Internet and that of terrorist organizations.

Part 3

Frames and Contexts

7

Critical Media Theory, Democratic Communication, and Global Conflict

Todd Fraley and Elli Lester Roushanzamir

The production of mass media content has largely been conceded to the global corporate environment. Despite points of contention over production and regulation issues, audiences tend to focus primarily on media content as the locus for critique. Mass communication audience research has tended to focus on how individuals receive messages. The concept of media literacy emerged within this framework as a way for audiences to analyze and clarify media messages.

However, since the mid-twentieth century and certainly after the September 11 attacks on the World Trade Center and the Pentagon, media literacy seems tame and passive. Sub- and supranational groups have proven adept at using both new (Internet) and older (audiocassette) technologies to further their goals and ambitions. Al-Qaeda, Hezbollah, Basque separatists, and Welsh movements are among the groups that count mass communication and mediated communication as a vital component of their resistance.

We propose an alternative concept, that is, *critical media consciousness*. Critical media consciousness retheorizes media literacy by expanding the critique to media production and regulation, opening up possible alternative forms of organization, and offering a reconceptualization of the audience. Critical media consciousness suggests possibilities for more democratic approaches to producing media content, including alternative ways of gathering information, different organizational arrangements, and so forth.

In the context of the twenty-first-century global political economy—one in which corporate superpowers thrive while national superpowers confront a drive toward smaller states based on ethnicity, religion, and the like—critical media consciousness can help revive the notion that democracy and social equality are still attainable goals. However, critical media consciousness alone cannot guarantee more progressive forms of media. Alternative media production and delivery can be and have been used for reactionary movements as well. In this chapter, we will highlight how the application of the concept of critical media consciousness may show ways of organizing outside the dominant corporate paradigm and how that concept can suggest more democratic media communication.

McWORLD OR JIHAD: WHITHER DEMOCRACY?

Currently, mainstream communications systems are naturalized as hierarchical and corporate structures that are unfavorable to a democratic model. But "there is nothing natural . . . about profit seeking, privately owned and operated communications media" (Keane 1993, 238). Changing this situation depends on an informed and participating citizenry. Many citizens are already laboring to create practical alternatives. Across the globe, progressive social movements incorporate a critical media consciousness in their attempts to sustain global democracy because they believe "we can make something better, if we have the courage to try" (Williams 1989, 31). For example, Centro de Mujeres Comunicadores Mayas (Guatemala) and Red de Informacion Indigena (Mexico) are groups in which indigenous peoples bypass corporate communication styles and messages.

However, as media saturate contemporary societies, becoming influential consciousness industries and therefore influencing politics and culture as well as the economy, communication technologies may serve different social groups. On the one hand, these technologies serve corporate and military constituencies, and on the other hand they may serve among the components for the development of global democracy.

In the post-9/11 world, the media's influence and usefulness form one of the battlegrounds on which war is waged. "McWorld" and jihadism are seemingly embedded within power structures; as Benjamin Barber (1992) observes, neither unbridled capitalism nor fundamentalism depends on or encourages participatory democracy. Certainly, on a global scale, that outcome remains jeopardized by media organizations and output.

Barber was prescient when he proposed the terms *McWorld* and *jihadism* as analogies for the world order of the twenty-first century. He explains that "the current world order pit[s] culture against culture [and] is falling precipitately apart and coming reluctantly together at the very same moment" (1992, 53). Cultures clash over social values within the framework of global inequality politically and economically. Within that environment, long-established political forms, not least of which is the nation-state, are eroded by both social approaches. McWorld's reliance on markets erodes national sovereignty through multinational corporate ownership, outsourcing of jobs, the dominance of American cultural images, and new regional organizations. Jihad serves as a shorthand for both subnational ethnic resistance and movements such as Pan-Islamism or Pan-Arabism, which have ravaged the Enlightenment values of individual liberty in partnership with democratic social formations. McWorld pursues markets with an eye toward favorable environments for return on investment; jihad pursues national dissolution, seeking smaller worlds sealed off from corrupt Western values.

Neither belief system is especially congenial for the furtherance of democratic institutions, nor is democracy a necessary condition for their success. Both McWorld and jihad work to fracture any progressive movements. And for both, the production, regulation, and content of the mass media fill a powerful role by advancing their positions as a propaganda tool.

Media are central to the success of corporate globalization and reactionary (sub-) nationalism. Therefore, progressive movements must also incorporate, rather than concede, a critical media consciousness as a core tool for the spread of global democracy. Communities, activist organizers, and others must press for access not least of all to provide and share crucial information necessary for informed deliberation (Kellner 1992).

MEDIA LITERACY/CRITICAL MEDIA CONSCIOUSNESS: CONCEPTS AND THEORY

Bill Walsh writing for the *Media Literacy Review* defines media literacy as "an attempt to make each of us more comfortable, more critical, and more conversant in various methods of communication" (Walsh n.d.). *Media Literacy Review* provides an overview of the literature that—admirable as the goal of educating people, especially young people, to be critical of mass media messages may be—still remains focused on how individuals use content (Walsh n.d.).

To reconceptualize media literacy as critical media consciousness is to more fully theorize. It helps illuminate the significance for individuals and for groups of learning how to access, create, and control media, as well as how corporate (and political) structures determine to a large extent what messages are produced, how they're distributed, and how they're received. Critical media consciousness broadens "media literacy" by fostering a critique of production, distribution, and regulation as well as media content. Critical media consciousness can contribute to an ideology of resistance and agency on the part of the heretofore dispossessed. Media participation, linked to social participation, can be one of the fundamental strategies in promoting a developed global democracy (or as discussed above, of global corporatism and reaction).

Len Masterman argues that "education in the technologies and the media should play an empowering and liberating role, helping prepare [individuals] for democratic citizenship and political awareness. Thus [individuals] should be given an understanding of the structures, mechanisms, and messages of the mass media . . . " (2001, 15).

In Masterman's framework, education leads to knowledge of media technologies as a first step in the process of developing critical media consciousness. He argues that control of mass media is intimately linked with and supported by the coalition of government and corporate entities. Furthermore, media play a vital hegemonic role in promoting the values of the powerful (Couldry 2000; Herman and Chomsky 1988). Through education, communities and progressive activists can begin to re-envision the role of mass media, realizing the potential role media may play in creating democracy and liberation without conceding it. Masterman, Nick Couldry, Edward Herman, Noam Chomsky, and Herbert Schiller, among others, present powerful arguments about how commercialized the public supply of information has become. Teaching critical media consciousness is a first step toward global resistance to the privatization of communication.

Masterman suggests that education prepares the way for understanding mediated communication as a potentially powerful liberating force. Participatory parity and access, production, and distribution of knowledge and information can dismantle the current status quo (Wasko 1992), that is, the evolution of media systems into "systems for the production, circulation, and appropriation of meaning" (Garnham 2000, 4). Progressive media systems have the potential to challenge hindrances to democracy due to concentrated ownership and control (Garnham 2000, 10). An expanding understanding of critical media consciousness reveals that communication systems are "not . . . irresistible steamrollers of the state, but . . . important sites for struggle" (Masterman 2001, 30).

Democratic citizenship goes hand in hand with political awareness. To establish—to even imagine—global democracy, democratic communication sites that enable individuals to access institutions that affect their lives must be established (Hagen 1992). Rational debate is increasingly negated as people lose the opportunities to express opinions; in short, they are effectively denied inclusion to the political process as crucial information disappears. As long as "gaps exist between those who have access to media and those who do not, those who have the power to define and those who are always defined, those who are allowed to speak about the world as they know and understand it and those whose experiences are inevitably framed by others" (Masterman 2001, 61), social equality and strong democracy will remain a naive ideal. Therefore, to ensure equality, democratization of the media must emerge and allow for democratization through the media (Hagen 1992).

Masterman's framework provides guidance for how to think about and develop a critical media consciousness: "[Individuals] should be given an understanding of the structures, mechanisms, and messages of the mass media" (2001, 15). However, that guidance, that education, does not alone guarantee progressive social movements or the promotion of democratic social formations.

TECHNOLOGICAL INDETERMINISM
AND HUMAN AGENCY

To say that critical media consciousness alone cannot always lead to democracy is to understate the point. Without making the connection of media consciousness to the larger theoretical framework of critical theory, mass communication media are used effectively by reactionary movements. Examples abound of how those forces, while delinking from corporate forms of media, sustain nonprogressive outcomes. Arnaud de Borchgrave (2005) writes:

> Iran's banned Tudeh (Communist) Party was based in East Berlin and the voice of "Free Iran" soon made itself heard courtesy of Wolf's minions. HVA operatives also concocted impersonations of the shah's voice and shipped the cassettes to small radio stations in the United States. These local broadcasts, trumpeted as hot exclusives, then were picked up by legitimate wire services and played back to Iran as "proof" that the shah was a "bloodthirsty tyrant." Simultaneously, Ayatollah Ruhollah Khomeini was recording antishah messages on cassettes that were smuggled into Iran and blared to the faithful in every mosque in the country.

Another example from the same source observes that Khomeini provided "a daily barrage of faxes and Internet E-mail reports that are a lethal mix of disinformation, information, innuendo, smear and rumor—kernels of truth laced with a tissue of falsehoods" (de Borchgrave 2005) that fostered links between anti-Western groups. The success of the Iranian Revolution of 1979 owes much to the understanding of how to manipulate mediated communication to achieve the revolutionaries' goals. It can be noted that of all the twentieth-century revolutions, the Islamic Republic of Iran is the only one to survive as a viable formation into the twenty-first century.

The resistance to the current Iranian government, while scattered globally, learned that mass and mediated communication are simply tools and not essentially reactionary. Many groups, including monarchists (who advocate a return of Pahlavi rule), liberal nationals, the Organization of the People's Mojahedin of Iran, and the Communist party of Iran (which recently split into two factions), promote their interests on the Internet and use videocassettes, audiocassettes, and so forth, which, in an effective distribution system, sends their messages around the world.

U.S. television news, along with other news sources (radio, newspapers, etc.), has itself been useful to al-Qaeda. Since the events of September 11, 2001, a steady stream of communication continues to use corporate media systems by effectively presenting extremists' points of view in prepared-for-Western-consumption sound bites and compelling visuals.

In Central America, indigenous peoples have used the Internet to develop political and cultural identities and to establish new communication and ties with other indigenous communities. Again the Masterman formula is applied, with education being the first step toward formerly disparate indigenous peoples connecting with others in their effort to have their concerns addressed.

Masterman's (2001) insights lie at the heart of moving from simply understanding the potential for media to be empowering and liberating to achieving a position of power and strength by using media. As Peter Bruck and Marc Raboy explain, "Strategies for social change and political action have to be comprehensive with regard to communication," including an understanding of who controls the means of production (1989, 12). Ultimately, critical media consciousness is a central component in constructing a democratic social formation, along with the more expected components such as organizing and linking smaller interest groups in a united front of larger movements for political and social change.

Too often, progressive activists view mass communication and mass media as already compromised institutions, in short taking on a dysfunctional belief in technological determinism. The wild hope for the Internet—that it would liberate communication from corporate hands—was quickly dashed. Only humans, whether individuals, groups, or classes, form and forge historical consequences. But the belief that one kind of media technology (e.g., the Internet or satellites) is crippling reduces consequential social change to the sum of technology plus access, directing attention to the implications of technology for people rather than the implications of, for example, how certain organizational frameworks lead to specific uses of that technology.

Today, the political content of news services is in many countries an essential basis for citizenship, providing the integrity of information flow upon which a degree of informed participation can occur (Corner 1999). According to Michael Schudson, the importance lies in the fact that "not everyone reads the paper but even those who fail to do are forced to follow the groove for their borrowed thoughts. One pen suffices to set off a million tongues" (1997, 7). The problem is that "news knowledge is almost by definition narrow and often superficial in character . . . allowing limited time for sustained development of any one item" (Corner 1999, 117).

According to Edward Herman (1995), commercial media structures leave access to privately owned media in the hands of the wealthy and powerful, allow government and business interests to penetrate these institutions either through direct control or indirect influence, and create a relationship between media and proponents of the status quo, fixing the boundaries of public discussion and repeatedly excluding fundamental dissent from news stories. In the United States, the day-to-day news-making process centers on a triangle of government officials, business leaders, and powerful institutions (Rodriguez 1995). The fact that these aspects of society are reported on with a cautious deference leads "self-censoring journalists" to produce uncritical news supportive of a dominant ideology that assists in setting the political agenda (Rodriguez 1995, 135). These accepted professional media codes—codes that claim to provide objectivity and truth—erect blockages to public expression (Downing 2001) and retard the development of an egalitarian and humanitarian form of globalization. Due to these shortcomings, the development of critical media consciousness is integral to the development of democracy.

Critical media consciousness seeks to expand the current concept of media literacy beyond its limited definitions. This alternative vision of media literacy understands the importance of empowering individuals to construct and distribute alternative representations as they expand public discourse and redevelop public life (Giroux, as cited in Cowie 2000). The goal is to move media from a system of commodified consciousness toward a system that offers the diverse, disagreeing, and contradictory environment that is essential to democracy.[1]

In this context, literacy becomes more than a tool for reading and writing. Rather, as Paulo Freire articulated, literacy establishes a way for individuals to fit into the world and more importantly to change it. This more critical and comprehensive approach to media literacy is essential to "preparing individuals to function as informed citizens in a democratic society" (Hobbs 2001, 165).

Media are more than simple conduits of information. Critical media consciousness ultimately enables individuals to analyze media as "sets of institutions with particular social and economic structures that are neither inevitable or irreversible" (Lewis and Jhally 1998, 109). The aim is to produce a media-savvy public of sophisticated citizens (as opposed to sophisticated consumers) with the potential to extend democracy (Lewis and Jhally 1998). A critical media consciousness focusing on all aspects of media is invaluable for those struggling to create global democracy. Ultimately, critical media consciousness provides the framework for discerning "media institutions as civic institutions," as well as the "potential for making technological innovations a means to enhance democratic citizenship" (Calabrese 2001, 77).

Critical media consciousness underscores the necessity of understanding, critiquing, and analyzing communication systems, communication forms, and mediated communication strategies that continue to influence the construction and presentation of reality. Mass communication seemingly offers numerous social benefits, but injustices, power struggles, isolation, and ignorance continue to plague the post-9/11 global environment. With continuous modifications to communications technologies, communication strategies and practices also change; nonetheless, democratic communication practices and political awareness are not guaranteed. Those engaged in conflict routinely utilize media to promote their agenda in lieu of engaging in beneficial discussions. Simply increasing the dissemination of diverse information does not ensure equality and understanding, but the fact remains that "communications options have the potential to transform both political organization and political power relations" (Bennett 2003, 19).

Humanitarian forms of globalization must "connect theories of democracy with theories of communication in order to allow new technologies to contribute to the expansion of democracy and the empowerment of more people" (Hacker 1996, 213). As Raymond Williams explained, the struggle for democracy and human liberation depends on the creation of democratic institutions that try to "extend the expression and exchange of experience on which understanding depends" (Williams 1968, 139). This view reflects media's symbolic status in a mediated society as well as illuminates key issues surrounding access, inequality, and the power to define.

A democratic social order, recognizing the existence of different groups and different interests, acknowledges the necessity of bargaining between segments of society with conflicting interests and the struggle of the disadvantaged and their allies against the injustice of privilege (Baker 1998). Therefore, democracy demands an inclusive, nonoppressive conception of society protecting numerous groups and offering a social order allowing for the development of differences in search of a noncoercive common good. This aim is only possible if groups have an adequate opportunity to develop their differing perspectives and have those perspectives fully voiced and given their due. In the end, a diverse media system, enabling open and varied discussion, is central to a global society based on understanding and acceptance.

Democracy empowers and requires all citizens to continually strive to create institutions that value and develop political equality, liberty, and moral self-development. An equitable global society must also contain powerful states, while enabling communication systems that tolerate and negotiate difference. The principle of autonomy emerges as an integral piece to this puzzle, by enabling citizens to remain free to determine the conditions of their own lives through free and equal participation in processes of debate and deliberation.

And communication emerges as essential to the establishment of liberty in a global world, because "if democracy is . . . government by discussion, government by rational and free public discussion . . . conversation must lie close to its heart" (Schudson 1997, 1).

Therefore, the creation of a democratic society requires adequate spaces and procedures for debate and decision making around issues to which citizens bring divergent views and interests (Held 1996, 312). In the end, democracy depends on discussion and an acceptance of the fact that democratic talk is not homogenous—it is public, and it is uncomfortable (Schudson 1997, 2).

McWORLD, JIHAD, OR DEMOCRATIC PRACTICE

Sadly, the mass media usually emerge as sites that disseminate propaganda and not as conduits for sharing, understanding, and agreement. Grounded in the idea that the creation of mediated forms of democratic communication is necessary and, more importantly, possible for the development of an equitable and just global world, we will now discuss the utilization of media by competing factions in the post-9/11 world, with specific attention to the media strategies of key players in what Barber has termed jihad vs. McWorld.

Historically and currently, the ideal of a truly egalitarian global society has been hindered by communication focusing on promoting ideologies and interests, as opposed to searching for agreement and common ground. Too often, organizations use media and communication technologies not for discussion and dialogue, but for "public diplomacy." Focusing on U.S. foreign policy, Nancy Snow explains public diplomacy as a way to "promote national interest[s] . . . through understanding, informing, and influencing foreign audiences" (2004, 55). The U.S. government has been involved in this process since the Voice of America was established to "spread democracy throughout the world" (Fortner, as cited in Napoli and Fejeran 2004, 2). This was followed by the creation of the Office of War Information and continues today with the Bush administration's creation of the Office of Global Communications (OGC) (Napoli and Fejeran 2004). Part of the goal of the OGC is to "co-ordinate . . . foreign policy messages and supervise America's image abroad" (Miller, Stauber, and Rampton 2004, 45).

During the 1990–91 Gulf crisis, CNN's worldwide presence, with virtually no competition from competing media outlets, allowed it to become the "newscast of record for the war" (Vincent 1992, 181). While that crisis was documented from an American point of view, individuals across the globe, and especially in the Arab world, mobilized to create new media outlets offering a variety of viewpoints (Rugh 2004). Currently, satellite TV, the Internet, and other communication technologies offer worldwide audiences instant access to conflicting perspectives and competing insights, and this has led to a war of information that remains central to the development of a flourishing global democracy. It remains an open question as to whether access will be trumped by corporatism.

The post-9/11 world is changing, and mediated forms of communication are key battlegrounds to those interested in disseminating views and legitimating ideologies to help determine the direction of this transformation. Today that conflict centers around "political tension[s] . . . between the forces of neoliberal economic globalization, seeking to expand the freedom of capital, and the forces of social resistance, seeking to preserve and to redefine community and solidarity" (Gills 2000, 3). To understand the communication currently taking place between the United States and its allies and the "axis of evil" (Barber's jihad vs. McWorld), we must accept that "media are part of the ideological struggle between social forces with conflicting and material interests" (Bruck 1992, 156). In the post-9/11 world, dialogue has taken a backseat to competing ideologies. The power and purpose of mediated communication is underscored as they function to propagate competing ideologies.

After 9/11, U.S. public diplomacy efforts included daily media strategy sessions among U.S. communication specialists (Miller, Stauber, and Rampton 2004). Public diplomacy after 9/11 also included meetings between U.S. and British officials to coordinate a consistent message and establish a news network that justified the fight against terrorism (Napoli and Fejeran 2004). Sometimes termed "information warfare" and more commonly understood as propaganda, for years this process has required "mainstream media [to] act as ciphers for the powerful" (Miller 2004, 6), while "failing to provide a coherent account of what happened, why it happened, and what would count as possible responses" (Kellner 2004, 144). These communication strategies are disappointing and detrimental, but they reveal the long-standing critical media consciousness of government officials, a consciousness that is currently being imitated by individuals and organizations resisting Western forms of globalization. Public diplomacy has traditionally been linked to nation-states, but the "evolution of global technologies . . . has brought public diplomacy among the range of options for groups or even individuals [wishing to] affect public opinion" (Napoli and Fejeran 2004, 1). Revealing their own critical media consciousness, Osama bin Laden, the Qaeda network, and media outlets such as al-Jazeera provide an excellent place to investigate the changes taking place within global discourse and new, though still disappointing, efforts at public diplomacy.

Indicative of the success of these strategies is the increased support of bin Laden, while the image of the United States continues to decline even with its public diplomacy efforts. A recent report by a Pentagon advisory panel explains, "The US is failing in its efforts to explain the nation's diplomatic and military actions to the Muslim world" (Shanker 2004). Simultaneously, while bin Laden has been forced into hiding and lacks the media access of U.S. government officials, many in the Arab world speak with admiration of this "lone hero able to stand up to superpower US" and his terrorist network continues to grow (Bowers and Tohid 2004). This reputation is partially the result of a sophisticated communications strategy, including the release of an audio- or videotape every six weeks since 9/11, Internet postings, and satellite television (Bowers 2004, 1).

Conscious of Yasir Arafat's success in transforming himself from wanted terrorist to recognized president of the Palestine Authority, bin Laden uses the media to "portray himself as a statesman" in a politically sophisticated way (Bowers and Tohid 2004). While some extremists use the Internet and media outlets to display executions and threats,[2] bin Laden circulates videos that discuss political concerns such as U.S. support of Israel, China, and Muslim tyrannies (Bowers and Tohid 2004). Disseminating this message is critical to al-Qaeda, as it serves as a form of public diplomacy countering that spread by the U.S. government via Western media outlets, as well as through the U.S.-run Iraqi Media Network. These messages also now spread beyond the Arab world and into Europe and North America and are emerging quickly and with a high quality (Bowers 2004).

Bin Laden has utilized different Arab satellite networks, including al-Jazeera, as well as different Arabic newspapers published in London (el-Nawawy 2004). With technology making it possible for almost anyone to afford digital cameras and editing equipment, al-Qaeda is able to produce complicated videos complete with scrolling messages, logos, sophisticated editing, and other production techniques similar to those found on many Western news outlets (Peters 2004). Assisted by media outlets the likes of al-Jazeera in airing these productions, terrorist organizations gain a potential audience of nearly forty million viewers, and at least 150,000 Americans (Auter 2004). This newfound reach, and the highly developed media consciousness displayed by groups like al-Qaeda, has caused alarm for the U.S. government because it presents a definite shift in public opinion and knowledge. As the Pentagon report states, America's diminished ability to persuade is the result of strategic communication problems that have left the United States without a credible channel of communication in the Muslim world (Shanker 2004). On the other hand, while bin Laden remains seemingly invisible, with the help of the Internet and al-Jazeera, the Arab world's most popular TV news channel, al-Qaeda has developed a communications strategy mirroring the public diplomacy efforts of traditional nation-states.

BE THE MEDIA

Effective use of mass-mediated forms of communication to promote an ideology does not represent the essence of critical media consciousness. The true benefit of critical media consciousness rests in its ability to understand mediated communication as an effective way to bring diverse groups together in search of common ground. As Barber explains, there is a "vast communications . . . network that can potentially give every person on earth access to every other person" (1992, 58).

Since the 1999 World Trade Organization meetings in Seattle, the independent ("indy") media network has evolved into an important arena for international discussions and devising resistance strategies (Downing 2003). This network of political activists/journalists "empower[s] individuals to become independent and civic journalists by providing a direct, unmoderated form of [communication] media" (Couldry 2003, 45). This "phenomenon . . . now encompasses a constellation of about 120 local collectives from Boston to Bombay," and it is referred to as a "democratic media outlet for the creation of radical, accurate, and passionate tellings of truth" (Beckerman 2003).

Described as a "giant leap forward in the struggle for communicative democracy" (Shumway 2003). The indy media network is slowly developing into a "day-to-day accounting of local and global concerns of social justice and anti-globalization advocates" (Beckerman 2003).

Within the indy media network, mass media systems are perceived as the heart of the struggle to spotlight the relationship between power and information in order to create a reciprocal power structure guided by responsive institutions. Information should, and in some instances does, flow more easily across social and geographical boundaries, and communications technologies have the potential to transform power relations (Bennett 2003, 19). Consistently, though, global citizens face difficulties for reaching a larger public, as communication by public-relations practitioners, professional journalists, and so-called experts replaces grassroots discussion (Manca 1989, 171). To offset these difficulties, Independent Media Centers (IMCs) promote the need for diversity of opinions and seek to overcome barriers to production, exhibition, and distribution as they try to achieve their goal of "provid[ing] an avenue for underrepresented groups to tell their own stories in their own voices, to get these voices out to the world quickly, and to move us all to action for social justice" (Perlstein 2001).

These efforts are sustained by the belief that power is the ability to successfully develop one's capacities through full participation and inclusion within the public arena. Therefore, communications technologies and forms offering the ability to produce and disseminate information become fundamental to critical media consciousness.

As Calabrese (2001) explains, the ability to participate as a listener and speaker is essential to competent citizenship. Since the inception of the indy media network, many individuals have realized their ability to organize, take action, and affect change by seeing themselves as part of a large and powerful community.

The indy media slogan, "Be the Media," offers a response to claims that "a movement that does not make it into the media does not exist" (Rucht, as cited in Bennett 2003, 17). By nurturing critical media consciousness, indy media sites have the potential to suggest and point the way toward a more democratic world and, further, to exist as the heart of that world.

Gal Beckerman (2003) describes the IMC process as "precarious, democracy teetering on the edge of anarchy," but others contend that indy media create "competent activist journalists . . . [e]mbodying the ethos of direct action, . . . telling the stories . . . for themselves . . . instead of waiting for them to be told by 'professionals.' The IMC Network is . . . a new paradigm for participatory activism."[3] Indy media are valuable as they create mediascapes focused on dialogue, sharing, and active participation that enable citizens to transform conflict into understanding—the essence of a strong democratic society. Critical media consciousness locates mediated communication—defined as a cultural form overcoming the limits of time and place through an extension of face-to-face dialogue—and its organization, development, and employment, at the center of the establishment of a strong global democracy.

Democracy depends upon open communication. In response, critical media consciousness calls for individuals to think critically about the democratic potential for media as they recognize that increasing the number of media outlets doesn't establish strong media or improve democracy. These connections highlight the importance of media power and expose ways in which mediated communication strategies and practices shape the existing world. In sum, critical media consciousness establishes strong media as diverse and unique citizens critically question mediated constructions and presentations that diminish, marginalize, and ultimately deny the reality of many.

CRITICAL MEDIA CONSCIOUSNESS

In tandem with progressive social organizations, critical media consciousness is vital for the development of the democratic communication structures required by democratic social formations. It assists in generating a public sphere constructed upon participatory parity among various segments of society. Of utmost importance to this project is accepting that communication strategies and systems are absolutely fundamental to establishing democracy on a global scale. With a correlation existing between information control and political power (Bruck and Raboy 1989), media power forms a connection with social conflict (Couldry and Curran 2003). Even as emerging technologies reveal the possibilities for democratic communications, "unofficial communicators" continue to face numerous obstacles hindering reception and transmission (Drew 1995, 73).

This recognition—conceptualizing critical media consciousness—theorizes how communication forms provide spaces where traditionally marginalized voices can share their unique interests, discuss differences, and arrive at mutually beneficial resolutions. If communication is understood as a foundation of society offering opportunities to create a just and humanitarian world, critical media consciousness is the concept that points the way. Mediated communication emerges as a cultural form extending participatory communication (dialogue) while suppressing forms of communication (monologue) that restrict access and limit deliberation by privileging certain voices, views, and ideologies.

To achieve an equitable global society, diversity of expression is legitimate and the ability of citizens to collectively determine issues depends on that expression. Ultimately, respectful communication forms a shared bond for "the development of a citizenry capable of genuine public thinking and political judgment and thus able to envision a common future in terms of genuinely common goods" (Barber 1984, 197).

As society expands and evolves, processes of communication add to its complexities. If we agree with Williams's idea that "general participation in common decision-making is the deepest principle in democracy itself" (as cited in Hagen 1992, 20) and that mass media are an essential component for effective and necessary communication in modern societies, then democratic communication systems must evolve beyond theoretical ideals, and global democracy and participatory parity cannot remain abstractions. Communications technologies are a given of globalization, and consequently, media are central to social coordination.

CRITICAL MEDIA CONSCIOUSNESS AND THE
PRACTICE OF DEMOCRACY

In theory, a media system existing in a democratic society should provide the potential for individuals to voice their policy preferences, concerns, and ideas, while also ensuring that informed and enlightened citizens have the ability to respond and act. Due to the size (geographic and population) and complexities of modern societies, public deliberation must be mediated, and democracy will work only if media provide full, accurate, and well-interpreted information to the public (Page 1996).

Critical media consciousness leads to an understanding of the barriers that currently exist for global democracy and of the implications of the current media structure. Simultaneously, such a consciousness provides an opportunity to affect change on such structures, creating an engaged, aware, informed, and connected individual.

Democratic communication is central to global democracy because it should "enable little people in big societies to send and receive a variety of opinions in a variety of ways" (Keane 1993, 239). A fully democratic communication system will also ensure that "great big dogmas and smelly little orthodoxies of all kinds are held in check and in which, thanks to the existence of a genuine plurality of media of communication, various individuals and groups could openly express their solidarity with other citizens' likes and dislikes, proposals, tastes, and ideals" (Keane 1993, 244).

Critical media consciousness returns agency to audiences so that they think about and analyze who they are in relation to their political context and take their lives into their own hands (Downing 1984). Historically this process has always been part of the process of creating alternatives that challenge existing authorities (Couldry 2003; Hamilton 2000, 2001). Frequently, individuals and groups create horizontal communication links, as opposed to the vertical process of communication that the mainstream media favor. While vertical communication creates a top-down form of communication moving from giant corporations (down) to ordinary people, horizontal communication allows for cross-community dialogue and provides an outlet for the discussion of important social and political realities lacking and overlooked by mainstream media (Downing 1995, 241). Thus, media can be used as an "effective instrument" in the democratic project (Anderson and Goldman 1993, 59).

Critical media consciousness is a concept that (contrary to media literacy) supplies a way to imagine a horizontal model for communication and in turn to imagine media beyond the constraints of commercialization; it is a way to transform the frustrations with commercialization into an ideology, a social practice. Answering Williams's call for the decapitalization, deprofessionalization, and deinstitutionalization of the media industry, critical media consciousness is a way to challenge the political and economic strength of corporate media. A people's media "tend[s] toward equality and emancipation" and replaces the reproducing relations of domination (Sparks 1993, 73) with a chorus of people's voices.

NOTES

1. Comment by Sut Jhally during a panel presentation at the National Conference on Media Reform, November 2003.
2. See Grindstaff and DeLuca 2004 for an excellent discussion of terrorism and media in relation to the Daniel Pearl execution.
3. Klein, n.d., from a pamphlet handed out at an Indy media conference.

REFERENCES

Anderson, K., and A. Goldson. 1993. Alternating currents: Alternative television inside and outside of the academy. *Social Text* 35:56–71.
Auter, P. J. 2004. Meeting the needs of multiple audiences: An examination of the Aljazeera and English Aljazeera Websites from the public relations perspective. *Global Media Journal* 2 (4). Available at http://lass.calumet.purdue.edu/cca/gmj/submitteddocuments/archivedpapers/fall2004/refereed/auter.htm (accessed June 6, 2005).
Baker, E. C. 1998. The media that citizens need. *University of Pennsylvania Law Review* 147 (317).
Barber, B. 1984. *Strong democracy: Participatory politics for a new age.* Berkeley: University of California Press.
———. 1992. Jihad vs. McWorld. *Atlantic Monthly*, March: 53–63.
Beckerman, G. 2003. Edging away from anarchy: Inside the indymedia collective, passion vs. pragmatism. *Columbia Journalism Review*, no. 5 (September/October). Available at http://www.cjr.org/issues/2003/5/anarchy-beckerman.asp (accessed June 6, 2005).
Bennett, L. 2003. New media power: The Internet and global activism. In *Contesting media power: Alternative media in a networked world*, ed. N. Couldry and J. Curran, 17–37. Boulder, Colo.: Rowman & Littlefield.
Bowers, F. 2004. Terrorists turn up the dial in global PR war. *Christian Science Monitor*, November 24.
Bowers, F., and O. Tohid. 2004. Osama bin Laden casts himself as Muslim elder statesman. *Christian Science Monitor*, November 1.
Bruck, P. 1992. Discursive movements and social movements: The active negotiation of constraints. In *Democratic communications in the information age*, ed. J. Wasko and V. Mosco, 138–58. Norwood, N.J.: Ablex.
Bruck, P., and M. Raboy. 1989. Introduction: The challenge of democratic communication. In *Communication for and against democracy*, ed. M. Raboy and P. Bruck, 3–16. Montreal: Black Rose Books.
Calabrese, A. 2001. Political significance of media literacy. In *Liberal democracy, citizenship, education*, ed. O. Luthar, K. McLeod, and M. Zagar, 68–86. Oakville, Ont.: Mosaic Press in cooperation with the Scientific Research Institute.

Calabrese, A., and M. Borchert. 1996. Prospects for electronic democracy in the United States: Rethinking communication and social policy. *Media, Culture, Society* 18:249–68.

Corner, J. 1999. *Critical ideas in television studies*. Oxford, U.K.: Clarendon.

Couldry, N. 2000. *The place of media power: Pilgrims and the witnesses of the media age*. London: Routledge.

————. 2003. Beyond the Hall of Mirrors: Some theoretical reflections on the global contestation of media power. In *Contesting media power: Alternative media in a networked world*, ed. N. Couldry and J. Curran, 39–54. Boulder, Colo.: Rowman & Littlefield.

Couldry, N., and J. Curran. 2003. The paradox of media power. In *Contesting media power: Alternative media in a networked world*, ed. N. Couldry and J. Curran, 3–16. Boulder, Colo.: Rowman & Littlefield.

Cowie, N. 2000. Media literacy and the commercialization of culture. Chapter 21 of *Critical studies in media commercialism*, ed. R. Anderson and L. Strate, 310–23. Oxford: Oxford University Press.

de Borchgrave, Arnaud. 2005. Warmonger spins evil yarns into fabric of Saudi society. Available at http://www.insightmag.com/media/paper441/news/1996/01/01/TheLastWord/Warmonger.Spins.Evil.Yarns.Into.Fabric.Of.Saudi.Society-212987.shtml (accessed June 6, 2005).

Downing, J. 1984. *Radical media: The political experience of alternative communication*. Boston: South End Press.

————. 1995. Alternative media and the Boston Tea Party. In *Questioning the media: A critical introduction*, ed. J. Downing, Ali Mohammadi, and Annabelle Sreberny-Mohammadi, 184–203. Thousand Oaks, Calif.: Sage.

————. 2001. *Radical media: Rebellious communication and social movements*. Thousand Oaks, Calif.: Sage.

————. 2003. The independent media center movement and the anarchist socialist tradition. In *Contesting media power: Alternative media in a networked world*, ed. N. Couldry and J. Curran, 243–58. Boulder, Colo.: Rowman & Littlefield.

Drew, J. 1995. Media activism and radical democracy. In *Resisting the virtual life: The cultural politics of information*, ed. J. Brook and I. Boal, 71–83. San Francisco: City Lights.

el-Nawawy, M. 2004. Terrorist or freedom fighter? The Arab media coverage of "terrorism" or "so-called terrorism." *Global Media Journal* 2 (4). Available at http://lass.calumet.purdue.edu/cca/gmj/submitteddocuments/archivedpapers/fall2004/refereed/elnawawy.htm (accessed June 6, 2005).

Garnham, N. 2000. *Emancipation, the media, and modernity: Arguments about the media and society*. Oxford: Oxford University Press.

Gills, B. K., ed. 2000. *Globalization and the politics of resistance*. New York: Palgrave.

Grindstaff, D. A., and K. DeLuca. 2004. The corpus of Daniel Pearl. *Critical Studies in Media Communication* 21 (4): 305–24.

Hacker, K. L. 1996. Missing links in the evolution of electronic democratization. *Media, Culture, and Society* 18:213–32.

Hagen, Ingunn. 1992. Democratic communication: Media and social participation. In *Democratic communications in the information age*, ed. J. Wasko and V. Mosco, 16–27. Norwood, N.J.: Ablex.

Hamilton, J. 2000. Alternative media: Conceptual difficulties, critical possibilities. *Journal of Communication Inquiry* 24 (4): 357–78.

———. 2001. Theory through history: Exploring scholarly conceptions of U.S. alternative media. *Communication Review* 4:305–26.

Held, D. 1996. *Models of democracy.* 2nd ed. Stanford, Calif.: Stanford University Press.

Herman, E. 1995. Media in the US Political Economy. In *Questioning the media: A critical introduction*, ed. J. Downing, Ali Mohammadi, and Annabelle Sreberny-Mohammadi, 77–93. Thousand Oaks, Calif.: Sage.

Herman, E., and N. Chomsky. 1988. *Manufacturing consent: The political economy of the mass media.* New York: Pantheon.

Hobbs, R. 2001. Expanding the concept of literacy. In *Information and Behavior*, vol. 6 of *Media literacy in the information age: Current perspectives*, ed. R. Kubey, 163–83. New Brunswick, N.J.: Transaction.

Keane, J. 1991. *The media and democracy.* Cambridge, U.K.: Polity.

———. 1993. Democracy and the media: Without foundations. In *Prospects for democracy: North, south, east, west*, ed. D. Held, 235–53. Stanford, Calif.: Stanford University Press.

Kellner, D. 1992. Public access television and the struggle for democracy. In *Democratic communications in the information age*, ed. J. Wasko and V. Mosco, 100–13. Norwood, N.J.: Ablex.

———. 2004. 9/11, spectacles of terror, and media manipulation. In *Tell me lies: Propaganda and media distortion in the attack on Iraq*, ed. D. Miller, 144–56. London: Pluto Press.

Lewis, J., and S. Jhally. 1998. The struggle over media literacy. *Journal of Communication* 48:109–20.

Macpherson, C. B. 1973. *Democratic theory: Essays in retrieval.* Oxford, U.K.: Clarendon Press.

Manca, L. 1989. Journalism, advocacy, and a communication model for democracy. In *Communication for and against democracy*, ed. M. Raboy and P. Bruck, 163–73. Montreal: Black Rose Books.

Masterman, L. 2001. A rationale for media education. In *Information and Behavior*, vol. 6 of *Media literacy in the information age: Current perspectives*, ed. R. Kubey, 15–68. New Brunswick, N.J.: Transaction.

Miller, D. 2004. Introduction to *Tell me lies: Propaganda and media distortion in the attack on Iraq*, ed. D. Miller, 1–11. London: Pluto Press.

Miller, L., J. Stauber, and S. Rampton. 2004. War is sell. In *Tell me lies: Propaganda and media distortion in the attack on Iraq*, ed. D. Miller, 41–51. London: Pluto Press.

Napoli, J., and J. Fejeran. 2004. Of two minds: U.S. public diplomacy and the Middle East. *Global Media Journal* 2 (4). Available at http://lass.calumet.purdue.edu/cca/gmj/submitteddocuments/archivedpapers/fall2004/refereed/napoli.htm (accessed June 6, 2005).

Page, B. 1996. *Who deliberates? Mass media in modern democracy.* Chicago: University of Chicago Press.

Perlstein, J. 2001. The independent media center movement: An experiment in media democracy. *MediaFile* 20 (1). Retrieved February 25, 2004, from http://www.media-alliance.org/article.php?story=20031109003144928.

Peters, G. 2004. "American" voice on new terror video. *Christian Science Monitor,* October 29.

Rodriguez, A. 1995. Control mechanisms of national news making: Britain, Canada, Mexico, and the United States. In *Questioning the media: A critical introduction,* ed. J. Downing, Ali Mohammadi, and Annabelle Sreberny-Mohammadi, 128–46. Thousand Oaks, Calif.: Sage.

Rodriguez, C. 1996. Shedding useless notions of alternative media. *Peace Review* 8 (1): 63–68.

———. 1998. Citizens' media and their potential in contexts of intense violence: Preliminary reflections. June. Retrieved November 4, 2003, from http://faculty-staff.ou.edu/R/Clemencia.Rodriquez-1/peacemedia.htm.

Rugh, W. A. 2004. How Washington confronts Arab media. *Global Media Journal* 2 (4). Available at http://lass.calumet.purdue.edu/cca/gmj/submitteddocuments/archivedpapers/fall2004/invited/rugh.htm (accessed June 6, 2005).

Schudson, M. 1992. Was there ever a public sphere? If so, when? Reflections on the American case. In *Habermas and the Public Sphere,* 6th ed., ed. C. Calhoun, 143–63. Cambridge, Mass.: MIT Press.

———. 1997. Why conversation is not the soul of democracy [Electronic version]. *Critical Studies in Mass Communication* 14 (4): 297–309.

Shanker, T. 2004. Panel cites many U.S. failures in dealing with Muslim world. *Seattle Post-Intelligencer,* November 26.

Shumway, C. 2003. Democratizing communication through community-based participatory media networks: A study of the independent media center movement. M.A. thesis, New School University. Available at http://chris.shumway.tripod.com/papers/thesis.htm (accessed February 25, 2004).

Snow, N. 2004. Brainscrubbing: The failures of US public diplomacy after 9/11. In *Tell me lies: Propaganda and media distortion in the attack on Iraq,* ed. D. Miller, 52–62. London: Pluto Press.

Sparks, C. 1993. Raymond Williams and the theory of democratic communication. In *Communication and Democracy,* ed. S. Spliko and J. Wasko, 69–86. Norwood, N.J.: Ablex.

Vincent, R. C. 1992. CNN: Talking to elites. In *Triumph of the image: The media's war in the Persian Gulf; A global perspective,* ed. H. Mowlana, G. Gerbner, and H. Schiller, 181–201. Boulder, Colo.: Westview Press.

Walsh, B. N.d. Expanding the definition of media literacy. Available at http://interact.
    uoregon.edu/MediaLit/mlr/readings/articles/expanddefml.html (accessed March 4,
    2005).
Wasko, J. 1992. Introduction. In *Democratic communications in the information age*,
    ed. J. Wasko and V. Mosco, 1–13. Norwood, N.J.: Ablex.
Williams, R. 1968. *Communications*. 2nd ed. London: Penguin.
———. 1989. *Resources of hope*. Ed. R. Gable. London: Verso.

8

Terrorism, Public Relations, and Propaganda

Nancy Snow

Ever since September 11, 2001, when outside terrorists attacked U.S. financial and military centers, the U.S. government has been immersed in a global information war to promote the interests, values, and image of the United States. Not since the Cold War has the government so engaged its persuasion industries to combat stereotypes, target enemy populations, and single out particular regions like the Middle East for widespread broadcast information campaigns to overcome negative perceptions and attitudes toward the United States. Within the matrix of this information war campaign, a number of terms have been resurrected to describe the U.S. effort, most notably *propaganda*, *public relations*, and *public diplomacy*.

The purpose of this chapter is to identify both the challenges and opportunities that public relations and public diplomacy offer in the post-9/11 environment. Against this backdrop, the ever looming charge of "it's all propaganda" casts a shadow on legitimate tools of persuasion that may benefit both the government and people of the United States.

The first part will delineate among public relations, propaganda, and public diplomacy to help clarify how each is used interchangeably within the information war context. The second part will single out a more balanced mutually beneficial symmetric model of persuasion as a counterparadigm to the dominant, Cold War-centric paradigm currently being used in the war on terrorism.

Public relations received a universal definition almost thirty years ago when a group of sixty-five public relations leaders took 472 definitions and came up with an eighty-eight-word sentence to describe what they do:

> Public relations is a distinctive management function which helps establish and maintain mutual lines of communications, understanding, acceptance, and cooperation between an organization and its publics; involves the management of

problems or issues; helps management to keep informed on and responsive to public opinion; defines and emphasizes the responsibility of management to serve the public interest; helps management keep abreast of and effectively utilize change, serving as an early warning system to help anticipate trends; and uses research and sound and ethical communication techniques as its principal tools. (Harlow 1976, 36)

Similarly, in 1980, the Public Relations Society of America came up with two short definitions that have remained popular to this day: "Public relations helps an organization and its publics adapt mutually to each other" and "Public relations is an organization's efforts to win cooperation of groups of people" (as quoted in Seitel 2001, 9). Embedded in the longer and shorter definitions is an emphasis on process, mutuality, and building credibility, all of which overlap with the concerns of persuasion and influence managers involved in the information wars since 9/11. The challenge is that to some, public relations at times amounts to nothing more than "spin," where words, facts, and images are twisted in order to better the outcome of the client, while a public diplomacy campaign to the Middle East may suffer the same characterization—as really nothing more than propaganda with a happy face. This may explain why public relations officials denounce the characterization of what they do as spinmeistering, while public diplomacy officials tend to eschew the word propaganda for what they do. Outside the United States, these delineations and defenses are not always accepted. In many circles, public relations, advertising, and marketing are used interchangeably with propaganda and do not carry the same negative, lying assumptions.

Within the U.S. context, propaganda carries a very negative connotation, even to this day, despite the word's original association with the Reformation period when Pope Gregory XV established a Congregation for the Propagation of the Faith to promote the Catholic faith against the rise of Protestantism in northern Europe. It is still widely accepted that *propaganda* refers to an information campaign of lies and deceptions to benefit the sponsoring institution. During World War II and the Cold War era, Americans generally thought of the government's enemies, be they Hitler, Stalin, or Khrushchev, as being engaged in propaganda, while the United States was only interested in promoting the truth. For instance, President Harry Truman launched a "Campaign of Truth" counteroffensive to Soviet aggression at the outbreak of war in Korea. His speechwriter at the time, Edward Barrett, wrote:

It was sure to cause headlines such as "Truman Declares Propaganda War." Happily, a new phrase came to mind. The American offensive was naturally to be based upon truth. Therefore, I suggested that the President call for a "Campaign of Truth." (Barrett 1955, 73)

Thereafter, Truman peppered his speeches with references to freedom, truth, and liberty, all used interchangeably to suggest the comparative advantage that the United States had in the struggle of ideas.

In order to understand propaganda's relationship to public diplomacy and public relations, it must be divested of its negative connotation. The U.S. government doesn't invariably inform and promote the truth while other countries, particularly those led by dictators, always engage in lies and deceit. Modern democracies, including the United States, generally shy away from the term because of its negative connotations, while modern dictatorships feel no need to do so. In place of "propaganda," democracies prefer to use euphemistic terms like "information" and "public diplomacy." This is why the United States first had a Committee on Public Information (World War I), then an Office of War Information (World War II) and the U.S. Information Agency (Cold War), and now an under secretary of state for public diplomacy and an Office of Global Communications (post-9/11). By contrast, the Soviets designated a Propaganda Committee arm of the Communist party, and the Nazis established a Ministry of Popular Entertainment and Propaganda.

It is more accepted outside the United States that virtually all governments, no matter the level of information control, engage in campaigns to influence the governed and their counterparts overseas, and these campaigns are assumed to carry with them both open and covert means of communication. As noted by Anthony Pratkanis and Eliot Aronson (1992, 11):

> The word *propaganda* has since evolved to mean mass "suggestion" or influence through the manipulation of symbols and the psychology of the individual. Propaganda is the communication of a point of view with the ultimate goal of having the recipient of the appeal come to "voluntarily" accept this position as if it were his or her own.

Robert Gass and John Seiter (2003, 11) identify five typical characteristics of propaganda:

1. It is strongly ideological in bent and does not serve strictly an information function. For example, a "just the facts, ma'am" function is not in and of itself, propaganda.
2. It is agenda-driven, which means that propagandists do not wish to be neutral or objective in intent or purpose.
3. It is institutional in nature, practiced by organized groups such as corporations, government agencies, religious groups, terrorist cells, or social movements, which is why we so often now associate propaganda with terrorism, defined at times as the "propaganda of the deed."

4. It must involve some type of mass persuasion campaign that targets a mass audience and relies on mass media to persuade that audience. The conversation around the company cooler is not propaganda.
5. Propaganda's bad reputation as a construct is based mostly on the ethics involved with the mass persuasion methods used. Propaganda tends to favor end results over ethics. Ethics are not excluded but are generally secondary to the end result sought by the propaganda campaign.

How is propaganda any different from the acceptable persuasion campaigns we call public diplomacy and public relations? I would argue that the difference is a semantic one over which scholars and practitioners continue to debate. Former United States Information Agency (USIA)/Worldnet TV Service director Alvin Snyder published a memoir in which he said that during the Cold War "the U.S. government ran a full-service public relations organization, the largest in the world, about the size of the twenty biggest U.S. commercial PR firms combined," and "the biggest branch of this propaganda machine is called the United States Information Agency" (1995, xi). What Snyder identifies as propaganda is preferably referred to these days by many diplomats as public diplomacy, defined by USIA's successors at the U.S. State Department as that which "seeks to promote the national interest and the national security of the United States through understanding, informing, and influencing foreign publics and broadening dialogue between American citizens and institutions and their counterparts abroad" (USIAAA 2002). The U.S. State Department has an under secretary for public diplomacy and public affairs, with former advertising executive Charlotte Beers serving in that position from just after 9/11 until the start of the war in Iraq in March 2003.

Like the term propaganda, the public relations industry carries negative associations, especially when associated only with spin and flacking for one's client. Joseph Duffey served as the final director of the USIA before its integration into the State Department. He told the U.S. Senate Foreign Relations Committee that U.S. public diplomacy must be distinguished from American public relations:

> Let me just say a word about public diplomacy. It is not public relations. It is not flacking for a Government agency or even flacking for America. It is trying to relate beyond government-to-government relationships the private institutions, the individuals, the long-term contacts, the accurate understanding, the full range of perceptions of America to the rest of the world, both to those who are friendly or inclined to be our partners or allies from one issue to another to those who are hostile, with some credibility or impartiality. (Duffey 1995)

What Duffey was describing is an ongoing problem for public diplomacy in the twenty-first century: it is difficult to define and scholars have few theories and models outside of propaganda and public relations on which to measure its effectiveness and practices.

If public diplomacy is linked to diplomatic history, it sits squarely in the midst of national security objectives and promoting national security interests:

> Public Diplomacy—the cultural, educational, and informational programs, citizen exchanges, or broadcasts used to promote the national interest of the United States through understanding, informing, and influencing foreign audiences.[1]
>
> Public diplomacy is as important to the national interests as military preparedness.[2]

At other times, the USIA has defined public diplomacy as a two-track process, both one-way informational and declaratory in purpose and two-way educational and mutual in outcome:

> Public diplomacy seeks to promote the national interest and the national security of the United States through understanding, informing, and influencing foreign publics and broadening dialogue between American citizens and institutions and their counterparts abroad. (USIAAA 2002)

The U.S. Information and Educational Exchange Act of 1948, also known as the Smith-Mundt Act, is one of the linchpins of U.S. public diplomacy. It has two-way communication strategies in its language: "The objectives of this Act are to enable the Government of the United States to correct the misunderstandings about the United States in other countries, which constituted obstacles to peace, and to promote mutual understanding between the peoples of the United States and other countries, which is one of the essential foundations of peace."[3] One of its authors, Karl Mundt, clearly viewed the act more as a one-way informational counter to Soviet propaganda. He wrote: "Immediately following the close of World War II when we realized that we were leaving a hot war only to enter a cold war, many of us recognized the importance of fashioning programs to meet effectively the non-military challenge confronting us. It was out of this era that the Smith-Mundt Act emerged." These Cold War weapons of words were needed because the United States faced "an alien force which seeks our total destruction" (Mundt, quoted in Glander 2000, 61).

The other U.S. public diplomacy linchpin, the Fulbright-Hays Act of 1961,[4] incorporated provisions of Senator J. William Fulbright's amendment in 1946 and the Smith-Mundt Act to establish a new educational and cultural exchange policy

> to increase mutual understanding between the people of the United States and the people of other countries by means of educational and cultural exchange; to strengthen the ties which unite us with other nations by demonstrating the educational and cultural interests, developments, and achievements of the people

of the United States and other nations, and the contributions being made toward a peaceful and more fruitful life for people throughout the world; to promote international cooperation for educational and cultural advancement; and thus to assist in the development of friendly, sympathetic, and peaceful relations between the United States and the other countries of the world. (Smith-Mundt Act, quoted in Snow 1998, 619)

This view of mutual understanding and mutuality in public diplomacy would likely emphasize very different approaches and measures of effectiveness than one placing public diplomacy squarely in the midst of a national crisis. Over the last fifty years, no single consensus has emerged to define the direction of U.S. public diplomacy aside from the goals and whims of the incumbent executive branch of the U.S. government. As Michael Holtzman (2003) observed in the *New York Times*:

United States public diplomacy is neither public nor diplomatic. First, the government—not the broader American public—has been the main messenger to a world that is mightily suspicious of it. Further, the State Department, which oversees most efforts, seems to view public diplomacy not as a dialogue but as a one-sided exercise . . . America speaking to the world.

Holtzman belongs to a school of thought on U.S. public diplomacy advanced by Senator Fulbright and Edward R. Murrow that suggests a far wider array of participants, practitioners, and perspectives than just those seen or heard in the armed forces or Foreign Service or inside the Washington beltway. As Murrow defined the field when appointed director of the USIA in 1963:

Public diplomacy differs from traditional diplomacy in that it involves interaction not only with governments but primarily with non-governmental individuals and organizations. Furthermore, public diplomacy activities often present many differing views represented by private American individuals and organizations in addition to official government views (quoted in Leonard, Stead, and Smewing 2002, 1).

Murrow's definition suggests that public diplomacy in practice is at much at home in corporate boardrooms, pop concerts, and peace rallies as it is inside the halls of Congress. Nevertheless, U.S. public diplomacy is still often assumed to be linked in some way, peripherally or dead center, with traditional diplomatic goals of national governments. As Christopher Ross, U.S. State Department special coordinator for public diplomacy and public affairs, writes:

The practitioners of traditional diplomacy engage the representatives of foreign governments in order to advance the national interests articulated in their own government's strategic goals in international affairs. Public diplomacy, by contrast, engages carefully targeted sectors of foreign publics in order to develop support for those same strategic goals. (2002, 75)

Whenever public diplomacy definitions are overtly linked to official outcomes of national governments (e.g., in the war on terror), this tends to connote a more negative interpretation linked to propaganda outcomes. In December 2004, the U.S.-based science and technology firm Battelle released a list of the top ten innovations for the war on terror. One innovation forecast to emerge in the coming decade (2005–2014) is twenty-first-century public diplomacy that requires nontechnical skills development in intercultural communication and advanced strategic communication. Battelle's team of experts included retired generals from the U.S. Army, Air Force, and Marine Corps as well as Ohio State University faculty. The team linked public diplomacy innovations directly to the U.S.-led war on terror that arose from the events of September 11, 2001:

> The war against terrorism is, in part, a war with extremists whose culture, worldview, and values conflict with those of the West. There are economic, religious, political, and ideological tensions between the Middle East and the West. As such, any discussion of tools for combating terrorism must include deploying mass communication to break down these barriers. The first step will be gaining a fuller understanding of opposing cultures and values so that the United States and its allies can develop more effective strategies to prevent terrorism. America needs to project a more balanced image of Western culture through strategic, positive communication. This could be achieved by communicating the Western message through targeted use of mass media, developing a next-generation Voice of America approach, perhaps supported with distribution of inexpensive, disposable TVs. (Battelle 2004)

While acknowledging the obvious strains in policy and projected images between the Middle East and the West, this definition of twenty-first-century public diplomacy offers primarily an asymmetric information model of public diplomacy that seeks to break down barriers in the Middle East to a Western worldview, message, and values. Western tension with the Middle East is causally linked to combating terrorism and overcoming oppositional cultures and values, but not linked to specific foreign policy disagreements with the United States. Gaining understanding of another culture is concerned primarily with comprehension in order to combat terrorism, not to building mutual understanding that may improve the foreign relations of the United States, its people, and its government with other nations and peoples.

This definition of twenty-first-century public diplomacy is an accepted dimension of public diplomacy, one identified in U.S. history as the tough-minded, Cold War–centric government information model whereby public diplomacy is defined as "the way in which both government and private individuals and groups influence directly or indirectly those public attitudes and

opinions which bear directly on another government's foreign policy decisions" (Signitzer and Coombs 1992, 138). The Battelle version belongs to
the political information side of public diplomacy that advocates the U.S.
case in particular and the Western civilization model in general. Within this
school of thought, it is most important that international publics gain a better
understanding of the United States and its culture, values, and institutions, primarily for securing U.S. foreign policy ends and defending national security
objectives.

Public diplomacy, in practice and conception, uses multifaceted approaches
to global communication. Like public relations, it can follow various tracks or
approaches to fulfill goals and objectives. Missing from the Battelle definition
is the intercultural communication dimension of public diplomacy identified
earlier, to foster "mutual understanding between the people of the United States
and the people of other countries" as advocated in the Fulbright-Hays Act. In
this framework, cultural comprehension is also sought, but not primarily for
unilateral advantage and outcome (which by definition stresses fast media such
as radio and television). Rather, long-term strategies for mutual benefit and
mutual trust are emphasized, including slower media such as films, exhibitions,
and educational and cultural exchanges (e.g., Fulbright scholars, International
Visitors Program).

Both public relations and public diplomacy can and do emphasize
relationship-building practices. It very much depends on the intended outcome
of the information campaign whether or not the relationship is tilted more to
the sponsoring organization's needs or to both the sponsor and the intended
recipient. One public relations textbook provides a widely accepted definition of international public relations as "the planned and organized effort of a
company, institution, or government to establish mutually beneficial relations
with the publics of other nations" (Wilcox 1989, 395). This definition allows
for two-way symmetric tactics of persuasion to be included in communication
outcomes.

The intercultural communication dimension in public diplomacy and public relations should not be sidelined but rather separated from the more
tough-minded battlefield tactics associated with counterterrorism. Unfortunately, the calamitous events of 9/11 have centered U.S. public diplomacy and
public relations strategies around strategic communication efforts to combat
terrorism as defined by and advocated primarily by the U.S. government generally, and the White House in particular. Most recently even these government
efforts have been criticized by the Defense Science Board (2004), a federal
task force comprised of an independent group of both academic and private
sector advisers that reports directly to the secretary of defense. The 102-page
unclassified text, finished in September 2004 but not released to the news media

until after the U.S. presidential election,[5] concluded that success in strategic communications means the following:

> We must understand that the United States is engaged in a generational and global struggle about ideas, not a war between the West and Islam. It is more than a war against the tactic of terrorism. We must think in terms of global networks, both government and non-government. . . . Strategic communication requires a sophisticated method that maps perceptions and influence networks, identifies policy priorities, formulates objectives, focuses on "doable tasks," develops themes and messages, employs relevant channels, leverages new strategic and tactical dynamics, and monitors success. This approach will build on in-depth knowledge of other cultures and factors that motivate human behavior. It will adapt techniques of skillful political campaigning, even as it avoids slogans, quick fixes, and mind sets of winners and losers. It will search out credible messengers and create message authority. It will seek to persuade within news cycles, weeks, and months. It will engage in a respectful dialogue of ideas that begins with listening and assumes decades of sustained effort. (Defense Science Board 2004, 2)

The Defense Science Board report concluded that U.S. credibility in the Middle East is at an all-time low and that American intervention in the Muslim world has increased the power and reputation of the most radical Islamists. According to the report, these Islamists, despite President Bush's claims, do not "hate our freedoms" or hate "freedom-loving peoples" but rather hate very specific policies, namely, what they perceive as uncritical, imbalanced support for Israel over Palestinian sovereignty and support for tyrannical regimes such as those in Egypt, Saudi Arabia, Jordan, and Pakistan, all of which receive varying levels of U.S. military and economic aid (Egypt is America's second-largest recipient of aid behind Israel).

A more troubling conclusion of the Defense Science Board report was the following: "Public diplomacy, public affairs, psychological operations (PSYOP), and open military information operations must be coordinated and energized." Further, leadership in strategic communications begins at the top: "A unifying vision of strategic communication starts with presidential direction." Both of these recommendations suggest that the government-led asymmetric model of public diplomacy will likely remain the dominant paradigm in global communications as advocated by leading think tanks, top government officials, and military experts. This would not bode well for more symmetric mutual understanding strategies in public diplomacy that may operate outside the dominant chambers of persuasion and influence in Washington, D.C.

Mark Leonard (2002, 8) of the London-based Foreign Policy Centre identifies three dimensions of public diplomacy: (1) news management; (2) strategic communications; and (3) relationship-building. These three dimensions may apply to domestic, bilateral, and global public diplomacy efforts. All three have dimensions that overlap with what public relations and public diplomacy officials do at varying times and intensities.

News management is cited as the first dimension of public diplomacy and involves management of day-to-day communication issues. Examples include the White House Office of Global Communications or the Coalition Information Centers (CICs) during the Afghanistan war period of 2001 and 2002. News management is reactive in minutes and hours and is mostly handled by traditional diplomacy institutions. In wartime, this dimension may operate at multiple levels, as pointed out by General Colin Powell during Operation Desert Storm:

> Remember when you are out there on television, communicating instantaneously around the world, we're talking to five audiences. One, the reporters who ask the question—important audience. Second audience, the American people who are watching. The third audience, 170 capitals who may have an interest in what the subject is. Fourth, you are talking to your enemy. It was a unique situation to know that your enemy was getting the clearest indication of your intentions by watching you on television at the same time you were giving that message. And fifth, you are talking to the troops. Their lives are on the line. (Quoted in Leonard 2002, 12–13)

Strategic communications refers to the totality of communications used to promote positive messages about the country—including those from government, business, tourism, finance sectors, and cultural institutions. While news management is more political and military in emphasis and has a reactive stance, strategic communications operates more in an economic realm and is proactive in process and purpose. All countries are interested in having a global competitive advantage that separates them from their competition. A country's reputation and national identity affects the bottom line where trading partners will buy services and goods. Strategic communications requires proactive campaigns that are refined and developed over weeks and months and those create a stake or buy-in for all public diplomacy institutions. Examples include the Shared Values Campaign of Charlotte Beers's tenure that used ninety-second "mini-documentaries" of five Muslim Americans in an attempt to open dialogue with the Muslim world and Muslims in the United States. While criticism rained down upon this campaign, one problem may have been that the State Department was trying to send too many messages. As Chris Powell, chairman of advertising company BMP DDB Needham (UK), says about strategic communication messages:

Have very few, preferably one, message. People are exposed to thousands of messages every day. They probably recall only a tiny fraction of these. The task is to cut through the fog by imagination and repetition. A contrast between diplomacy and advertising is that in advertising an enormous amount of work goes into the preparation—boiling ideas down into very, very simple concepts, and then repeating that message over and over again until you are thoroughly bored with it. When you are so bored with it that you feel like giving up, the listener may just have begun to register the message. So stick to it. (Quoted in Leonard 2002, 15–16)

Strategic communications will enhance or detract from a country's reputation. No country can get its way unless it is favorably perceived in the global environment. Within strategic communications, countries are wise to play upon their strengths: The national image for Germany to play up might be brand quality and luxury, as signified in BMW and Mercedes. Great Britain is known for tradition, which helps heritage brands that stress the past. Norway, home to the Nobel Peace Price, has a national reputation in international mediation, which signals to countries involved in civil conflict that it can be a neutral and honest broker. The Pew Global Attitude Survey in 2002, which measured attitudes toward the United States, suggests that while many foreign publics condemn U.S. government action in the world, there is strong support for U.S. values of technical expertise, entrepreneurialism, and openness. While these value traits are indeed positive, they may not be effective if the values are not associated with the sponsoring country due to an overarching negative image or brand—that of the world's sole military, economic, and cultural superpower:

Despite the widespread hostility toward the United States and many of its policies, the ideals it has long promoted are widely popular. Freedom of speech, fair elections, an impartial judiciary are prized goals for people around the world. Even globalization and expanded trade are widely supported. Ironically, these ideals are winning converts globally not because they are associated with the U.S., but in spite of that connection. (Kohut 2003)

Relationship-building is the most long-term of the three dimensions of public diplomacy and the one most oriented toward mutuality and exchange among peers and equal partners. It is, in my opinion, the dimension of public diplomacy that should be receiving the greatest emphasis so that we can overcome our Cold War mentality, which continues to emphasize an asymmetric one-way communication model elevating explanation and influence of our superiority over a climate of mutual understanding.

The two-way symmetric model of public diplomacy is characterized by international exchanges, cultural diplomacy, international conferences and seminars, and face-to-face and virtual networks. Examples include the International Visitor and Fulbright exchange programs in the United States, the Japan Exchange and Teaching (JET) program in Japan, Sister Cities International, Rotary International, and exchange programs of the British Council. Relationship-building in public diplomacy places an emphasis on engaging populations rather than winning arguments or selling a brand. Engaging requires that your public diplomacy strategy increase contact and interaction impacts that enhance others' appreciation for one's country in the long term. This includes strengthening educational, scientific, and sports ties and increasing tourism, international study, trade, and support for your values. Relationship-building will not be measured in terms of weeks or months but years. This dimension is the most public-targeted and public-involved of the three dimensions. As Mark Leonard writes:

> Public diplomacy is about building relationships: understanding the needs of other countries, cultures and peoples; communicating our points of view; correcting misperceptions; looking for areas we can find in common cause. The difference between public and traditional diplomacy is that public diplomacy involves a much broader group of people on both sides, and a broader set of interests that go beyond those of the government of the day. Public diplomacy is based on the premise that the image and reputation of a country are public goods which can create an enabling or a disabling environment for individual transactions. (Leonard 2002, 8–9)

Along similar lines, but more crisis oriented, is a model of public diplomacy that researchers John Arquilla and David Ronfeldt describe as "netwar." In their book *In Athena's Camp: Preparing for Conflict in the Information Age*, they link crisis communications to doing public diplomacy:

> Netwar refers to information-related conflict at a grand level between nations or societies. It means trying to disrupt, damage, or modify what a target population "knows" or thinks it knows about itself and the world around it. A netwar may focus on public or elite opinion, or both. It may involve public diplomacy measures, propaganda and psychological campaigns, political and cultural subversion, deception of or interference with local media, infiltration of computer networks and databases, and efforts to promote a dissident or opposition movements across computer networks. Thus designing a strategy for netwar may mean grouping together from a new perspective a number of measures that have been used before but were viewed separately. (1997, 14)

From Arquilla and Ronfeldt's perspective, crisis events mean that the value of human and social capital will become even more important in the information age, along with the need to train our own and allies' information-age warriors.

Information is viewed as a "fourth dimension of national power—an element in its own right, but still one that, like the political, economic, and military dimensions, functions synergistically to improve the value and effects of the others" (Arquilla and Ronfeldt 1997, 419).

Signitzer and Coombs note a distinction in public diplomacy between the so-called tough-minded who "hold that the purpose of public diplomacy is to exert an influence on attitudes of foreign audiences using persuasion and propaganda" and the "tender-minded" school, which "argues that information and cultural programs must bypass current foreign policy goals to concentrate on the highest long-range national objectives. The goal is to create a climate of mutual understanding" (Signitzer and Coombs 1992, 140). Neither school of thought can stand entirely on its own; they must be synthesized.

A further breakdown from tough and tender is what practitioners of public diplomacy engage in on two tracks: political communication, is administered by a section of the foreign ministry, embassy, or (in the U.S. context) State Department; and cultural communication, which may be administered not only by a cultural section of the foreign ministry, embassy, or State Department but also by quasi-governmental or nongovernmental bodies (e.g., the British Council, Sister Cities International, or National Council of International Visitors). Signitzer and Coombs also distinguish between two types of cultural communication: cultural diplomacy, which aims to present a favorable national image abroad; and cultural relations, which have mutual information exchange and no unilateral objective in mind, just "an honest picture of each country rather than a beautified one" (1992, 140).

U.S. foreign policy makers are criticized for being intransigent on core policies, for example, unfailing support for Israel, with no evidence that dialogue about policy is even possible. While the U.S. policy of supporting Israel is not likely to change, there is certainly room for U.S. policy makers to show more sympathy for Palestinian deaths as often as the United States condemns the killing of Israelis. The avenues by which goodwill and dialogue can be strengthened are through citizen diplomacy and international exchanges. While the ultimate purpose of official U.S. public diplomacy and the government marketing campaign to foreign publics is to present U.S. foreign policy and national security objectives in the best light, an important secondary source for America's public diplomacy campaign is citizen diplomacy. This calls on the American public to play its part and not watch foreign policy making from the sidelines.

For too long, and perhaps in part due to our incredible comparative advantage in communications technology, the United States has emphasized amplification over active listening, telling America's story to the world over promoting international dialogue. Anti-Americanism and general ill will toward the United States is driven by perceptions that the United States is quick to talk and explain but last to listen or understand. For a change, it wouldn't take much for the United States to listen first and talk second. It certainly wouldn't make things worse if we tried harder to be citizen-diplomats in our relations with our overseas counterparts. This is what international educational and cultural exchanges expect from those who travel across national boundaries. Why haven't we tapped these alumni, including Fulbright, Rotary, and Peace Corps volunteers as citizen-ambassadors? We're simply not doing as much as we could.

There is so much we still don't know, and we need to unite partnerships among government, the private sector, and universities to study social influence, changes in mindsets, how to teach tolerance and mutual respect, and methodologies that will measure current public diplomacy programs in an effort to find best practices. We could start by undertaking efforts to identify the best public diplomacy and public relations practices used by other countries. Some of the world's leaders in so-called soft power diplomacy (as opposed to hard power military domination) include the Scandinavian countries such as Denmark and Norway, as well as the Netherlands, Japan, and the United Kingdom.

Finally, to have a lasting and effective public diplomacy that places mutual understanding at its core, the United States must consider its legacy of strategies of truth. The short-lived and ill-conceived Office of Strategic Influence (OSI) was a here-today, gone-tomorrow debacle in 1992, but there remains plenty of concern in 2004 that some within the Department of Defense would just as soon continue to use such strategies of deception under the "whatever works" rubric. It is one thing to use deception against the enemy, but the OSI sought to use deception to plant false stories in reputable overseas news markets. Any approach based on falsehoods and deception will not have long-lasting, enduring outcomes but only short-term, tactical advantages.

My public diplomacy experience at the USIA and my propaganda research have convinced me that the more transparent and genuine U.S. public diplomacy strategies are, the better off long-term strategic and mutual interests will be, both from government and public perspectives. We learned from the Soviets and others that psychological operations based on falsehoods can be effective, but in the long run are likely to damage a country's credibility in the eyes of the world. Arquilla and Ronfeldt argue that "an approach based on falsehoods will more likely have only short-term, or tactical effects—not enduring strategic ones. Therefore, truth must be the polestar of American strategic public diplomacy, and uses of information as 'propaganda' must be eschewed" (1999, 65). Practitioners of public relations and public diplomacy may wish to take heed of that last recommendation as they seek to adopt and use each other's strategies and tools in their efforts to build influence, trust, and credibility among their international customers, clients, and publics.

NOTES

1. As quoted in "Building America's Public Diplomacy through a Reformed Structure and Additional Resources," a U.S. government planning report for integration of USIA into the State Department, 2002. (Washington, D.C.: United States Advisory Commission on Public Diplomacy).

2. Report of the United States Advisory Commission on Public Diplomacy, 1990, as quoted in Kunczik 1997, 228.

3. U.S. Congress, House Committee on Foreign Affairs, *United States Information and Educational Exchange Act of 1947* (Washington, D.C.: United States Government Printing Office), 3.

4. The Fulbright-Hays Act is also known as the Mutual Educational and Cultural Exchange Act of 1961, P.L. 87–256. The purpose of the Fulbright Program is to increase mutual understanding between the people of the United States and the people of other countries.

5. For more on this, see Sidney Blumenthal, "The New Pentagon Paper," *Salon.com*, December 2, 2004.

REFERENCES

Arquilla, John, and David Ronfeldt. 1997. *In Athena's camp: Preparing for conflict in the information age*. Santa Monica, Calif.: Rand.

———. 1999. *The emergence of Noopolitik: Toward an American information strategy*. Santa Monica, Calif.: Rand.

Battelle. 2004. Battelle panel's top ten innovations for the war on terror headed by technology advances to support better intelligence, decision-making: Scientists, academicians also call for non-technical advance-communication to foster cultural understanding. May 10. Available at http://www.battelle.org/news/04/5-10-04TopTenTerrorInnova.stm (accessed June 7, 2005).

Barrett, Edward W. 1955. *Truth is our weapon*. New York: Funk & Wagnalls.

Coombs, Philip H. 1964. *The fourth dimension of foreign policy: Education and cultural affairs*. Ed. John C. Campbell. Council on Foreign Relations Policy Book Series. New York: Harper and Row.

Defense Science Board. 2004. *Report of the Defense Science Board Task Force on Strategic Communication*. September. Washington, D.C.: Office of the Under Secretary of Defense for Acquisition, Technology, and Logistics. Available at http://www.acq.osd.mil/dsb/reports/2004-09-Strategic_Communication.pdf (accessed June 8, 2005).

Duffey, Joseph. 1995. Comments before the U.S. Senate Committee on Foreign Relations, Subcommittee on International Operations. *Reorganization and revitalization of America's foreign affairs institution.* S. Hrg. 104–215. 104th Cong., 1st sess. March 23.

Gass, Robert, and John Seiter. 2003. *Persuasion, social influence, and compliance gaining.* Boston: Allyn & Bacon.

Glander, Timothy. 2000. *Origins of mass communications research during the American Cold War: Educational effects and contemporary implications.* Mahwah, N.J.: Lawrence Erlbaum Associates.

Harlow, Rex F. 1976. Building a public relations definition. *Public Relations Review* 4 (Winter).

Holtzman, Michael. 2003. Washington's sour sales pitch. *New York Times.* October 4.

Kohut, Andrew. Anti-Americanism: Causes and characteristics. December 10. Washington, D.C.: Pew Research Center for the People and the Press. Available at http://people-press.org/commentary/display.php3?AnalysisID=77 (accessed June 8, 2005).

Kunczik, Michael. 1997. *Images of nations and international public relations.* Mahwah, N.J.: Lawrence Erlbaum Associates.

Leonard, Mark, with Catherine Stead and Conrad Smewing. 2002. *Public diplomacy.* London: Foreign Policy Centre.

Pratkanis, Anthony, and Eliot Aronson. 1992. *Age of propaganda.* New York: W. H. Freeman & Co.

Ross, Christopher. 2002. Public diplomacy comes of age. *Washington Quarterly* 25 (2): 75–83.

Seitel, Fraser. 2001. *The practice of public relations.* 8th ed. Upper Saddle River, N.J.: Prentice-Hall.

Signitzer, Benno H., and Timothy Coombs. 1992. Public relations and public diplomacy: Conceptual convergences. *Public Relations Review* 18 (2): 137–47.

Snow, Nancy. 1998. The Smith-Mundt Act of 1948. *Peace Review* 10 (4): 619–24.

Snyder, Alvin A. 1995. *Warriors of disinformation: American propaganda, Soviet lies, and the winning of the Cold War.* New York: Arcade.

USIAAA (U.S. Information Agency Alumni Association). 2002. What is public diplomacy? September 1. Available at http://www.publicdiplomacy.org/1.htm (accessed June 7, 2005).

Wilcox, D. L., Phillip H. Ault, and Warren K. Agee. 1989. *Public Relations: Strategies and Tactics.* 2nd ed. New York: Harper and Row.

9

September 11, Social Theory, and Democratic Politics

Douglas Kellner

Momentous historical events, such as the September 11 terrorist attacks and the subsequent Terror War, test social theories and provide a challenge to give a convincing account of the event and its consequences.[1] In the following analyses, I want first to suggest how certain dominant social theories were put in question during the momentous and world-shaking events of September 11. I take up the claim that "everything has changed" in the wake of September 11 and attempt to indicate both changes and continuities to avoid one-sided exaggerations and ideological simplicities. I conclude with a few reflections on the implications of September 11 and the subsequent Afghanistan and Iraq Terror War for critical social theory and democratic politics, envisaging a new global movement against terrorism *and* militarism and *for* democracy, peace, environmentalism, and social justice.

SOCIAL THEORY, FALSIFICATION, AND THE EVENTS OF HISTORY

Social theories generalize from past experience and provide accounts of historical events or periods that attempt to map, illuminate, and perhaps criticize dominant social relations, institutions, forms, trends, and events of a given epoch. In turn, they can be judged by the extent to which they account for, interpret, and critically assess contemporary conditions or predict future events and developments. One dominant social theory of the past two decades, Francis Fukuyama's *The End of History* (1992), was strongly put into question by the events of September 11 and their aftermath.[2] For Fukuyama, the collapse of Soviet communism and triumph of Western capitalism and democracy in the early 1990s constituted "the end of history." This signified for him "the end point of mankind's ideological evolution and the universalization of Western liberal democracy as the final form of human government" (1992, 4). While there may be conflicts in places like the Third World, overall for Fukuyama liberal democracy and market capitalism have triumphed and future struggles will devolve around resolving routine economic and technical problems, and the future will accordingly be rather mundane and boring.

Samuel Huntington polemicizes against Fukuyama's "one world: euphoria and harmony" model in his *The Clash of Civilizations and the Remaking of World Order* (1996). For Huntington, the future holds a series of clashes between "the West" and "the rest." Huntington rejects a number of models of contemporary history, including a "realist" model—that nation-states are primary players on the world scene and will continue to form alliances and coalitions that will play themselves out in various conflicts—as well as a "chaos" model that detects no discernible order or structure.

Huntington asserts that the contemporary world is articulated into competing civilizations that are based on irreconcilably different cultures and religions. For Huntington, culture provides unifying and integrating principles of order and cohesion, and he delineates seven or eight different civilizations that emerge from within certain cultural formations and are likely to come into conflict with each other, including Islam, China, Russia, and the West.

While Huntington's model seems to have some purchase in the currently emerging global encounter with terrorism and has become an influential conservative ideology, it tends to overly homogenize both Islam and the West, as well as the other civilizations he depicts. Moreover, his model lends itself to pernicious misuse and has been deployed to call for and legitimate military retribution against implacable adversarial civilizations by conservative intellectuals, including Jeane Kirkpatrick, Henry Kissinger, and members of the Bush administration.

Huntington's work provides too essentialist a model that covers over contradictions and conflicts both within the West and within Islam. Both worlds have been divided for centuries into dueling countries, ethnic groups, religious factions, and complex alliances that have fought fierce wars against each other and that continue to be divided geographically, politically, ideologically, and culturally. Islam itself is a contested terrain, and in the current situation there are important attempts to mobilize more moderate forms of Islam and Islamic countries against Osama bin Laden's al-Qaeda terror network and Islamic extremism.

Hence, Huntington's binary model of inexorable conflict between the West and Islam is not only analytically problematic but also covers over the crucial battle within Islam itself to define the role and nature of the religion in the contemporary world. It also decenters the important challenge for the West to engage the Islamic world in a productive dialogue about religion and modernity and to bring about more peaceful, informed, and mutually beneficial relations between the West and Islam. Positing inexorable conflicts between civilizations may well describe past history and present challenges, but it does not help produce a better future and is thus normatively and politically defective and dangerous.

Globalization includes a homogenizing neoliberal market logic and commodification, cultural interaction, and hybridization, as well as conflict between corporations, nations, blocs, and cultures. Benjamin Barber's book *Jihad vs. McWorld* (1996) captures both the homogenizing and conflictual elements of globalization. Barber divides the world into modernizing, homogenizing, Westernizing, and secular forces of globalization, dominated by multinational corporations, opposed to premodern, fundamentalist, and tribalizing forces at war with the West and modernity. The provocative "jihad" in the title seems to grasp precisely the animus against the West in Islamic extremism. But jihad scholars argue that the term has a complex history in Islam and often privilege the more spiritual senses as a struggle for religion and spiritualization or a struggle within oneself for spiritual mastery. In this view, bin Laden's militarization of jihad is itself a distortion of Islam that is contested by mainstream Islam.

Barber's model also oversimplifies present world divisions and conflicts and does not adequately present the contradictions within the West or the "jihad world," although he postulates a dialectical interpenetrating of both forces and sees both as being opposed to democracy. His book does, however, point to problems and limitations of globalization, noting serious conflicts and opponents, unlike Thomas Friedman's harmonizing duality of *The Lexus and the Olive Tree* (1999), which suggests that both poles of capitalist luxury and premodern roots are parts of the globalization process. In an ode to globalization, Friedman assumes the dual triumph of capitalism and democracy, à la Fukuyama, while Barber demonstrates contradictions and tensions between capitalism and democracy within the New World (Dis)Order, as well as the antidemocratic animus of jihad.

Dominant dualistic theories that posit a fundamental bifurcation between the West and Islam are thus analytically suspicious in that they homogenize complex civilizations and cover over differences, hybridizations, contradictions, and conflicts within these cultures. Positing inexorable clashes between bifurcated blocs à la Huntington and Barber also fails to illuminate specific discord within the opposing spheres and the complex relations between them. They fail as well to articulate the complexity in the current geopolitical situation, which involves highly multifaceted and intricate interests, coalitions, and conflicts that shift and evolve in response to changing situations within an overdetermined and constantly evolving historical context. Consequently, the events of September 11 and their aftermath suggest that critical social theory needs models that account for complexity and the historical roots and vicissitudes of contemporary problems like terrorism rather than abstract theoretical generalizations. Critical social theory also needs to articulate how events like September 11 produce novel historical configurations while articulating both changes and continuities in the present situation.[3]

SEPTEMBER 11 AND TERROR WAR: HAS EVERYTHING CHANGED?

In the aftermath of September 11, there was a wealth of commentary arguing that "everything has changed," that the post-September 11 world is a different one, less innocent, more serious, and significantly altered, with momentous modifications in the economy to the polity to culture and everyday life. There were some doubters, such as historian Alan Brinkley, who stated in a *New York Times* interview, "I'm skeptical that this is a great rupture in the fabric of history."[4] Time alone will tell the depth of the magnitude of changes, but there are enough significant changes that have occurred already to see September 11 as a *transformational event* that has created some dramatic alterations in both the U.S. and global society, signaling shifts and novelties in the current world.

In the context of U.S. politics, September 11 was so dramatic, so far-reaching, and so catastrophic that it flipped the political world upside down, put new issues on the agenda, and changed the political, cultural, and economic climate almost completely overnight. To begin, there was a dramatic reversal of the fortunes of George W. Bush and the Bush administration. Before September 11, Bush's popularity was rapidly declining. After several months of the most breathtaking hard-right turn perhaps ever seen in U.S. politics, Bush seemed to lose control of the agenda with the defection of Vermont Republican senator Jim Jeffords, who became an Independent in May 2001. Jeffords's defection gave the Democrats a razor-thin majority in Congress and the ability to block Bush's programs and to advance their own (see Kellner 2001, chap. 11). Bush seemed disengaged after this setback, spending more and more time at his Texas ranch. He was widely perceived as incompetent and unqualified, and his public support was seriously eroding.

With the terror attacks of September 11, however, the bitter partisanship of the previous months disappeared and Bush was the beneficiary of a remarkable outburst of patriotism. Support for the Bush administration was strongly fueled by the media, which provided 24/7 coverage of the heroism of the firemen, police, and rescue workers at the World Trade Center. The response of ordinary citizens to the tragedy showed American courage, skill, and dedication at its best, as rescue workers heroically struggled to save lives and deal with the immense problems of removing the Trade Center ruins. New York City and the country pulled together in a remarkable display of community, heroism, and resolve, which the media focused on in their ongoing coverage of the tragedy. There was an explosion of flags and patriotism and widespread desire for military retaliation, fanned by the media.

There was also a demonizing coverage of bin Laden and his al-Qaeda network of terrorists and a demand for strong military retaliation. The anthrax attacks, unsolved as I write in summer 2005, fueled media hysteria and mass panic that terrorism could strike anyone at any time and any place. Bush articulated the escalating patriotism, vilification of the terrorists, and demand for stern military retaliation, and a frightened nation supported his policies, often without seeing their broader implications and threat to democracy and world peace.

There was a brief and ironical ideological flip-flop of Bush administration policy, in which it temporarily put aside the unilateralism that had distinguished its first months in office in favor of a multilateral approach. As the Bush White House scrambled to assemble a global coalition against terrorism with partners such as Pakistan, China, and Russia that it had previously ignored, or in the case of China even provoked, illusions circulated that the United States would pursue a more multilateral global politics. With the collapse of the Taliban and the de facto conclusion of the intense military phase of the war in Afghanistan by December 2001, however, the Bush administration arguably reverted to its old unilateralism. Thus, the "Bush doctrine" articulated in his January 2002 State of the Union address projected an "axis of evil" threatened by U.S. military action, called for unprecedented military action and buildup, and evoked an image of an era of war via U.S. military intervention throughout the world for the foreseeable future.

Prior to September 11, the Bush administration had been rabidly pro–"free market" and antigovernment, but it was forced by the September 11 events to recognize the need for stronger government programs. There was widespread consensus that federal funds and programs were necessary to help rebuild New York, provide increased domestic security, and regulate industries such as air travel, which showed itself to be woefully lacking in security measures. Yet it should be noted that the main government interventions undertaken by the Bush administration were in the areas of "homeland security" and a gigantic military buildup. These included a highly illiberal right-wing law-and-order program of unleashing government agencies to surveil, arrest, and detain those suspected of being terrorists in what many see as the most outrageous assault on civil liberties and the open society in U.S. history. There have been no serious initiatives in the area of investing to rebuild infrastructure of cities, highways, or the public health system. Moreover, Bush's proposed "economic stimulus" package largely consisted of tax breaks for the wealthy rather than new government programs to help the poor and those losing their jobs during a severe economic downturn.

Moreover, government bailouts went mainly to Bush administration allies such as the airline industry, with no funds for job retraining and support for workers laid off. Hence, although September 11 created a remarkable reversal of fortune for George W. Bush, it has so far not produced any fundamental re-structuring of the U.S. economy or polity, outside of right-wing law-and-order programs and tightened airport and domestic security. The September 11 terror attacks and subsequent anthrax attacks did, however, point to a vulnerability to terrorism and danger not previously experienced by Americans on U.S. soil. Bush continued to exploit the 9/11 attacks to legitimate his invasion and occu-pation of Iraq in 2003, and as recently as June 2005, in a televised speech at Fort Bragg, Bush repeatedly associated the Iraq intervention as part of a "war on terror" that was justified by the September 11 attacks.

The new vulnerability caused a reversal of priorities, both national and per-sonal, for many people, and made it clear that the United States had to address problems of globalization and terrorism—issues that were far from the hearts and minds of the average U.S. citizen. For a while, irony was out and seri-ousness was in, and a new sobriety replaced the usual American concern with triviality and diversion. Americans, like people in most of the world, had to learn to live with finitude, contingency, risk, and other concepts that were pre-viously philosophical categories but were now realities of everyday life. There was a sudden sense that everything could change within days or weeks, and that technologies that were part and parcel of everyday life, such as airplanes or mail delivery, could be weapons of destruction. Furthermore, fears circu-lated that technological weapons of mass destruction threatened Americans anywhere and anytime, creating new forms of insecurity and anxiety that the media fueled with hysterical coverage of the anthrax attacks, endless accounts of terrorist networks, and highly dramatized reports of the Afghanistan war.

Crucially, the September 11 events dramatized the facts that globalization is a defining reality of our time and that the much-celebrated flow of people, ideas, technology, media, and goods could have a downside as well as an upside, and expensive costs as well as benefits. For the first time, the American people were obliged to perceive that they had serious enemies throughout the globe and that global problems had to be addressed. No longer could the United States enjoy the luxury of isolationism; it was now forced to actively define its role within a dangerous and complex global environment.

The terror attacks of September 11 have put in question much conventional wisdom and have forced U.S. citizens and others to rethink the continued viability of key values, practices, and institutions of a democratic society. In particular, the events of September 11 force us to rethink globalization, new technology, democracy, and national and global security. September 11 and its aftermath demonstrate the significance of globalization and the ways that global, national, and local scenes and events intersect in the contemporary world. The momentous tragedy of September 11 also points to the fundamental contradictions and ambiguities of globalization, undermining one-sided pro- or antiglobalization positions.

September 11 was obviously a global event that could only happen in a global world, a networked society that is interconnected, where technology is available for anyone, where there is a constant global flow of people, products, technologies, ideas, and the like. September 11 could also only be a megaevent in a global media world, a society of the spectacle, where the whole world is watching and participates in global media spectacle or what Marshall McLuhan called a "global village." Thus, September 11 dramatized the interconnected networked globe and the important role of the media, in which individuals everywhere can simultaneously watch events of global significance unfold and thus participate in the dramas of globalization.

Already, Bill Clinton had said before September 11 that terrorism is the downside, the dark side, of globalization, and after September 11 Colin Powell interpreted the terrorist attacks as part of the dark side of globalization that had to be dealt with globally. Worldwide terrorism is threatening in part because globalization relentlessly divides the world into have and have nots, promotes conflicts and competition, and fuels long simmering hatreds and grievances— as well as bringing people together and creating new relationships, interactions, and hybrid culture. This, I would argue, is the objective ambiguity of globalization that both brings people together and brings them into conflict, that creates social interaction and inclusion, as well as hostilities and exclusions, and that potentially tears regions and the world apart while attempting to pull things together. Moreover, as different groups gain access to technologies of destruction and devise plans to make conventional technologies, such as the airplane, instruments of destruction, the dangers of unexpected terror events, any place and any time, proliferate and become part of the frightening mediascape of the new millennium.

Tragically, the main response of the Bush administration to the threats of terrorism has been largely unilateral military action with the support, so far, of a large majority of the American people. The intervention in Afghanistan seemed to indicate that U.S. military power was the most efficacious way to go after terrorism. President Bush warned just before the New Year that 2002 would be "a year of war," and his January 2002 State of the Union address expanded the Bush doctrine to indicate that the United States is ready to go it alone against the "axis of evil" and envisages military action as the solution to the problem of terrorism—action that he took in 2003 in an invasion of Iraq with apparently catastrophic results.

Bush articulated his "doctrine" by declaiming "either you're with us, or against us" in the war on terrorism, suggesting that whoever did not follow his lead was an enemy. Few remarked that his position was a resurrection of National Socialist theorist Carl Schmidt's doctrine of "friend" and "enemy," which defined politics as coalitions against enemies and with friends. There was also a religious fundamentalist dimension to the Bush doctrine. The administration's discourse of a perpetual war against evil evokes a Manichean theological mindset that divides the world into a battle between good and evil and takes for granted that one's own side is the "good" one. Such a doctrine is simplistic, moralizing, absolutistic, and highly dangerous. It is absolutistic, assuming that one's enemy is evil and must be destroyed, privileging military action. It is also opportunistic, portraying the enemy of the moment as part of a matrix of evil that requires destruction. Believing that we can eradicate evil from the world, as Bush has claimed is his administration's goal, is not only unrealistic but could envelop the world into perpetual global war of the sort envisaged by George Orwell.

By contrast, I would argue that terrorism is a complex global problem that requires a set of global solutions, and that the unilateralism that marked Bush administration policy both before September 11 and as of 2002 is a dangerous route to take. Obviously, defeating global terrorism requires a multilateral effort on a variety of fronts—economic, financial, diplomatic, political, judicial, and military. So far, some of the most effective blows against al-Qaeda's network have come from local and national police and intelligence forces arresting al-Qaeda members and foiling terrorist plans. Blocking terror network finances, breaking up local cells, limiting the international travel of terrorists, and using legal and, if necessary, military power on a global scale is the solution to defeating a global network of terrorists.

There is the danger, however, that unilateral U.S. military action itself will breed more terrorist cells, will increase the wave of anti-Americanism, and will result in more deadly terrorist attacks against the United States. Bush administration unilateralism, then, which prides itself on "realism," is realistically perilous and reckless. It is a form of unilateralist "crackpot realism" that fails to see clearly that a global problem like terrorism requires a unified and multilateral effort and coalition, not just U.S. military action. In regard to limiting weapons of mass destruction, it is apparent that there is a burning need for global arms control, controlling nuclear, chemical, and biological weapons as well as land mines, cluster bombs, small weapons, and the like. So far, the Bush White House has opposed every international treaty concerning arms control and the United States has long been the major force in the international arms trade industry (see Kellner 2001 and 2003).

Moreover, the Bush administration should not be trusted to serve as the world's global policeman against terrorism, since many members of this administration and previous U.S. administrations have themselves engaged in state terrorism and supported terrorist movements.[5] Further, instead of containing terrorism, the president's aggressive championing of military solutions to terrorism is legitimating other repressive regimes to suppress human rights and democracy and to themselves use military methods to deal with their respective regime's opponents and critics—as is evident in the India-Pakistan dispute, the intensification of the Israeli-Palestinian conflict, and numerous other actions around the world.[6] In this situation, it is thus important to defend democracy and to criticize both militarism and terrorism.

FOR DEMOCRACY AND AGAINST TERRORISM
AND MILITARISM

I conclude that in light of the Bush administration's attacks on democracy and the public sphere in the United States and elsewhere in the name of a war against terrorism, there should be a strong reaffirmation of the basic values and institutions of democracy, especially as they come under attack by regimes like Bush's. Furthermore, there needs to be a global movement *against* terrorism, militarism, and social injustice and *for* democracy, peace, environmentalism, human rights, and social justice. Rather than curtailing democracy in the naming of fighting terrorism, we need to strengthen democracy in the name of its revitalization and indeed the survival of the planet against the forces of violence and destruction. Rather than absolve the current administration's domestic and foreign policy from criticism in the name of patriotism and national unity, as its supporters demand, we need more than ever a critical dialogue on how to defeat terrorism and how to strengthen democracy throughout the world.

Democracy is in part a dialogue that requires dissent and debate as well as consensus. Those who believe in democracy should oppose all attempts to curtail democratic rights and liberties and a free and open public sphere. Democracy also involves the cultivation of oppositional public spheres, and as in the 1960s, on a global scale there should be a resurrection of the local, national, and global movements for social transformation that emerged as a reaction to war and injustice in the earlier era. This is not to call for a return to the 1960s, but for the rebirth of a global movement for peace and justice that builds on the lessons of the past as it engages the realities of the present.

In addition to reaffirming democracy, we should be against terrorism and militarism. This is not to argue for a utopian pacifism but to argue against militarism, in the sense that the military is offered as the privileged solution to the problem of terrorism and in which the military is significantly expanded, as in the Bush administration's massive military buildup, and used for unilateral military action. Thus, while I would argue that military action against terrorism is legitimate, I would oppose U.S. unilateral militarism outside of the bounds of recognized military conventions and law and would favor more multilateral action in the context of global law and coalitions.

There is little doubt that bin Laden and al-Qaeda terrorists are highly fanatical and religious in their ideology and actions, in a way hard to comprehend by Western sensibilities. In their drive for an apocalyptic jihad, they believe that their goals will be furthered by creating chaos, especially war between radical Islam and the West. Obviously, dialogue is not possible with such groups, but, equally as certain, an overreactive military response that causes a large number of innocent civilian deaths in a Muslim country could trigger precisely such an apocalyptic explosion of violence as was dreamed of by the fanatic terrorists. It would seem that such a retaliatory response was desired by the bin Laden group that carried out the terrorist attacks on the United States. Thus, to continue to attack Arab and Islamic countries could be to fall into the bin Laden gang's trap and play their game—with highly dangerous consequences.

Further, we need to reflect on the global economic, social, environmental, and other consequences of promoting militarism and an era of warfare against terrorism. Evoking and fighting an "axis of evil," as called for by the Bush administration, is highly dangerous, irrational, and potentially apocalyptic. It is not clear that the global economy can survive the constant disruption of warfare. Nor can the environment stand constant bombardment and warfare, when ecological survival is already threatened by unrestrained capitalist development (see Kovel 2002 and Wilson 2002). To carry out continued military intervention, whether against an "axis of evil" or against any country that is said to support terrorism, risks apocalypse of the most frightening kind. The large-scale bombing of Iraq, Iran, or any Arab country could trigger an upheaval in Pakistan, or war with India, with conceivable turmoil in Saudi Arabia and other Muslim countries. It could also help produce a dangerous escalation of the Israeli-Palestinian conflict, already at a state of white-hot intensity, whose expansion could engulf the Middle East in flames.

Thus, while it is reasonable to deem international terrorism a deadly threat on a global scale and to take resolute action against terrorism, what is required is an intelligent multifaceted and multilateral response. This would require a diplomatic consensus that a global campaign against terrorism is necessary that requires the arrest of members of terrorist networks, the regulation of financial institutions that allow funds to flow to terrorists, the implementation of national security measures to protect citizens against terrorism, and the worldwide criminalization of terrorist networks that sets international, national, and local institutions against the terrorist threat. Some of these measures have already begun and the conditions are present to develop an effective and resolute global campaign against terrorism.

There is a danger, however, that excessive unilateral American military action could split a potential coalition, creating uncontrollable chaos that might destroy the global economy and create an era of apocalyptic war and misery such as Orwell evoked in *1984*. We are living in a very dangerous period and must be extremely careful and responsible in appraising responses to the events of September 11 and the other terrorist attacks that are bound to happen. This will require the mobilization of publics on a local, national, and global level to oppose both terrorism and militarism and to seek productive solutions to the social problems that generate terrorism, as well as to terrorism itself.

Consequently, while I would support a global campaign against terrorism, I believe that we cannot depend on war or large-scale military action to solve the problem of global terrorism. Terrorists should be criminalized, and international and national institutions should go after terrorist networks and those who support them with the appropriate legal, financial, judicial, and political instruments. Before and during the U.S. military intervention in Afghanistan, an intelligent campaign was under way that had arrested many participants and supporters of bin Laden and other terror networks, that had alerted publics throughout the world to the dangers of terrorism, and that had created the conditions of possibility for a global campaign against terror. But we need global movements and institutions to oppose purely militarist attacks on terrorism that legitimate the suppression of democracy in the name of the war against terrorism.

In terms of modern/postmodern epistemological debates, I would argue against absolutism and universalism and for providing a contextual and historical account of terms such as "terrorism." There were times in history when "terrorism" was an arguably defensible tactic used by those engaged in struggles against fascism, such as during World War II, or in national liberation struggles, as in the movements against oppressive European and later U.S. empire and colonialism. In the current situation, however, when terrorism is a clear and present danger to innocent civilians throughout the world, it seems unacceptable to advocate, carry out, or defend terrorism against civilian populations because of the lethality of modern weapons, the immorality of indiscriminate crime, and the explosiveness of the present situation, when terror on one side could unleash a genocidal, even species-cidal, retaliatory response.

It is therefore the time for neither terrorism nor reckless unilateral military intervention, but for a global campaign against terrorism that deploys all legal, political, and morally defensible means to destroy the network of terrorists responsible for the September 11 events, but also one that is for democracy. Such a global response would put terrorist groups on notice that their activity will be strongly opposed, and that "terrorism" will be construed as a moral and political malevolence not to be accepted or defended. But a progressive global campaign should also not accept militarism, the erection of a police-military state, and the undermining of democracy in the name of fighting terrorism.

Thus, while I would support a global campaign against terrorism, especially the Qaeda network, that might include military action under UN or other global auspices, I would not trust unilateral U.S. military action due to previous U.S. failures in the region and its sustained history of supporting the most reactionary social forces (see Kellner 2003 and 2005). Indeed, one of the questions of the current crisis, and of globalization itself, is whether the U.S. empire will come to dominate the world, or whether globalization will constitute a more democratic, cosmopolitan, pluralistic, and just world without domination by hegemonic states or corporations. Now more than ever, global institutions and movements are needed to deal with global problems, and those who see positive potential in globalization should renounce all national solutions to the problem of terrorism and seek global ones. Consequently, while politicians such as Clinton and Powell have deemed terrorism "the dark side of globalization," it can also be seen as an unacceptable response to misguided and destructive imperial national policies which themselves must be transformed if a world without terror is possible.

Furthermore, this will require the anticapitalist globalization movement to rethink its nature, agenda, and goals. There may well be a "clash of civilizations" occurring today between the globalizing forces of transnational capital and resistance to global capitalism by heterogeneous configurations of individuals, groups, and social movements. But in its first stages the movement against capitalist globalization tended to be defined more by what it was against than what it was for, hence, the common term "antiglobalization movement." A new progressive anticorporate globalization and peace movement must, however, define itself by what it is *for* as well as against. In the wake of September 11, local, national, and global democratic movements should be for democracy, peace, environmentalism, and social justice and against war, militarism, and terrorism, as well as the multiplicity of injustices that social movements are currently fighting. Now, more than ever, we are living in a global world and need new global movements and politics to address global problems and achieve global solutions. Finally, a democratic politics should be animated by a cosmopolitan and multilateral globalization.

COSMOPOLITAN GLOBALIZATION

In the light of the contested and controversial 2000 and 2004 U.S. elections (see Kellner 2001 and 2005), U.S. democracy needs to be rethought and radicalized, with increased solidarity with democratic forces and struggles throughout the world and development of theories and practices of cosmopolitan globalization.[7] On a global level, the largely unilateralist and militarist Iraq intervention clearly shows the dangers and destructive effects of the Bush administration's preemptive-strike doctrine, and the need for strong multilateralism and genuinely global solutions to problems like terrorism, dangerous weapons, and rogue regimes. For many, the Bush doctrine of preventive wars and preemptive strikes embedded in the Iraq invasion contravenes international law. In particular, the invasion of Iraq and use of military force to overthrow the Iraqi regime violated sections 3 and 4 of Article 2 of the United Nations Charter, which stipulates: "All members shall settle their international disputes by peaceful means in such a manner that international peace and security, and justice, are not endangered [and shall] refrain in their international relations from the threat or use of force against the territorial integrity or political independence of any state."[8]

In addition, the so-called Bush doctrine has alienated the United States from its key allies and large segments of the world that increasingly oppose U.S. policy.[9] Bush administration and Pentagon ideologues believed that with the collapse of the Soviet Union, the United States was the regnant military power and should use U.S. military power to enforce its will and interests. The Bush/Cheney gang's Iraq fiasco clearly demonstrates the limitations of this position, making evident the follies of preventive wars, preemptive strikes, and unilateralism.

The debacle in Iraq discloses the fallacious assumptions upon which the Bush doctrine of preventive war was predicated. For preventive war to work, there must be solid intelligence upon which military action can be taken, and the Iraq case revealed deep flaws in U.S. intelligence capabilities. Secondly, launching preventive war requires that U.S. military power be sufficiently superior to guarantee victory and minimal losses, while the Iraq debacle shows that U.S. military power does not ensure victory and that military power alone does not guarantee successful resolutions to difficult political problems.[10]

The Iraq case suggests that multilateral solutions are needed for global problems and that, as with Bosnia, Kosovo, Haiti, and other recent political crises, global and multilateral alliances and forces are necessary. With

Immanuel Wallerstein (2004), I would agree that this should not be taken as an endorsement of "weak multilateralism," defined as a U.S.-dominated system of alliances whereby the United States dictates to allies, controls the United Nations and global institutions, and imposes its will on the world. Such a form of "weak multilateralism" is top down and not truly multilateral, but merely conceals control and hegemony of the United States and global corporate domination. Clinton pursued such a weak multilateral strategy, and it is likely that John Kerry might have pursued a similar type of multilateralism.

This form of what I would call "neoliberal globalization" should be opposed to a strong or genuine multilateralism that is multipolar, involves autonomous partners and alliances, and is radically democratic. Such a democratic and global multilateralism would include nongovernmental organizations, social movements, and popular institutions, as well as global institutions such as the United Nations. A democratic and multipolar globalization would be grounded philosophically in Enlightenment cosmopolitanism, democracy, human rights, and ecology, drawing on notions of a cosmos, global citizenship, and genuine democracy.[11]

The need for cosmopolitan multilateralism and globalization shows the limitations of one-sided antiglobalization positions that dismiss globalization out of hand as a form of capitalist or U.S. domination. Taking this position is admitting defeat before you've started, conceding globalization to corporate capitalism and not articulating the contradictions, forms of resistance, and possibilities of democracy grounded in globalization itself. Rather, a U.S.-dominated or corporate globalization represents a form of neoliberal globalization that, interestingly, Wallerstein claims is "just about passé" (2004: 18). The argument would be that Bush administration unilateralism has united the world against U.S. policies, so that the United States can no longer push through whatever trade, economic, or military policies it wishes without serious opposition. Wallerstein points to the widely perceived failures of International Monetary Fund and World Trade Organization policies; the collapse of the recent Cancun and Miami trade meetings, which ended with no agreement as strongly united so-called southern countries opposed U.S. trade policy; and finally, global opposition to the Bush administration's Iraq intervention. He also points to the rise of the World Social Forum as a highly influential counterpoint to the Davos World Economic Forum, which has stood as an organizing site for a worldwide antineoliberal globalization movement.

Cosmopolitan globalization thus overcomes the one-sidedness of a nation-state and national interest–dominant politics and recognizes that in a global world the nation is part of a multilateral, multipolar, multicultural, and transnational system. A cosmopolitan globalization driven by issues of multipolar multilateralism, democratization, and globalization from below would embrace women's, workers', and minority rights, as well as strong ecological perspectives. Such cosmopolitan globalization thus provides a worthy way to confront challenges of the contemporary era ranging from terrorism to global warming.

The intervention in Iraq showed the limitations of militarist unilateralism and that in a complex world it is impossible, despite awesome military power, for one country to rule in a multipolar globe. The failures of Bush administration policy in Iraq suggest that unilateralist militarism is not the way to fight international terrorism or to deal with issues such as "weapons of mass destruction," but is rather the road to an Orwellian nightmare and an era of perpetual war in which democracy and freedom will be in dire peril and the future of the human species will be in question.

At this moment of history, the United States is confronted with the question of whether it wants to preserve its democratic republic or attempt to expand its imperial empire, a project likely to create new enemies and alienate old allies.[12] Global problems require global solutions, and Bush administration unilateralism and its quest for empire have arguably created new enemies, overextended U.S. military power, and weakened international alliances. These are frightening times, and it is essential that all citizens become informed about the fateful conflicts of the present, gain clear understanding of what is at stake, and realize that they must oppose at once international terrorism, Bushian militarism, and an Orwellian police state in order to preserve democracy and make possible a life worthy of a human being.

NOTES

1. This chapter draws on research from Kellner 1992, 2001, 2003, and 2005. Thanks to Rhonda Hammer and Richard Kahn for continuous support and critical analysis of my September 11 and Terror War studies. I am using the term "Terror War" to describe the Bush administration's "war against terrorism" and its use of aggressive military force and terror as the privileged vehicles of constructing U.S. hegemony in the current world (dis)order. The Bush administration has expanded its combat against Islamic terrorism into a policy of Terror War in which it has declared the right of the United States to strike any enemy state or organization presumed to harbor or support terrorism and to eliminate "weapons of mass destruction" that could be used against the United States—a policy undertaken in the invasion of Iraq. Members of the Bush administration seek to promote Terror War as the defining struggle of the era, coded as an apocalyptic battle between Good and Evil, used to legitimate the U.S. invasion and occupation of Iraq and any subsequent military adventures.

2. Fukuyama's 1992 book was an expansion of his 1989 article published in the conservative journal *National Interest*. His texts generated a tremendous amount of controversy and were seen by some as a new dominant ideology proclaiming the

triumph of Western ideals of capitalism and democracy over all of their opponents. With a quasi-Hegelian gloss, Fukuyama thus proclaimed the victory of the ideas of neoliberalism and the "end of history," and his work prompted both skepticism ("it ain't over 'til it's over") and impassioned critique. If terrorism and the Bush administration militarism soon pass from the historical scene and a neoliberal globalization driven by market capitalism and democracy returns to become the constitutive force of the new millennium, Fukuyama would end up being vindicated after all, but in the current conflictual situation, his views appear off the mark and irrelevant to the present situation.

3. I provide my own historical and theoretical account of the background to the events of September 11 in Kellner 2003. Put abstractly, a critical theory of the post–September 11 world would combine the Hegelian-Marxian perspectives of a globalized world and the vicissitudes of capitalism and the contemporary era with concrete historical study of specific events, such as the September 11 terrorist acts and the lessons for contemporary social theory and democratic politics.

4. Alan Brinkley, interview in *New York Times*, September 14, 2002.

5. See Kellner 2001, as well as Chomsky 2001 and his volumes of other writings that have demonstrated U.S. complicity in terrorism over the past several decades. As my forthcoming study (see Kellner 2005) will indicate, the United States has also arguably involved itself in state terrorism in the Afghanistan intervention, and thus cannot be trusted to stop terrorism and violence, which its actions are likely to perpetuate and intensify.

6. Human Rights Watch (2002) has released a report that documents how a wide spectrum of countries have used the war against terrorism to legitimate intensified repression of their domestic opponents and military action against foreign adversaries. For an overview, see http://www.hrw.org/press/2002/02/usmil0215.htm.

7. This concluding section is an extract from Kellner 2005. Thanks to Dean Birkenkamp and Alison Sullenberger for support with this project, and to Melanie Stafford and Rhonda Hammer for discussion and editing of the text.

8. Cited in Cox 2004: 153. Author and former Justice Department prosecutor William J. Cox lays out in detail the ways that the Bush administration's Iraq invasion contravenes several articles of the UN Charter and has no legal justification, thus constituting an "illegal use of force" (2004, 153ff). Cox also documents the administration's "illegal detention of prisoners" (154ff) and how, by violating the norms of international law, Bush could be subject to impeachment (157ff).

9. The PEW Research Center's global attitude reports over the last several years document dramatically increasing anti-Americanism and disgust with Bush administration policies. See http://people-press.org/pgap/.

10. This argument is made by Ivo H. Daalder and James M. Lindsay (2004), who also argue that "Bush's conception of preemption far exceeded responding to an imminent danger of attack. He instead advocated preventive wars of regime change. The United States claimed the right to use force to oust leaders it disliked long before they could threaten its security."

11. On cosmopolitanism, see Cheah and Robbins 1998 and the special issue of *Theory, Culture and Society* on "Cosmopolis," vol. 19, nos. 1–2 (February 2002).

12. On the dangers of perpetual war and threats to the U.S. democratic republic in the expansion of empire, see Vidal 2002 and 2003 and Mann 2003. On the dangers

of Bush administration unilateralist militarism and the need for global solutions to global problems, see Kellner 2003 and 2005, Barber 2003, and Clark 2003. General Wesley Clark warns that the Bush administration has planned a series of wars against the "axis of evil" to promote U.S. hegemony and to use U.S. military power to further a neoconservative agenda of control of the Middle East.

REFERENCES

Barber, Benjamin R. 1996. *Jihad vs. McWorld*. New York: Ballatine Books.

———. 2003. *Fear's empire*. New York: Norton.

Cheah, Pheng, and Bruce Robbins. 1998. *Cosmopolitics*. Minneapolis: University of Minnesota Press.

Chomsky, Noam. 2001. *9-11*. New York: Seven Seals Press.

Clark, Wesley. 2003. *Winning modern wars: Iraq, terrorism, and the American empire*. Washington, D.C.: Public Affairs Books.

Cox, William J. 2004. *You're not stupid! Get the truth: A brief on the Bush presidency*. Joshua Tree, Calif.: Progressive Press.

Daalder, Ivo H., and James M. Lindsay. 2004. Shooting first: The preemptive-war doctrine has met an early death in Iraq. *Los Angeles Times*. May 30.

Friedman, Thomas. 1999. *The Lexus and the olive tree*. New York: Farrar, Straus, Giroux.

Fukuyama, Francis. 1992. *The end of history*. New York: Avon Books.

Human Rights Watch. 2002. Dangerous dealings: Changes to U.S. military assistance after September 11. February. Available at http://hrw.org/reports/2002/usmil/.

Huntington, Samuel. 1996. *The clash of civilizations and the remaking of world order*. New York: Touchstone Books.

Johnson, Chalmers. 2000. *Blowback: The costs and consequences of American empire*. New York: Henry Holt.

Kellner, Douglas. 1992. *The Persian Gulf TV war*. Boulder, Colo.: Westview Press.

———. 2001. *Grand theft 2000*. Lanham, Md.: Rowman and Littlefield.

———. 2003. *From September 11 to terror war: Dangers of the Bush legacy*. Lanham, Md.: Rowman and Littlefield.

———. 2005. *Media spectacle and the crisis of democracy*. Boulder, Colo.: Paradigm Press.

Kovel, Joel. 2002. *The enemy of nature: The end of capitalism or the end of the world?* London: Zed Books.

Mann, Michael. 2003. *Incoherent empire*. London and New York: Verso.

Vidal, Gore. 2002. *Perpetual war for perpetual peace: How we got to be so hated*. New York: Thunder Mouth Press/Nation Books.

———. 2003. *Dreaming war: Blood for oil and the Cheney-Bush junta*. New York: Thunder Mouth Press/Nation Books.

Wallerstein, Immanuel. 2004. Soft multilateralism. *Nation* (February 2): 14–20.

Wilson, E. O. 2002. *The future of life*. New York: Knopf.

10

International Communication after Terrorism: Toward a Postcolonial Dialectic

Anandam P. Kavoori

This chapter focuses on "postcolonial" theory in the fields of cultural studies, comparative literature, anthropology, and historiography and its relevance for a cultural perspective on the study of media and terrorism. Postcolonial analytical strategies are discussed and related to the subject matter of terrorism by (1) disarticulating the semantic and political field behind traditional categorizations of international communication (culture, nation, and theory) and suggesting how these are reworked in the semantic space of contemporary terrorism and (2) articulating issues of globality, identity, and reflexivity and seeing how these are animated and disseminated in contemporary, pre- and post-9/11 strategies of mediated terrorism.

INTRODUCTION

Periodic reviews of the field of international communication (e.g., Mowlana 1986, 1994) have shown a persistence of a limited conceptual model for understanding complex global relationships based on (or devolved from) dependency or developmentalist approaches and focused narrowly on media content or institutional issues. Writing a decade ago, Hamid Mowlana called for a conceptual framework for international communication that moves beyond the "sense of International Communication as interactions among states or policy making elites" (1994, 15) and for increased understanding of a cultural approach to global issues both at the "topical, substantive level as well at the epistemological level" (27). In that same time period, Annabelle Sreberny-Mohammadi identified the emergent paradigm of "cultural revisionism" as the direction of the future—a future that she pointed out is still searching for a coherent theoretical shape (1992, 119).

Part of that coherence has now arrived, thanks to congruent trends in the literature on international/global issues in disciplines such as anthropology, comparative literature, and history and in the interdisciplinary concern of cultural studies. In each of these fields, a concern with global issues, framed in cultural terms, have coalesced around a contested term *postcolonialism*. Meanwhile, our understanding of the relationship between media and terrorism has undergone a sea change, with the events of 9/11 serving as the liminal event that has transferred "terrorism" as a niche, regional phenomenon to a defining concept and circumstance that challenges contemporary social, cultural, and political order.

In this chapter, I theorize the connections between these two developments and strike a path for future studies of international communication, a field that, I will argue, needs to understand emergent postcolonial dialectics as they intersect with terrorism into new, more mobile and reflexive communication pedagogies. Simply put, the chapter seeks to point the direction for international communication after terrorism.

THE POSTCOLONIAL PERSPECTIVE:
COMPLEXITY AND POWER

What is postcolonialism? There are two immediate referents that the term recalls. It attempts to identify conditions of contemporary globality as something that has links with processes of historical and contemporary colonialism and imperialism—a historical process that has provided spatial, social, and cultural maps for most, if not all, contemporary societies. It is also an attempt to define the contours of contemporary social formations that live in the aftermath of colonialism and struggle to define alternate sets of maps as they function in new global structures.

The postcolonial project in literary and historical studies (which saw numerous writings from the mid- to late 1990s) as relevant to the study of international communication is an attempt to move beyond the theoretical binary of development/dependency that has determined the course of research in the last four decades. It is an attempt, as Richard Rouse puts it, to make sense of a confused world, a world made up of

> criss-crossed economies, intersecting systems of meaning, and fragmented identities. Suddenly, the comforting modern imagery of nation-states and national languages, of coherent communities and consistent subjectivities, of dominant centers and distant margins no longer seems adequate.... We have all moved irrevocably into a new kind of social space (1991, 8).

In looking at how the world is put together, both the developmentalist and dependency approaches focus on issues of cultural determination as a subset or derivative of economic forces. In the words of Hanno Hardt, "The aspect of dependence, as an aspect of a more comprehensive theory of imperialism, has been used to account primarily for the economic structures and relationships among developed and underdeveloped countries" (1992, 136). In addition, the developmentalist (and to a lesser extent the dependency) approach continues the ethnocentric use of the characteristics of West European and North American society as goal states from which calibrated indices of underdevelopment can be constructed (Golding 1977, 39). The range and complexity of global relationships is inadequately dealt with in both of these approaches, which are in the end predominantly modernist in orientation.

Developmentalist approaches link issues of the world to those of modernity and dependency approaches to a critique of modernity as a basis for categorization and modernism as a synonym for Western culture and practices. The media appear in these debates either as constructors of Western dominance or as agents of social change. Terrorism operates at the margins—questioning the integrity of states or as impediments to their development. International communication here is an arena for contestation, but one limited by the framework of states as actors and agents of mobilization—media texts about terrorism are framed in reference to their positionality about the viability of the agents of terrorism—as seen, for example, in news coverage about the Mau Mau in Africa, the Sandinistas in Nicaragua, and an entire generation of news coverage about "coups, dictators and droughts," that is, as part of a larger fabric of developmentalist/dependency-driven cultural and media frames.

Postmodernism, the other dominant framework through which global cultural issues are currently being framed, works against both developmentalist and dependency approaches in its rejection of the Enlightenment project, universalist rationality, and progressivism. Ironically, however, postmodernist interpretations of globality focus on the emergence of a common culture of consumption and style (Ferguson 1992, 71) and see global social fragmentation along lines of neotribalism as evidence that social coercion and state powers are replaced by individualized acts of collectivizing will. Terrorism appears here too at the margins, as a kind of niche identity politics, even as a modernist reaction to postmodernism, but always as a kind of shorthand for identity politics—where terrorism becomes both conflated and reduced to one of many sites for the articulation of cultural conflict—not substantially different from conflicts over race, gender, class, and sexuality.

I would argue that these three approaches are a legacy to a transcendent vision of globality, specifically, a perspective at its core driven by notions of unreflexive dominance and its natural result: cultural homogenization. Terrorism is, in the end, placed in the specific diacritical space of localism, with only two options available to it: assimilation or defiance. Little attention is given to the range, diversity, and possibilities of multiple mediations of globality. Drawing on my earlier critical engagement with postcolonial research (Kavoori 1998), I suggest that this body of scholarship points the way to a more kaleidoscopic view of globality, focused on issues of culture and made up, on the one hand, by issues of *power* and, on the other, by *complexity*. It is this dual focus that will provide International Communication, the direction that I suggest it have in the context of terrorism.

The issue of power in postcolonial theory goes beyond that framed in terms of either cultural imperialism or dependency theory but rather in the "specifically anti or post-colonial discursive purchase in culture, one which begins in the moment that the colonizing power inscribes itself onto the body and space of its others and which continues as an often occluded tradition into the modern theater of neo-colonialist international relations" (Williams and Chrisman 1994, 13).

The issue of complexity is not only about the changes in the conditions of contemporary globality that Rouse indicates above but also, as ArifDirlik suggests (in his discussion of the Three Worlds model), is a crises of our categories:

> Post-coloniality represents a response to a genuine need, the need to overcome a crisis of understanding produced by the inability of old categories to account for the world. The metanarrative of progress that underlies two centuries of thinking is in deep crisis. Not only have we lost faith in progress but also progress has had actual disintegrative effects. The crisis of progress has brought in its wake a crises of modernization, more in its Marxist than in its bourgeois guise, and called into question the structure of the global as conceived by modernizationalists and radicals alike in the decades after World War II that is, as three worlds. Whether they be fixed geographically or structurally, in bourgeois or in Marxist social theory, the Three Worlds are indeed no longer tenable. The globe has become as jumbled up spatially as the ideology of progress has temporally (1994, 352).

The two centuries of thinking Dirlik suggests resonates through developmentalist, dependency, and postmodernist theorists in their use of such key semantic/ethnographic totalizations as "culture," "nation," "gender," and even "theory." Where does terrorism lie within these totalizations? In the sections to follow, I will argue that the answer lies in mapping a direction already undertaken by the postcolonial project—to interrogate the stability and consequences of totalizing frames and then to examine how terrorism as a concept and as reality has been implicated in the collapse of such categories.

DISARTICULATING TOTALIZATIONS: CULTURE, NATION, THEORY

One of the aims of the postcolonial approach has been a deconstruction of common truths that have assumed the aura of factuality. These facts, or "totalizations," are critiqued for the political and cultural constructs. In this section, I take a closer look at these constructs that are sometimes uncritically assumed in the international communication literature and then examine their consequences for an understanding of the relationship between media and terrorism.

Culture

"Culture" has always been a problematic term, but it is even more problematic in today's complex world. As Michael Agar puts it, the confusion over the term comes from a lack of understanding over how the world works now.

> In the old days, scholars invented an idea of what they studied. The idea defined a research object, one that was isolated in space, one that by and large provided a life from birth to death. [Scholars] entered this closed spatio-temporal world. What they came up with, the results of their exploration, they called "culture." The definition was a philosophical nightmare. In retrospect, we realize that this story about what we studied was a fiction even then. But now, in the modern or postmodern era, the idea looks ridiculous. The former traditional community has lost whatever edges it had, and, therefore, the term "culture" that we used to label it has lost its referent as well. (Agar 1992, 5–7)

Once, cultures could be prefigured visually—as objects, theaters, or texts (Clifford 1986, 12). Today, culture is always relational, an inscription of communicative processes that exist historically between subjects in relations of power (Clifford 1986, 15). The issue of what "culture" is then needs to be differently constituted by the international communication research community. Instead of seeing an essentialist fixity to totalizing categories of culture such as "French" or "Indian," there is a need to see that what has come to be called "culture" is in fact many things, including a multiply authored invention, a historical formation, an enactment, a political construct, a shifting paradox, an ongoing translation, an emblem, even a trademark.

Terrorism appears at the margin of contemporary discourse about culture—as part of its relational matrix rather than of its central constitutive nature. Terrorism is not, I would argue, an oppositional discourse or even a restitutive one (to often older, patriarchal forms of identity) but rather a constitutive one. It drives contemporary forms of identity politics, seen most closely in how culture is internally constituted. This history is not new—it played an important role in how nationalist politics were constructed by colonial powers in contexts as distinct as the British experience in India and the French one in Algeria. In the early seventies and eighties, it reappeared as primarily a cultural prescription against state-centered identity formations, such as in the case of Northern Ireland or in Turkish/Greek constructions of terrorism in Cyprus. Today, it emerges primarily as a consequence of cultural essentialisms, as seen in the Bush administration's narrow reading of American cultural identity, following an earlier imprint established by the Thatcher administration in England, and the decade-long rule of the Hindu Bharatiya Janata party in India. In each case, the careful rearticulation of a media-centered essentialist identity starkly contrasts with the purported death of essentialism in the literature of postcolonial studies.

For international communication, the idea of essentialism needs to be tackled by identifying the process by which such "cultures" are manufactured. First, culture is often tied to a historical reconstruction of self—American, French, German—a process that is not only a fiction in the sense of a collective imagination (fostered by state elites) but also a politics by virtue of how it structures and relegates the world into a division made up of benevolent selves and malevolent others.

The late Edward Said has probably done the most both to identify the nature of this process in understanding the dynamics of orientalism and then to argue that understanding "culture" cannot be divorced from processes of historical and contemporary colonialism. The two terms often thought of separately— "culture" as the process of community beliefs and "colonialism" as a political and social framework for appropriating others (economically, culturally)—are brought together. As Said argues:

> Essences such as Englishness and Orientalisms, modes of production such as Asiatic and Occidental, all of these in my opinion testify to an ideology whose cultural correlatives well precede the actual accumulation of imperial territories worldwide. (quoted in Jewsiewicki and Mudimbe 1994, 35)

Said thus locates culture and colonialism as part of a single practice. Culture is in a sense manufactured through colonial frameworks of categorization and appropriation. The importance of this idea is not limited to older colonial discourses such as Orientalism, but is also relevant to contemporary discourses about terrorism as it surfaces in news reports, popular culture, policy papers, government documents, and a variety of media products and texts. The issue of power in such a culture/colonization schema then draws on Foucauldian notions of discourse rather than on the traditional frameworks of cultural imperialism.

Drawing on this background our understanding of terrorism is tied into what Raka Shome (1996) calls "discursive imperialism." She writes:

> The question that is perhaps most central to the postcolonial project is: How do western discursive practices, in their representations of the world and of themselves, serve to legitimize the contemporary global power structures? To what extent do the cultural texts of nations such as the United States and England reinforce the neo-imperial political practices of these nations? These are very important questions to investigate for they illustrate how in the present times, discourses have become the prime means of imperialism. Whereas in the past, imperialism was about controlling the "native" by colonizing her/him territorially, now imperialism is more about subjugating the "native" by colonizing her/him discursively. (1996, 505)

While this strand in postcolonial structuration of culture/colonialism/terrorism sees a world that is limited, hegemonic, and restricted by issues of power, the idea of complexity is present in the idea that discourse is not monolithic. Rather, "discourses are tactical elements or blocks operating in the field of force relations; there can exist different or even contradictory discourses within the same strategy. . . . [Power is] a multiple and mobile field of force relations wherein far-reaching, but never completely stable, effects of domination are produced" (Foucault 1980, 100).

Understanding processes of cultural and colonization, then, is not limited to the constitutive powers of colonizers over the colonized (by the articulation and rearticulation of culture), but also includes processes of culture/colonization/terrorism that are multiply structured, variously localized, and differentially articulated.

One major strand here is the development of a historiography focused on the "subaltern." The subaltern is a figure produced by historical programs of modernity and domination but nevertheless provides a mode of reading history in a different way from that inscribed in elite accounts. The aim is one of retrieving the autonomous will and consciousness of the subaltern (Prakash 1992, 8–9). At issue is how the

> subaltern may have played a constitutive rather than a reflective role in colonial and domestic imperial discourse and subjectivity. Rather than being that other onto which the colonizer projects a previously constituted subjectivity and knowledge, native presences, locations, and political resistance need to be further

theorized as having a determinacy or primary role in colonial discourses, and in
the attendant domestic versions of these discourses. In other words, the movement may have been as much from "periphery" to "center" as from "center" to
"periphery." (Williams and Chrisman 1994, 16)

Terrorism can be seen structurally, if not ideologically, as part of the larger
construct of nativism and decolonization. While its subalternity is suspect, its
self-derived notions of authenticity (as seen in speeches by Osama bin Laden)
can place it within this same discursive space—a space that it actively manip-
ulates through news channels such as al-Manar and al-Jazeera and numerous
websites.

Issues of culture and terrorism—framed in terms of complexity and power—
are also present in discussions of how culture can be framed in terms of issues
of "cultural politics." If the totalization "culture" is critiqued for its role in
the colonial formation, it is also implicated in its dealing with its constituent
social subjectivities—ethnicity, gender, and sexuality, among others. What,
for example, happens to issues of differential experience and exploitation of
women from men in colonial/neocolonial conditions? Here the answer that
postcolonial criticism provides is that they are submerged by that master label
for culture—"nation."

Nation

Nationalism is a force that is contradictory—once generative, today it aggres-
sively asserts the boundaries and mythos of its own creation. The preeminent
imagined community, it has defined both the theoretical and political practices
of international communication. Aijaz Ahmad argues that this is tied in closely
to the structuration of the world according to the Three Worlds model and the
oppositional binary of colonialism–nationalism.

> There is a very tight fit between the Three Worlds theory, the over-valorization
> of nationalist ideology, and the assertion that "national allegory" is the primary,
> even exclusive, form of narrativity in the so-called Third World. If this "Third
> World" is constituted by the singular experience of colonialism and imperialism
> and if the only possible response is a nationalist one, then what else is there that
> is more urgent to narrate than this experience? In fact there is nothing else to
> narrate. (1992, 102)

The ideas of nationalist cultures and interactions between nation-states have
dominated issues of international communication. Much of the cultural imperialism debate reflects a primacy accorded to issues of the nation-state. As

Ernest Gellner puts it:

> In the struggles that are fought out around this issue in many parts of the world today, the structural changes brought about by the transnationalization of media flows are often assessed and officially defined in terms of a threat [such as terrorism] to the autonomy and integrity of "national identity." However, such a definition of the problem is a very limited and limiting one, because it tends to subordinate other, more specific and differential sources for the construction of cultural identity to the hegemonic and seemingly natural one of nationality. After all, nations are themselves artificial, historically constituted politico-cultural units; they are not the natural destiny of pre-given cultures, rather their existence is based upon the construction of a standardized "national culture" that is a prerequisite to the functioning of a modern industrial state. (quoted in Ang 1991, 252)

It is now commonplace to argue that the nation-state is in danger, not only by the forces of globalization but equally by terrorism. In sum, nationalism as the doctrine holding states together is both internally and externally contested. Arjun Appaduari notes, "One important feature of global cultural politics . . . is that state and nation are at each other's throats, and the hyphen that links them is now less an icon of conjuncture than an index of disjuncture" (1990, 34). Equally significant, issues of internal contestation can be examined by how the hegemonic cultural identity of nationality gets constructed at the cost of those based upon class, locality, gender, generation, ethnicity, religion, politics, and so forth.

These issues have been dealt with extensively by feminist historiography within the postcolonial project, which examines the question of "why it is that nationalism achieves the ideological effect of an inclusive and putatively macro-political discourse, whereas the women's question—unable to achieve its own autonomous macro-political identity—remains ghettoized within its specific and regional space" (Radhakrishnan 1992, 78).

The space of contemporary terrorism seems to have exacerbated this ghettoization, in the emergence of a patriarchally centered nationalism on both sides of the imperial formation—the cult of George W. Bush and that of Osama bin Laden. International communication needs to be reoriented to a critical global literacy that examines the discursive forces that create, legitimize, and accord "normalcy" to this new resurgent patriarchy in a variety of new and popular texts. Of special relevance may be the feminist postcolonial approach that attempts to extend the feminist project macropolitically. As Radhakrishan suggests, "The category of gender in its particularity resonates with a general or universal potential for meaning, and the task is not to eschew universality or globality in favor of pure difference or heterogeneity, but to read and interpret carefully the many tensions among the many forms of the particular-universal categorical claims" (1992, 79).

The idea, then, is to continue to redeploy issues of power not by replacing issues of patriarchal nationalism/terrorism by gender (in its structuration as a micropolitic) but to produce an occluded set of relationships that tie together issues of culture and identity, nation and gender, politics and empowerment. Radhakrishnan, again, provides the full complement:

> What does it mean to speak of "one" politics in terms of an "other"? How is a genuine nationalist consciousness [possible]? Is it inevitable that one of these politics must form the horizon for the other, or is it possible that the very notion of a containing horizon is quite beside the point? Isn't the so-called horizon itself the shifting expression of equilibrium among the many forces that constitute and operate the horizon: gender, class, sexuality, ethnicity, etc.? If one specific politics is to achieve a general significance, it would seem that it has to possess a multiple valence, i.e. enjoy political legitimacy as a specific constituency and simultaneously make a difference in the integrated political or cultural sphere. (1992, 78–79)

What future can one accord the political field around the term "nation" for the study of international communication? Addressed in our scheme of complexity and power, the nation is internally hegemonic, as we have discussed. It is also, however, externally hegemonic in its perpetuation of Western, Eurocentric, colonialist patterns. Nationalist/terrorist resistance to imperialism, for example, itself derives its notion of "nation" and of national self-determination from the Western culture that is being resisted. Seen from this perspective, nationalism/terrorism is a product of imperialism, and as Gayatri Spivak remarks, it only succeeds "in changing the geo-political conjuncture from territorial imperialism to neo-colonialism" (quoted in Young 1990, 168). The idea of complexity belies the idea of modern states as multiply constituted by different social subjectivities, but also by nationalism itself, which is a complex historical and cultural movement. To allow for both power and complexity, nationalism can be seen as a "contradictory discourse and its internal contradictions need to be unpacked in their historical specificity. The historical agency of nationalism [and terrorism] has been sometimes hegemonic though often merely dominant, sometimes emancipatory though often repressive, sometimes progressive though often traditional and reactionary" (Radhakrishan 1992, 82).

Theory

Just as "culture" and "nation" need to be deconstructed in the study of international communication, so does the totalization "theory" (including the capitalized "Postcolonial Theory"!). "Theory" is seen by some in the postcolonial project as a synonym for certainty, for science, for imperialism. Postcolonial critics argue that totalizing theory is the product of a post-Enlightenment European construction of history and is therefore Eurocentric. Postcolonial criticism takes the critique of Eurocentricism as its central task (Dirlik 1994, 334), including both the modernist and postmodernist frames of reference. While it shares with postmodernism its incredulity toward metanarratives and a criticism of antecedent (modernist, patriarchal, elitist) claims to a certain exclusivity of insight (Appiah 1991, 342), it nevertheless sees postmodernism

> as operating as a Euro-American western hegemony, whose global appropriation of time and place inevitably proscribes certain cultures as backward and marginal while co-opting to itself certain of their cultural "raw" materials. Postmodernism is then projected onto these margins as normative, as a neo-universalism to which "marginal" cultures may aspire, and from which certain of their more forward looking products might be appropriated and "authorized." (Williams and Chrisman 1994, 13)

The difference between the two approaches is also present in their different political agendas. Vijay Mishra and Robert Hodge suggest that if for postmodernism the object of analysis is the subject as defined by humanism, with its essentialism and mistaken historical verities, its unities and transcendental presence, then for postcolonialism the object is the imperialist subject, the colonized as formed by processes of imperialism (1991, 405).

Where does that leave terrorism? Is it merely a variant of postmodernist politics or of Eurocentricism? The options that the postcolonial project offers is that of localized, politicized, and reflexive narrativization of postcolonial conditions combining issues of both power and complexity. Terrorism would perhaps be placed within such a theoretical fabric. The central theoretical impulse that postcolonial theory assumes is to straddle a politics of opposition and struggle while retaining issues of power, domination, and asymmetry. At issue, however, is how a post-foundational, subaltern, and localized theory can coexist against the very Western, imperial, and global processes that make postcolonialism a marketing success in the metropolitan academe.

Given the postcolonial project's focus on issues of power and complexity, the totalizations "postcolonialism" and "postcolonial" themselves have been critiqued. If the theory promises a decentering of history, the singularity of the term effects a recentering of global history around the rubric of European time. Colonialism returns at the moment of its disappearance (McClintock 1992, 86). Ella Shohat (1992) similarly argues that the totalization "postcolonialism" provides a dubious spatiality in its application to different colonial experiences and dubious temporality in its universal application to all post-colonial situations and progressions. Anne McClintock provides perhaps the most important critique when she suggests that the "singular category 'post-colonial' may license too readily a panoptic tendency to view the globe within the generic abstractions voided of political nuance" (1992, 87). The very aim of historical and contemporary critique may be then offset as the project "throws up comparisons of another totalizing form of scholarship, orientalism" (Mishra and Hodge 1991, 401).

Despite these inherent tensions, postcolonial criticism does provide alternate possibilities in our understanding of global and international communication issues. Most of all, it provides a "proliferation of historically nuanced theories and strategies which may enable us to engage more effectively in the politics of affiliation, and the currently calamitous dispensations of power" (McClintock 1992, 97).

We now turn to a discussion of some of these concerns as we elaborate on the postcolonial take on issues of global cultural formations, the politics of location, and the politics of comparative research as these concerns are implicated in our global understanding of media and terrorism.

POSTCOLONIAL ARTICULATIONS: GLOBALITY, IDENTITY, REFLEXIVITY

Globality

Current theorizations of globality are mired in debates around the term "glob-alization." I do not wish to spend too much time in the shark-infested waters around this term, pointing out only that the term has little analytical coher-ence left, given its application in a multiplicity of contexts and its wide use simultaneously by modernizationalists, politicians, postmodernists, and radi-cals. Marjorie Ferguson points out that globalization is a teleological doctrine that promotes, explains, and justifies an interlocking system of world trade. A term, in other words, that has moved rapidly from prophecy to assumption (1992, 69, 87).

Postcolonial critics address issues of globalization by focusing less on issues of grand development or progress but rather on the absences, multiplicities, inequities, and displacements, the in-betweenness and the transience of hu-man experience in an age of unprecedented technological, economic, political, and cultural connectedness. Terrorism appears in and through each of these changes—framed differently depending on perspective. For some, terrorism is not just the prerogative of nonstate actors working against the process of inex-orable connectedness; they see the entire system of globalization as predicated on violence—in policy, discourse, and process, and in the end on the body, directly through incarceration of "terrorists" but equally through the specific opiate of entertainment media and through a wider fabric of a global medical-state-culture complex that structures contemporary cultural consciousness. The relationship between media and terrorism, then, has to be duplicated in terms of its institutional correlates that exist in all those realms that are traditionally separated: technology, politics, markets, and so on. It is this process that needs to be explicated, intervened in, and, to the extent possible, radicalized by the next generation of international communication scholars and practitioners.

At the core of such an exercise is a refitting of our conceptual lenses. For many postcolonial critics, issues of globality are framed not in linear communicative terms but by complexity. Appadurai, in an often quoted analysis, sees the issues of media globality as one part of the global cultural economy that is structured by a "complex, overlapping, disjunctive order" (1990, 296). This disjunctive order, in his view, is constituted by the interaction of five "scapes" of interaction: the *ethnoscape*, *technoscape*, *infoscape*, *financescape*, and *mediascape*, which are interconnected and even overlapping. (Appadurai adds, "The conditions under which the current global flows take place are through the growing disjunctures. . . . People, machinery, money, images, and ideas now follow increasingly non-isomorphic paths" (1990, 301).

To these, we can now add the notion of a "terrorscape" that is simultaneously an objective presence (intersecting with these others scapes) but also a discursive one. The emergence and intersection of such presences exist through the range of news media, from neonationalist American media, through al-Hura and al-Jazeera, to the very niched manifestations of webcasting and rejuvenated traditional media (radio, video cameras, cassette recorders). In addition, new hybrids have emerged that expand the relationship between the objective and the discursive (such as blogging and cell phones) and those that create new analogies for violence through both role modeling and recreation (such as gaming); these are used for recruitment in equal measure by institutions established for regulated violence (the U.S. Army, for example, uses video war games as a recruiting tool) and by cyberwatchers/terrorists and hackers as they close the gap between the material and the discursive.

This restructuring of globality has implications for how the world is being reshaped. Appadurai, for example, develops what Anthony Giddens calls "time-space distanciation" (1990, 64); another example is David Harvey's notions of how globality helps to create complex relations between local involvements and interactions across distance. Of equal relevance is Ulf Hannerz (1991) who sees the role of the media as a "machinery of meaning" that culls images and referents globally and constitutes a process termed "creolization" leading to the emergence of a new global "ecumene which is characterized both by an organization of diversity and a diversity in organization" (261). Hannerz also emphasizes issues of power and argues that issues of globality are not constituted just by diversity (complexity) but by

> issues of social distribution—the ways in which collective cultural inventory of meanings and meaningful external forms [such as media] are spread over a population and its social relationships. The distribution of culture within the world is affected by a structure of asymmetrical relationships; these relationships affect cultures by shaping the material and power conditions to which cultures adapt even in their more autonomous cultural processes. . . . That influx does not enter into a vacuum, or inscribe itself on a cultural tabula rasa, but enters into various kinds of interaction with already existing meanings, and meaningful forms, however these may be socially distributed, in cumulative historical processes. (261–63)

Contemporary cultural processes—and terrorism is now being increasingly constructed as a contemporary process—need to be rethought by the next generation of international communication scholars. This new model for the distribution of culture must include others besides "terrorism." Masai Miyoshi, for example, identifies six of these:

> There are six interrelated developments in post–World War II history, none of which should or could be considered in isolation. It is indeed possible to argue that any one of these developments needs to be studied in close conjunction with every other. They are: (1) The cold war (and its end); (2) decolonization; (3) transnational corporatism; (4) high-tech revolution; (5) feminism; (6) the environmental crises. There are adjacent cultural coordinates such as postmodernism, popularization of culture, cultural studies, de-disciplinization, ethnicism, economic regionalism and so on. The relationship between the two groups is neither homologic nor causal, but its existing nature requires further examination in a different context. (1993, 728)

To this we may add a conceptual endnote: These processes and history of ideas are open-ended; they are not derived from the end of history or even the end of terrorism (through a new global/imperial U.S. foreign policy) but through a process of reimagination that is happening in places initially hard to identify as providing change. In fact, one of the few givens is that such processes are rarely identified as pivotal. The contemporary ambivalence in media institutions and industries over the issue of piracy is one such example of a paradigmatic misplacement. A second is our befuddlement over the emergence of citizen-journalists/provocateurs from the web into blogging. A third and perhaps most critical and problematic one is the expected emergence (within a decade) of a biotechnological communication system that is predicated on the body (the first steps of which are chips/devices for communication in the body) and of a wider articulation of the body as devices for collective communication rather than just individuation. These developments will parallel (and disjunctively connect with) those in the seemingly disconnected realms of terrorism, state violence, and the continued corporatization of democracy.

Identity

The two themes of complexity and power are also evident in the postcolonial notions of "diaspora" and "hybridity"—both of central significance to the issue of cultural identity and terrorism in the world today. "Diaspora" refers to the process of what Appadurai calls "deterritorialization," where not only do money, commodities, and persons unendingly chase each other around the world but also group imaginations of the modern world find their fractured and fragmented counterpart. "Hybridity" refers to the idea, discussed earlier, that ideas of essentialism are of little service in understanding issues of identity. Rather, identity in the postcolonial world is marked by indeterminacy. As Shome puts it:

> Post-colonialism is about borderlands and hybridity. It is about cultural indeterminacy and spaces in-between. Resisting attempts at any totalizing forms of cultural understanding (whether imperialistic or nationalistic), the post-colonial perspective argues for a recognition of the "hybrid location of cultural values." (Shome 1995, 9, quoting Bhabha 1992, 439)

One of the implications of such a framework is to see that conditions of contemporary terrorism lead not only to a range of complex cultural identity formations described variously as "cosmopolitans," "ex-centric natives," or "mimics" (Bhabha 1992) but equally to the more central idea that "in the increasingly integrated world system there is no such thing as an independent cultural identity [as in 'the terrorist'] but that every identity [the plural, terrorist(s)] must define and position itself in relation to the cultural frames affirmed by the world system" (Ang 1991, 253). The central task as seen by postcolonial critics is to extend this analytic by a focus on issues of "politics of location," where issues of both complex identity articulation and interpolation by constituent power relations are manifest, across traditional lines of identity affiliation (class, race, nation), and those centered around violence (terrorists, militants, hijackers, hackers).

Chandra Mohanty argues that developing a politics of location requires exploration of the "historical, geographical, cultural, psychic and imaginative boundaries which provide ground for political definition and self-definition" (1987, 3). Location is not seen as something rigid but a "temporality of struggle" (40) characterized by multiple locations and asynchronous processes of movement between cultures, languages, and complex configurations of meaning and power (Mani 1989, 26). In locating such a province for understanding identity rather than the totalizing one of national identity, international communication needs to develop the idea formulated by Stuart Hall that "identity is neither continuous nor continually interrupted but constantly framed between the simultaneous vectors or similarity, continuity and difference (quoted in Frankenberg and Mani 1993, 295). This has important, problematic implications for traditional categories of "terrorists," both in its contemporary structuration as a category defined by its antipathy to nation-states and historically as the generator of nationalist movements. Today, such a politics of location needs to be simultaneously placed within the life-space of postmodern nation-states and their multiple identity formations; the cooptation of postnationalist identities by a global corporate citizenship and by the lack of fixity that categories such as terrorists hold in the mobile landscape of contemporary culture.

Simply put, one can view postcolonial structurations of terrorism as co-constructed with other axes of domination and resistance. Discussing the response to the Salman Rushdie case in Great Britain, Lata Mani and Ruth Frankenberg (1987) argue that issues of identity formulation not only are articulated along the colonization–decolonization axis but are equally shaped by other axes, among them gender, race, religion, sexuality, and political orientations. Similarly, in discussing issues of African-American identity, they suggest that "the struggle of African-Americans in the USA becomes a political resource for forging imagined diasporic communities. The engagement of colonization/decolonization thus has transnational dimensions, its local expressions multiply inflected by regional and global affinities and considerations, in turn crosscut by class, race, gender, sexuality, etc." (Mani and Frankenberg 1987, 303).

Terrorism seen across regional contexts (African, Asian, or Latin American rather than its usual referent, Arab or Middle Eastern) confronts international communication with multiple axes, conjunctures, and politics of location simultaneously imprinted by concerns of transnational power, even as their media representations remain those narrowly imprinted by concerns of religion (Islam), masculinity, and Arab ethnicity.

Reflexivity

The last concern relevant to the field of international communication is that of reflexivity. A concern central to the cultural studies project, it has been focused on extensively by postcolonial critics. The central issue seems to be that the politics of location of subjects studied needs to be connected with the subject position of the researcher and the archive of which he or she is part. This has its roots, perhaps, in what Edward W. Said first outlined in *Orientalism:* "The starting point in critical elaboration is the consciousness of what one really is ... as a product of the historical process to date, which has deposited in you an infinity of traces, without leaving an inventory" (1979, 25).

Taking this maxim to heart, postcolonial critics (and *their* critics) pay a good deal of attention to the ideological basis and the position of the field of postcolonialism in the social formation. The tension lies in straddling the balance between their position as First World academics, their subject matter, and their avowed aim of elaborating and making possible strategies of empowerment. A similar concern is emergent in contemporary analysis of terrorism, both in terms of the experts who frame "terrorism" and the subjects of terrorism.

A starting point for a reflexive understanding of terrorism can draw on the continuing debate about the "postcolonial." Critics of postcolonial theory have considered the emergent popularity of the term "postcolonial," and they may find equal interest in "the terrorist." They have pointed out that the term "postcolonial" is problematic because it may be a more palatable label for metropolitan administrators than, say, "neocolonialism" or "neoimperialism" or that the term is less about hegemony and more about the emergent power of postcolonial critics in western academe—that is, the term may have more to do with marketing than analysis. The word "terrorist" is a term, we may surmise, marked simultaneously by its ambiguity and its specificity. It has cachet as a shorthand for an Arab mentality and as a catch-all for the culture of the globally disaffected. Like "postcolonial," it reappears even as the triumph of globalization appears all but immanent.

Academic fashion notwithstanding, the reflexive consideration of terms such as "terrorist" and "postcolonial" represents an important methodological step: The politics of location/practice must be foregrounded in fundamental ways to relationships between the subjects studied and those who study them. Elizabeth Lester-Massman points out that such awareness is all but absent in comparative research in communication. Discussing calls for increased comparative research, she points out that the "fundamental contradiction in that call for comparative work in communication studies is that the intellectual laborers refuse to recognize the power disparities, not simply in the object of their research but in the subject—that is, in and among themselves" (1991, 92).

Focusing on some of the complexities of the power disparities and conceptual frames as this chapter has attempted to do is perhaps the first step in framing the field of international communication after global terrorism.

REFERENCES

Agar, M. 1992. The intercultural frame. Paper presented at the Conference of Intercultural Communication at the LAUD Symposium, Duisburg, Germany.

Ahmad, A. 1992. *In theory: Classes, nations, literatures*. London: Verso.

Ang, I. 1991. Desperately seeking the audience. London: Routledge.

Appadurai, A. 1990. Disjuncture and difference in the global cultural economy. *Theory, Culture, and Society* 7:295–310.

Appiah, K. 1991. Is the post in post-modernism the post in post-colonial? *Critical Inquiry* 17:346–57.

Bhabha, H. 1992. Post colonial criticism. In *Redrawing the boundaries: The transformation of English and American literary studies*, ed. S. Greenblatt and G. Gunn. New York: Modern Language Association of America.

Clifford, J. 1986. *Writing culture*. Berkeley: University of California Press.

Dirlik, A. 1994. The post-colonial aura: Third World criticism in the age of global capitalism. *Critical Inquiry* 20:328–56.

Ferguson, M. 1992. The mythology about globalization. *European Journal of Communication* 7:69–93.

Foucault, M. 1980. The eye of power. In M. Foucault, *Power/knowledge: Selected interviews and other writings, 1972–1977*, ed. C. Gordon. New York: Pantheon.

Giddens, A. 1990. *The consequences of modernity*. Stanford, Calif.: Stanford University Press.

Golding, P. 1977. Media professionalism in the Third World: The transfer of an ideology. In *Mass Communication and Society*, ed. J. Curran, M. Gurevitch, and J. Woollacott. London: Open University.

Hannerz, U. 1991. Scenarios for peripheral cultures. In *Culture, globalization, and the world system*, ed. A. D. King. London: Macmillan.

Hardt, H. 1992. *Critical communication studies: Essays on communication, history, and theory in America*. New York: Routledge.

Jewsiewicki, B., and V. Mudimbe. 1994. For Said. *Transition* 63:34–50.

Kavoori, A. 1998. Getting past the latest "post": Assessing the term "post-colonial." *Critical Studies in Mass Communication* 15:195–212.

Lester-Massman, E. 1991. The dark side of comparative research. *Journal of Communication Inquiry* 15:92–106.

Mani, L., and R. Frankenberg. 1987. The challenge of orientalism. *Economy and Society* 14 (2).

McClintock, A. 1992. The angel of progress: Pitfalls in the term "post-colonialism." *Social Text* 31/32:84–89.

Mishra, A., and B. Hodge. 1991. What is post-colonialism? *Textual Practice* 5:400–11.

Miyoshi, M. 1993. A borderless world? From colonialism to transnationalism and the decline of the nation-state. *Critical Inquiry* 19 (4): 726–51.

Mohanty, C. 1987. Under Western eyes: Feminist scholarship and colonial discourses. *Feminist Review* 30 (Autumn): 61–88.

Mowlana, H. 1986. *Global information and world communication: World frontiers in international relations*. White Plains, N.Y.: Longman.

———. 1994. Shapes of the future: International communication in the 21st century. *Journal of International Communication* 1:14–32.

Prakash, G. 1992. Postcolonial criticism and Indian historiography. *Social Text* 31/32:8–19.

Radhakrishnan, R. 1992. Nationalism, gender, and the narrative of identity. In *Nationalisms and Sexualities*, ed. A. Parker, M. Russo, D. Sommer, and P. Yeager, 77–95. New York: Routledge.

Rouse, R. 1991. Mexican migration and the social space of postmodernism. *Diaspora* 1:8–23.

Said, E. 1979. *Orientalism*. New York: Vintage.

Shohat, E. 1992. Notes on the post-colonial. *Social Text* 31/32:99–113.

Shome, R. 1995. Postcolonial interventions in the rhetorical canon: An "other" view. *Communication Theory* 6:40–59.

———. 1996. Race and popular cinema: The rhetorical strategies of whiteness in City of Joy. *Communication Quarterly* 44 (4): 502–18.

Sreberny-Mohammadi, A. 1992. The global and the local in international communications. In *Mass Media and Society*, ed. J. Curran and M. Gurevitch, London: Edward Arnold.

Williams, C., and P. Chrisman. 1994. *Colonial discourse and postcolonial theory: A reader*. New York: Harvester.

Young, R. 1990. White mythologies: Writing history and the West. London: Routledge.

Discussion Questions for Part 3

1. In chapter seven, Fraley and Roushanzamir say: "The aim is to produce a media-savvy public of sophisticated citizens (as opposed to sophisticated consumers) with the potential to extend democracy." In what ways can ordinary citizens successfully challenge the corporatization of television programming?
2. Based on your reading of chapter eight, follow an unfolding media event (e.g., a terrorist event, a public diplomacy initiative, a presidential speech, a scandal) and identify the relationship between public relations and propaganda.
3. Why are dualistic theories (such as those offered by Fukuyama and Huntington in chapter nine) so popular in broadcast news media coverage?
4. How would you implement a "cosmopolitan globalization driven by issues of multipolar multilateralism, democratization, and globalization from below"? Discuss. (See chapter nine.)
5. How are contemporary nations "constructs"? What is the relationship between older uses of the term "culture" and postcolonial ones? Discuss these questions with reference to chapter ten.
6. What is the relationship of "terrorscape" to daily news coverage? What is the difference between the U.S. news media and channels such as al-Jazeera in articulating "terrorscapes"? Discuss these questions with reference to chapter ten.

Index

About the Contributors

Simon Cottle is professor of media and communication in the School of Journalism, Media and Cultural Studies at the University of Cardiff, Wales (from 2006). Previously he was director and inaugural professor of the Media and Communications Program at the University of Melbourne, Australia. He has researched and authored many books and articles on media production and the mediatization of conflicts, including *TV News, Urban Conflict, and the Inner City* (1993); *Television and Ethnic Minorities: Producers' Perspectives* (1997); *The Racist Murder of Stephen Lawrence: Media Performance and Public Transformation* (2004); and *Mediatized Conflict: New Directions in Media and Conflict Studies* (2005). His edited collections include *Ethnic Minorities and the Media: Changing Cultural Boundaries* (2000); *Media Organization and Production* (2003); and *News, Public Relations and Power* (2003). He is currently preparing a new book, *Global Crises, Global Reporting*.

Todd Fraley is assistant professor of communication in the School of Communication, East Carolina University, Greenville, N.C. He received his master's degree (2000) and Ph.D. (2004) in journalism and mass communication from the University of Georgia, Athens. His research interests are in popular culture, the politics of representation, political economy, and democratic communication.

Marion Herz works practically and theoretically in the fields of biotechnology and psychoanalysis, feminism and queer theories, film, art, and literature in Munich, Germany. Her upcoming Ph.D. dissertation is "PornoGRAPHIE: Eine Geschichte" (Pornography: A history).

Anandam P. Kavoori is associate professor of telecommunications and broadcast news at the Grady College of Journalism and Mass Communication, University of Georgia, Athens. He has a Ph.D. in journalism and mass communication from the University of Maryland, College Park (1994), and a master's in cultural anthropology from Brandeis University (1992). Dr. Kavoori is a specialist in the comparative cultural analysis of media texts, with a special focus on television news. His work on television news has focused on European, American, and Asian television. In addition to the edited book *The Global Dynamics of News* (2000), he has published scholarly articles in most major international journals, including *Media, Culture and Society*; the *Journal of Communication*; *Critical Studies in Mass Communication*; the *Journal of Broadcasting and Electronic Media*; *Communication Monographs*; the *International Journal of Cultural Studies*; the *Journal of International Communication*; and *Jump Cut*. Dr. Kavoori is the coordinator of the University of Georgia–CNN World Report Program and has been a consultant to CNN International and the Discovery Channel. He helped design and train journalists for India's most successful twenty-four-hour news channel, *Aaj Tak* News.

Douglas Kellner is the George Kneller Chair in the Philosophy of Education at UCLA. He has authored many books and essays on social theory, politics, history, and culture, including *Grand Theft 2000*, *The Persian Gulf TV War*, *Media Culture*, and *Media and Cultural Studies: Keyworks* (with Meenaskshi Gigi Durham).

Bruce Klopfenstein is professor and director of the Dowden Center for New Media Studies at the Grady College of Journalism and Mass Communication at the University of Georgia. He has a master's (1981) and Ph.D. (1985) from Ohio State University. Dr. Klopfenstein studies the adoption and diffusion patterns for emerging media technologies. He is currently focusing on interactive television.

Teresa La Porte is professor of international communication and vice dean in the School of Communication of the University of Navarre, Spain. She is the director of the research project "Globalizatión and Pluralism in the European Public TV," financed by the Spanish government, and is also collaborating as an expert on global media and public diplomacy in another project, "The Social Experience of Time," funded by the BBVA Foundation. La Porte has been a research scholar at the London School of Economics and at the Center for International Affairs at Harvard University. She has also been a scholar at NATO. Most of La Porte's research is related to the analysis of international news in the media. In this field, her published work includes *The Bosnian War* *in Spain: The Media's Representation of a Distant Violent Conflict, Le sommet à Nice : Entre la globalisation et la diversité, Foreign News in Spain: Reporting One's Own Image of the World, Media Effect on International Controversies,* and *What Kind of European Information to Bridge the Knowledge Gap?* In addition, she is the author of the book *The Foreign Policy of Franco's Regime, 1957–1963.*

Elli Lester Roushanzamir's research uses critical cultural studies approaches to investigate the relationships between media images and media political-economy with a particular focus on international communication. She has taught and conducted research in Innsbruck, Austria; Addis Ababa, Ethiopia; and Oxford, England and has published articles in the *Journal of Communication Inquiry, Argumentation, Critical Studies in Media Communication, Journalism and Mass Communication Monographs, Journalism and Mass Communication Quarterly,* and the *International Journal of Hospitality and Tourism.*

Teresa Sádaba is associate professor in the School of Communications at the University of Navarre, Spain. She is also the vice director of the master's program on political and corporate communication, a program in collaboration with George Washington University, Washington, D.C. The focus of Sádaba's research and teaching is on political communication. She is a former visiting professor at the University of Texas, Austin, and a Fulbright fellow in Salzburg, Austria. She teaches a course at the University of Paris XII and University Complutense in Madrid and is the editor of *Periodistas ante conflictos* (1999) and several works about communication and terrorism.

Antje Schuhmann is assistant professor at the Institute of American Cultural Studies at the University of Munich. She works as an activist and researcher in the fields of antiracist feminism, critical whiteness, and nationalism and postcolonialism. Her next publications will be "Whose Burden? The Significance of the Israel-Palestine Conflict in German Identity Politics" in *Media and Myth*, a publication of the German Jewish Studies Centre of the University Sussex, England (2005) and the book *Race-Gender-Class: On the Postcolonial Culture of the National; A Feminist Critique* (2006).

Nancy Snow is assistant professor of communications at California State University, Fullerton, and adjunct professor at the Annenberg School for Communication, University of Southern California (USC). She is a senior research fellow in the USC Center on Public Diplomacy. Dr. Snow is the author of *Propaganda, Inc.: Selling America's Culture to the World* and *Information War* and coeditor of *War, Media and Propaganda: A Global Perspective.* She worked for the U.S. Information Agency and U.S. State Department from 1992 to 1994.

Daya Kishan Thussu is professor of international communication at the University of Westminster in London. He is the founder and managing editor of a new Sage journal, *Global Media and Communication*. A former associate editor of Gemini News Service, a London-based international news agency, he has a Ph.D. in international relations from Jawaharlal Nehru University, New Delhi. Dr. Thussu is the coauthor of *Contra-Flow in Global News* (1992), editor of *Electronic Empires: Global Media and Local Resistance* (1998), author of *International Communication: Continuity and Change* (2000), and coeditor of *War and the Media: Reporting Conflict 24/7* (2003).